Now & Then

Also by Robert Hass

POETRY
Time and Materials: Poems 1997–2005
Sun Under Wood
Human Wishes
Praise
Field Guide

ESSAYS
Twentieth Century Pleasures

TRANSLATIONS
Czeslaw Milosz, *The Separate Notebooks*
(with Robert Pinsky and Renata Gorczynski)
Czeslaw Milosz, *Unattainable Earth* (with the author)
Czeslaw Milosz, *Collected Poems* (with the author and others)
Czeslaw Milosz, *Provinces* (with the author)
Czeslaw Milosz, *Facing the River* (with the author)
Czeslaw Milosz, *Treatise on Poetry* (with the author)
Czeslaw Milosz, *Road-side Dog* (with the author)
Czeslaw Milosz, *Second Space: New Poems* (with the author)
The Essential Haiku: Versions of Bashō, Buson, & Issa

EDITOR
Robinson Jeffers, *Rock and Hawk: A Selection of Shorter Poems*
Tomas Tranströmer, *Selected Poems: 1954–1986*
Into the Garden: A Wedding Anthology (with Stephen Mitchell)
The Addison Street Anthology: Berkeley's Poetry Walk (with Jessica Fisher)
Poet's Choice: Poems for Everyday Life

Now & Then

The Poet's Choice Columns
1997–2000

Robert Hass

SHOEMAKER & HOARD

Library of Congress Cataloging-in-Publication Data

Hass, Robert.
    Now & then : the Poet's choice columns, 1997–2000 / Robert Hass.
          p. cm.
    Includes indexes.
    ISBN-13: 978-1-59376-146-2 (alk. paper)
    ISBN-10: 1-59376-146-5 (alk. paper)
    1. English poetry—History and criticism. 2. American poetry
—History and criticism. I. Title. II. Title: Now and then.

PR503.H27 2007
811'.54—dc22

                                    2007003474

Book design by Gopa & Ted2, Inc.
Printed in the United States of America

Shoemaker ⟨SH⟩ Hoard
www.shoemakerhoard.com

10 9 8 7 6 5 4 3 2 1

For Finn, Josephine, Cole, Ella, Hazel & Fionna
—when you want, someday, to read a poem

Contents

A Note to Readers xi

1997

December 7   Wallace Stevens and Joni Mitchell 3

December 14   In Memoriam: James Laughlin 6

December 21   Nativity Poems:
              William Butler Yeats and Louise Glück 9

December 28   A New Year's Poem
              from the Korean *Sijo* Tradition 10

1998

January 4   A Korean Poet: Ko Un 13

January 11   In Memoriam: Denise Levertov 16

January 19   In Memoriam: William Matthews 18

January 25   Frank Bidart 19

February 1   A Polish Poet: Adam Zagajewski 21

February 8   A Question of Decency: Walt Whitman 24

February 15   Stanley Plumly 26

February 22   Sonia Sanchez 29

March 1   Marie Howe 30

March 8   John Koethe 32

March 15   Sylvia Plath 34

March 22   Ted Hughes 37

March 29   Spring, and a New Translation of Horace 39

April 5   Passover: Linda Pastan 41

April 12   Easter: Mary Karr 44

April 19   An Irish Poet: Derek Mahon 45

April 26   Audubon's Birthday: Birds by Robert Frost,
              W. C. Williams, and Robinson Jeffers 47

May 3   In Memoriam: Octavio Paz......................... 49
May 10   Mother's Day: Dorianne Laux..................... 51
May 17   Agha Shahid Ali................................. 53
May 24   Margaret Atwood................................. 55
May 31   Memorial Day and Shakespeare.................... 56
June 7   Summer and Baseball: Linda Gregerson............ 60
June 14   Encompassing Nature:
               Sappho, Lady Komachi, and an Irish Bard......... 61
June 21   Father's Day: Cornelius Eady.................... 64
June 28   Joseph Stroud and Larissa Szporluk.............. 66
July 5   Independence Day: Ralph Waldo Emerson........... 68
July 12   Patriotism and Public Memory: Robert Lowell..... 70
July 19   Susan Wheeler................................... 74
July 26   D. A. Powell.................................... 76
August 2   Arthur Sze...................................... 78
August 9   The Villanelle:
               Theodore Roethke and Elizabeth Bishop........... 79
August 16   In Memoriam: Zbigniew Herbert................... 81
August 23   Something Old, Something New: Charlotte Mew... 84
August 30   Yusef Komunyakaa................................ 85
September 6   Labor Day: Gary Snyder.......................... 87
September 13   May Swenson..................................... 88
September 20   Donald Justice.................................. 90
September 27   Presidents, Poets, and Shame: James Wright...... 92
October 4   Filipino Poetry: *Returning a Borrowed Tongue*...... 95
October 11   John Ashbery.................................... 97
October 18   Sterling Brown.................................. 99
October 25   Robert Bly..................................... 102
November 1   Chase Twichell................................. 104
November 8   A Canadian Poet: Roo Borson.................... 106
November 15   A Portuguese Poet: Fernando Pessoa............. 107
November 22   Thanksgiving:
               Harriet Maxwell Converse and Iroquois Song..... 109
November 29   A Swedish Poet: Tomas Tranströmer.............. 111
December 6   Czeslaw Milosz: The Poet as a Road-side Dog..... 114
December 13   Israeli Poems on War and Peace: Yehuda Amichai... 116

December 20   Christmas: Mark Doty 117
December 27   A Poem for the End of a Thousand Years:
              W. H. Auden 120

1999

January 2   A Scottish Poet for New Year's Day:
              George Mackay Brown 123
January 10   In Memoriam: Margaret Walker 124
January 17   In Memoriam: Janet Lewis 127
January 24   Philip Larkin. 130
January 31   A Spanish Poet: Rafael Alberti 131
February 7   George Herbert. 132
February 14   Valentine's Day: Kenneth Rexroth 134
February 21   An Irish Poet: Paul Muldoon 136
February 28   Ben Jonson 138
March 7   Pattiann Rogers 140
March 14   An Italian Poet: Eugenio Montale 142
March 21   Claudia Rankine 144
March 28   Gerard Manley Hopkins. 146
April 4   Easter: Charles Wright 148
April 11   Richard Wright and Langston Hughes 152
April 18   Wang Ping 155
April 25   Michael Ondaatje 156
May 2   Forrest Gander. 160
May 9   A Serbian Poet: Vasko Popa 162
May 16   Adrienne Rich. 165
May 23   Malena Mörling. 167
May 30   Memorial Day: Jaime Sabines 170
June 6   The Poetics of Travel: Elizabeth Bishop. 173
June 13   Paul Beatty 175
June 20   Father's Day: Li-Young Lee 177
June 27   Poetry and Weddings: Benjamin Saenz 180
July 4   Independence Day: Rita Dove 182
July 11   Fanny Howe. 183
July 18   Lee Ann Brown 187
July 25   A Serbian Epic: *The Battle of Kosovo*. 189

August 1   Denise Levertov. 193
August 8   Summer Shakespeare 196
August 15   Louise Glück 199
August 22   In Memoriam: Sherley Anne Williams. 202
August 29   Naomi Shihab Nye. 205
September 5   Labor Day: Willam Blake and Debra Allbery. 207
September 12   One Thousand Years of Poetry in English:
                A Millennium Gathering. 210
September 19   Rainer Maria Rilke: *Herbsttag*. 221
September 26   Rainer Maria Rilke Translated by
                Galway Kinnell and William Gass. 224
October 3   Andrew Hudgins. 227
October 10   Heather McHugh 229
October 17   Dean Young 232
October 24   John Clare. 237
October 31   Halloween: John Keats and Lynne McMahon 240
November 7   Czeslaw Milosz: An Argument About Imperialism . . 243
November 14   Wallace Stevens 245
November 21   Thanksgiving: Daniel Halpern 250
November 28   A Peruvian Poet: César Vallejo 253
December 5   Bad Words: Stephen Berg. 256
December 12   Seamus Heaney's *Beowulf* as an Ecological Epic. 259
December 19   Snow: Emerson, Lowell, Dickinson,
                Longfellow, Whittier, and Stevens. 261
December 26   Christmas: Ira Gershwin and Cole Porter. 267

2000

January 2   New Year's Day:
                Tessa Rumsey and Harryette Mullen. 271
January 9   Charlotte Smith. 274
January 16   Rita Dove. 277

Epilogue   Ezra Pound. 281

Copyright Acknowledgments 287

Index 297

A Note to Readers

THIS IS A BOOK of poems and small essays about them written over a period of about two years. It came about because Nina King, then literary editor of the *Washington Post,* invited me to write a weekly column for the *Post's Book World.* The idea was that I would, each week, select a poem and comment on it. The aim was to introduce poetry to people who had never read it at all; to reintroduce it to people who had read it in school but had gotten out of the habit and, having an impulse to find their way back to it, didn't know where to start; and to give people who did read poetry some poems and ideas about poems to think about.

The column was a novelty. Nothing quite like it had been done in an American newspaper in many decades, if ever, and it was immediately popular with readers of *Book World.* In very little time it was syndicated nationally in more than twenty-five newspapers, including the *San Francisco Examiner,* the *Seattle Times,* the *Miami Herald,* the *Atlanta Journal,* the *Chicago Sun-Times,* the *Detroit News,* and the Philippines' principal English-language paper, the *Manila Times.*

I wrote the column for four years. Since then it has continued to thrive in the hands of Rita Dove, Edward Hirsch, and Robert Pinsky. For the first two years of working on it, my task was mainly to pick a poem and provide the briefest framing by way of commentary. But in late 1997 the format of *Book World* changed, and I had a little more space to work with, which allowed me sometimes to present two poems rather than one, or a longer poem, or to let my note turn into a very short essay. Sometimes I found myself writing a little long and then cutting, and I have been able to reproduce the uncut versions here. In two or three places, for various reasons, I've patched and filled—rewritten a column or written a new one in the spirit of the ones I was writing at that time. This book's predecessor, *Poet's Choice: Poems for Everyday Life,* is basically an anthology. *Now & Then* is more nearly a book of essays about poems and poets. It covers the period from the early winter of 1997 to midwinter 2000 , and, like its predecessor, it is attentive to seasons and holidays, to the turning wheel of the year. Because of this, I was surprised, rereading the assembled pieces, by how much it resembled a Book of Hours. The reader of it watches the year turn, and the form invites short readings, meditations to be undertaken daily or weekly in quiet times. And, of course, it would be pleasing to me if it were read that way, since that's the way in which I myself read poetry.

I wrote the columns this way because the sense of time in them is one of the things I like about newspapers. In my childhood three newspapers came into our house every day, the local paper of our small California town, the *San Rafael Independent-Journal,* and the morning paper from the city, the *San Francisco Chronicle,* both of which were delivered by newsboys on bicycles, and an evening paper, the *San Francisco Call-Bulletin,* which my father brought home from his weekday commute. The papers mattered to my siblings and me for their comics and, when we were a little older, their sports pages. In the comics, time did not exist. On the sports pages there were three seasons, football, basketball, and baseball, only dimly related to the weather in California. My older brother and I spent hours in the evenings imitating the styles of the sports cartoonists in the papers. The artist for the *Chronicle* cast figures like the University of California's football coach, Pappy Waldorf, and the manager of the San Francisco Seals, Lefty O'Doul, in the heroic mode, like the serious comics *Prince Valiant* and *Terry and the Pirates.* The *Call-Bulletin* artist drew comedy like *Blondie* or *The Katzenjammer Kids:* round noses, whiskers, and squiggly lines behind the baseball that skittered right through the legs of the clueless shortstop. We labored over our productions, each in its season, now in one style, now in the other. And our eyes must have drifted over to the rest of the paper. I have a distinct memory of the *Call-Bulletin* calling up a world full of dangerous Communist spies; in the *Chronicle,* movie stars of the period like Franchot Tone or Monica Freeman were spotted dining in what would be the last of the city's supper clubs.

And there were other ways in which we were instructed in seasons: stories on how to buy a pumpkin or to carve it, recipes for Thanksgiving stuffing, Christmas ads, recipes for cranberry relishes. The comic pages would have make-your-own valentines in February that could be colored with crayons and cut out with scissors, and they would start doing Easter stories in early April. I see now that this insistence was not unconnected to advertising revenues. In fact, I think I saw it then. My daily walk to grammar school took me down the four blocks of the main commercial street of our town, and many of the merchants were parents of my schoolmates. I knew that back-to-school shoes were a very good thing for the Chapman family, and so were summer sandals, and that they did good business in dress shoes in the weeks before proms; and that one bought basketball shoes and baseball cleats from Mr. Brusati in the sporting goods store, each in its season, and new mitts as one's hands grew larger. I went to a Catholic school and we wore uniforms on weekdays, so at Mass on Sundays one noticed, at a certain age and in a certain season, that the girls had begun to wear sweaters, as if the world had suddenly burst into Technicolor. The sweaters were exactly the colors of the ones in the ads run by the local department stores, in those years red, orange, goldish-orange, and dull yellow, so that they made an equivalent to fall foliage when our long, mild Indian summers came to an end and the air began to cool in mid-October.

Newspapers imbed us in time—from the date on page one to the smallest details of format. I have a vivid memory of one day helping a friend to fold papers for his paper route and coming to what seemed like the metaphysical realization that each day's newspaper represented a day. They came and went, like days. And—another leap—the Sunday papers with their fat formats and their color comics represented weeks. It was an idea that I couldn't even think of a way to communicate to my friend, but it made me slightly dizzy, as if I had glimpsed some truth about the great wheeling movement of the stars and the planets and the world of events that the papers treated as a matter of such urgency.

So this, it turns out, is a book about time. I put off assembling these columns for several years because, in truth, I was tired of them after four years of weekly deadlines. But assembling them now, I was surprised by how this work of just a few years ago feels almost as if it belongs to another era: here in September of 1998 is Mark McGwire, rounding the bases after having broken the single season home run record. And here is the United States bombing of the city of Belgrade. Here is the moment when it seemed to the world that Israel and the Palestinian Authority were within a hairsbreadth of a peace agreement. Here is a young Pakistani-American poet writing about the Arabic language and the inability of the West to see the Muslim world (in 1999). Here is the story of the White House intern and the impeachment trial of the president of the United States.

And here is the coming and going of the millennium. There are essays here on summer Shakespeare and the Christmas music in department stores. There is—for the millennium—a mini-history of poetry in the English language. The book has, in the flow of time, a curious air of normality, of life and its interests and brutalities going about their business.

I am one of those people who did not believe that the world changed on September 11, 2001, who think that the idea that the world changed was a propaganda tactic of the militarist wing of the Republican Party, a hijacking of the meaning of the hijacking to recreate a Cold War mentality in our country. In 1998 and 1999 we were already at war with Iraq. That war consisted in establishing no-fly zones over the Kurdish regions of northern Iraq and the Shia regions of southern Iraq to protect those populations from the predations of Sadaam Hussein. Meanwhile, we imposed an economic embargo on the Sunni dictator's regime, and the United Nations monitored his armaments, a policy of containment that, from our present vantage point, seems remarkably clear-headed. In any case it was, for Americans, a quiet war, and you will not find it here. There are no Iraqi poets in the pages that follow. They were not on my radar and, though Penguin Books had published a volume of modern Arabic poetry, there was no book in translation then available of Iraqi poetry. There is now, *Iraqi Poetry Today,* edited by Saadi Samawe and Daniel Weissbort and published by the Modern Poetry in Translation series of King's College, London. It appeared in 2003.

But the time in these pages was not without its dangers and anxieties. At the center of the book is W. H. Auden's great elegy for William Butler Yeats. It was written in the winter of 1939, and it carries in it the cold and terror of a violent century. What one gets from it now is a deep sense of moral intelligence, a sense of what language is like in the hands of a poet at a time of genuine crisis. It is level, a little cool, passionately engaged, but engaged in the act of finding both measure and accuracy in speech. It made me aware that we have been living, not in a time of increased dangers (except for the ways in which the recklessness of our incursion into Iraq has made the world more dangerous), but in a time of enormously heightened rhetorical violence, in which the politicians and the press, particularly the television news channels, have collaborated. This realization had the effect for me of making the poems, as I reread them, seem admirably measured and sane. They do not always succeed—I was trying to give people a sense of the breadth and range of poetry, both old and new, and I often turned to whatever came into my hands—but most of the poems were trying to get the weight and shape of experience right.

All through the book readers are invited to the quiet and intensity of reading, not exactly as if it were the blessed water in a medieval baptismal font in an old church, the entire violence of the world carved onto the outside of the font—that is the great Swedish poet Tomas Tranströmer's figure for the wish of poetry—but something more like a haiku of the eighteenth-century master Buson. It is a poem about a particular kind of Book of Hours, a cheaply printed, cheaply bound farmer's almanac. The poem goes like this:

> This old almanac
> Gladdens my heart
> Like a sutra.

It would be pleasant if a book of this kind shared the qualities of almanac and sutra, in the way that poetry can seem both to penetrate time and penetrate our days, more deeply than our walking-around consciousness usually does, and to lift us out of it, out of the turning wheel for a moment, so that we can see ourselves and the life around us more clearly. It's my hope that this book will in a small way serve both these purposes for its readers, and that it will encourage some readers to read, now and then, more widely and deeply in the enormously exhilarating range of available poetries.

I was very lucky in my collaborators at the *Washington Post,* Jennifer Howard, who made sure I did not miss a deadline, and Maria Arana, *Book World*'s current editor, herself a distinguished writer whose eye to my often hurried prose was a great gift. I need to thank them here and to thank Jack Shoemaker for encouraging me to make this book, Roxanna Font for bringing it into existence, and Kristen Sbrogna for the patient work of proofreading and permission gathering.

Now & Then

DECEMBER 7

Wallace Stevens and Joni Mitchell

It is getting on to winter, and I almost cannot say so to myself without thinking of that lyric from Joni Mitchell's *Blue:*

> It's coming on Christmas
> They're cutting down trees
> They're putting up reindeer
> And singing songs of joy and peace—

With its surprising chords and its sudden, unexpected leap to the chorus:

> Oh I wish I had a river
> I could skate away on.

It is a song about romantic loss and about Christmas blues. People of my generation will also remember that it is about the mood of the country during the Vietnam War, when so many of the young felt helpless before the violence their government had unleashed across the world.

The season and that leap in the song made me think of one of the most haunting American poems of the twentieth century. It's Wallace Stevens's "The Snow Man." It comes differently to its unexpected conclusion. It seems to arrive there almost inevitably, in the unwinding of its syntax, and leaves most readers blinking at what they have come to. Here it is:

The Snow Man

One must have a mind of winter
To regard the frost and the boughs
Of the pine-trees crusted with snow;

And have been cold a long time
To behold the junipers shagged with ice,
The spruces rough in the distant glitter

Of the January sun; and not to think
Of any misery in the sound of the wind,
In the sound of a few leaves,

Which is the sound of the land
Full of the same wind
That is blowing in the same bare place

For the listener, who listens in the snow,
And, nothing himself, beholds
Nothing that is not there and the nothing that is.

This comes from a really splendid new edition of Wallace Stevens, *Collected Poetry and Prose,* published by the Library of America. It's the best single volume of his work to appear, though it isn't as beautiful as the old Knopf hardback *Collected Poems.* But all the poems are in the Library of America edition, and the essays on poetry, and selections from the letters, and the aphorisms, the best known of which, I suppose, are "Money is a kind of poetry" and "The greatest poverty is not to love in the physical world." But there are others: "The tongue is an eye." "A poem is a pheasant." It would make a resplendent holiday gift.

That takes care of my seasonal duties. Now look back at that wintry poem, bright as ice. In college, I remember, we argued for hours about what those last lines meant, as if the chill of the poem and its enormous clarity would not quite let go of us. In the way that Joni Mitchell's song has its historical context, so, I suppose, does Stevens's poem. He belonged to the generation of writers—all of the modernists did—who had to address the ways in which the Christian idea, or at least the Protestant and transcendentalist idea, of a divinity in nature had lost its hold on their imagination. "We live," the woman in his poem "Sunday Morning" muses, "in an old chaos of the sun." When Stevens went to college in the early 1900s, aestheticism was in the air. He was a boy from solid Lutheran and German stock—Pennsylvania Dutch, as it was called—and his mother could still speak the Pennsylvania Dutch dialect to the farm women who came to Reading to sell their produce on Saturdays. He has what must be a poem to his mother, explaining his conversion to French poetry:

Explanation

Ach, Mutter
This old, black dress,
I have been embroidering
French flowers on it.

Not by way of romance,
Here is nothing of the ideal,
Nein,
Nein.

It would be different,
Liebchen,
If I had imagined myself,
In an orange gown,
Drifting through space,
Like a figure on a church-wall.

He was going to have to manage in a world without angels, and he thought about this subject for the rest of his long life as a poet and an executive of the Hartford Insurance Company. He was sure that the solution to the problem of the loss of what he called the "romance" of the ideal was imagination, which in one of his rare essays he calls "the Necessary Angel."

In Hartford this autumn, a friend drove me by the offices of the Hartford Insurance Company and the house where Stevens lived. I had read that he walked to work, and, taking what seemed the shortest way, I tried to walk his walk to work. It led through a park, and I thought that

I had, perhaps, come to the ground of that frosty place where, in a fierce New England January, Stevens, sometime in the teens of the century, had turned in his mind the rhythms of a poem that was a single long sentence, about not projecting anything onto the landscape and seeing what is there and seeing what is not there.

But this paraphrase hardly settles the mystery of those last few lines. They stay in the mind, like Joni Mitchell's song. Away, away, she says. Here, here, the poet says, and he says it takes a mind of winter to say it. But where and what is *here* is the question he has been teasing us with ever since.

DECEMBER 14

In Memoriam: James Laughlin

James Laughlin died last month. He was the publisher of New Directions, which he started in the 1930s when he was still a student at Harvard. He published Ezra Pound, William Carlos Williams, Tennessee Williams, Henry Miller, Kenneth Rexroth. He was probably the most important literary publisher of this half century. And he was a poet, schooled on the classics, which he studied in school—the frank, practical, sharp-witted and plain-spoken poets of the Greek anthologies and the Roman empire—and on the writers he published. His last book, *The Country Road* (Zoland Books), appeared in 1995.

It contains poems, mostly, of aging, spoken by himself or by imagined speakers coping with the afflictions of their late years. Some of them, like this one, have a bluntness that can be a little startling.

The Least You Could Do

> he told her, would be to forget
> your pride of ownership for an hour
> and let her come to sit by my bed
> for that fraction of time.
> What could we say in an hour
> that would hurt you, or would take

anything away from what you've had?
What looks could we exchange
that would harm you in any way?
It's more than ten years
since we were lovers; in ten years
we haven't seen each other.
Is it so strange that we want
to meet again for a last time,
to look at each other, to listen to
each other's voices, ever
so gently to touch hands?
It's the least you could do.

What makes me sit up and take notice is not the implied narrative of the poem or its aggrieved tone, but that I can't tell how much it's *intended* to wound the wife to whom I guess it's spoken and how much it's a portrait of a desperately vulnerable yearning that doesn't care whom it wounds. Whatever else the poem does, it certainly renders a living voice.

Among the poems in his *Collected Poems* is "Byways," a sequence of casually written anecdotal pieces. It is not innovative verse-making. I think Laughlin must have borrowed its plain, straightforward style from his friend Kenneth Rexroth, and it allowed him to tell stories from a long and eventful literary life. Here is a passage about sneaking with another of his authors, the Trappist monk and poet Thomas Merton, back into his famous Kentucky monastery in the middle of some night in the late 1950s. Merton had gotten leave for the day, which they spent talking about Henry Miller and Djuana Barnes. They ended in a roadhouse consuming "a red-eye ham, / I think they called it, with a bottle of / St. Emilion to wash it down / And a few nips of cognac / To settle the stomach."

When we got back to Gethsemani
There wasn't a light in the place.
Brother Gatekeeper was long gone
To his cot in the dormitory.
What to do? I remember, said Tom,
A place on the other side near

The cemetery where the wall
Isn't quite as high as it is here.
Tom was right, the wall was lower.
I got down on all fours
And had Tom stand on my back.
Can you reach the top? I asked.
Just with my fingertips, he said.
OK, hold on if you can,
I'll get up and push up your legs.
Tom was up, lying on the wall but
I couldn't reach his dangling hand.
I thought of my belt. I took it off
And tossed one end up to him.
Brace your legs around the wall
And I'll climb with my legs
The way Rexroth taught me on
Rock faces in the mountains.
Believe it or not, it worked.
We lay in the grass on the far side
Of the wall and laughed and laughed
And laughed. We have done the Devil's
Work today, Tom, I told him.
No, he said, we've been working for
The angels; they are friends of mine.
Keeping very quiet, Tom went off to
His bishop's room, I to my bed
In the wing for retreatants.

James Laughlin's *Collected Poems* is also in print, as well as volumes of his correspondence with his authors. Like many Americans of my generation, I got a good part of my literary education from reading the books he published. He was an immense presence, and he will be missed.

DECEMBER 21

Nativity Poems:
William Butler Yeats and Louise Glück

Probably the best known modern poem about the Nativity story is one by the Irish poet William Butler Yeats:

The Magi

Now as at all times I can see in the mind's eye
In their stiff, painted clothes, the pale unsatisfied ones
Appear or disappear in the blue depth of the sky
With all their ancient faces like rain-beaten stones,
With all their helms of silver hovering side by side,
And all their eyes still fixed, hoping to find once more,
Being by Calvary's turbulence unsatisfied,
The uncontrollable mystery on the bestial floor.

This comes from his book *Responsibilities,* published in 1914. He wrote it, he once remarked, one day when he "looked up at the blue of the sky and suddenly imagined, as if lost in the blue of the sky, stiff figures in procession. I remembered that they were the habitual image suggested by the blue sky, and looking for a . . . fable called them 'The Magi.'" "The bestial floor," I've always supposed, is the stable at Bethlehem, and these wise men are, in Yeats's version, forever hunting for it as they march across the sky.

A contemporary American poet, Louise Glück, in *The First Four Books of Poems* (Ecco), has written what must be, at least partly, a response to Yeats:

The Magi

Toward world's end, through the bare
beginnings of winter, they are traveling again.
How many winters have we seen it happen,
watched the same sign come forward as they pass
cities sprung around this route their gold

engraved on the desert, and yet
held our peace, these
being the Wise, come to see at the accustomed hour
nothing changed: roofs, the barn
blazing in darkness, all they wish to see.

I'm not sure I get this poem entirely. "The sign" must be the star at
Bethlehem. The "we" in this poem, the ordinary folk who watch the
Magi pass by, seem to be speaking with some irony. At least the linebreak
"these / being the Wise" makes you wonder how wise they are. And I
like it in this world of the ordinary mysteries—"roofs, the barn blazing /
in darkness"—that the townsfolk hold their peace. Peace to you in this
season and happy holidays.

DECEMBER 28

A New Year's Poem
from the Korean *Sijo* Tradition

Here's a New Year's poem from eighteenth-century Korea:

A boy comes by my window
            shouting that it's New Year's.
I open the eastern lattice—
            the usual sun has risen.
Look, kid! It's the same old sun.
            Wake me when a new one dawns!

This is the classic type of the Korean lyric poem. It's called a *sijo*. I've
adapted it as well as the following from the translation by Richard Rutt
in *The Bamboo Grove: An Introduction to Sijo*, which was published by the
University of California Press in 1971 and is still, as far as I know, the
best study of the form in English. Like the English lyric, the *sijo* began
as a song form. The earliest ones date from the fourteenth century, and
contemporary Korean poets still write them. They're basically three line

poems of about fifteen syllables to a line. The rhythm comes from the patterning of phrases within the line.

And they get used for all kinds of purposes. Here's a poem, probably from the sixteenth century, that uses nature imagery to talk about wrangling politicians:

> Can a swarm of these tiny insects
> > devour a whole great spreading pine?
> Where is the long-billed
> > woodpecker? Now we could really use one.
> When I hear the sound of falling trees
> > I cannot contain my sorrow.

The woodpeckers, of course, eat insects. Here's one from a beautiful sequence called "The Nine Songs of Kosan." It was written in the sixteenth century by the great Korean Confucian philosopher Yi I. The songs were composed after he had retired from government service and was living in Kosan, a place equivalent perhaps to the Blue Ridge mountains. Here is the last poem in the sequence:

> Where shall we find the ninth song?
> > Winter has come to Munsan;
> The fantastic rocks
> > are buried under snow.
> Nobody comes here for pleasure now.
> > They think there is nothing to see.

Confucian maybe, but it seems very much like a Buddhist joke. Here's hoping that there's much to see in the New Year.

A Korean Poet: Ko Un

Modern Korean poetry, like the poetry of Eastern Europe, is inextricably entangled with the country's history in the twentieth century: Japanese military occupation from 1905 to 1945, during which time efforts were made to eradicate the Korean language; a devastating civil war, made more devastating because the war and the peninsula became a pawn in the Cold War; the division of the country; a series of military dictatorships in the South, the Republic of Korea, accompanied by continued Cold War tensions with the North; a U.S. military presence; a remarkable economic recovery; and an intense grass-roots democracy movement that often fought the government in the streets.

The conflict between the protesters and the government culminated in a massacre in the southern city of Kwangju in 1979 in which over five hundred people, mostly students, were killed. It was the Tiennamen Square of that decade. To get a sense of the magnitude of it: there are forty million Koreans, so it was as if the U.S. National Guard had shot down 2,500 students at Kent State in 1971 instead of four. After Kwangju, the memory of that event became the focus of the pro-democracy movement, which finally bore fruit in 1992 when the Republic elected a president, Kim Young Sam, who exposed financial scandals and prosecuted the perpetrators of the massacre. Last week the leader of the movement for decades, Kim Dae Jung, was elected to the presidency. It's a remarkable story, it's not only a story about the Korean economy, and it's not over. And Americans, who bear some responsibility for the violent turns in modern Korean history, know very little about it.

One of the prominent literary figures in the movement to resist government suppression of the Kwangju incident and to bring about democratic reforms was a poet named Ko Un. In the 1970s and 1980s he was arrested four times, imprisoned, tortured—as a result of which he lost his hearing in one ear—and ultimately pardoned. He had been a student in the years of Japanese occupation, a Buddhist monk when he began to write, and, after his return to secular life, another of the twentieth century's alienated urban poets until he joined the democracy movement and became an active dissident. While he was in prison, he conceived one of his major projects, to write a poem about every person he had ever known. Called *Ten Thousand Lives,* two volumes of this monumental work have been published. Only a handful of the poems have appeared in English translation, but they are remarkably rich. Anecdotal, demotic, full of the details of people's lives, they're not like anything else I've come across in Korean poetry. It's to be hoped that a fuller translation of them will appear.

In the meantime a book of Ko Un's short Buddhist poems is just out from Parallax Press, *Beyond Self: 108 Korean Zen Poems,* translated by Kim Young Moo and Brother Anthony. Here are a few of these brief, tough-minded poems in the "crazy wisdom" tradition:

Echo

To mountains at dusk:
What are you?

What are you are you . . .

A Drunkard

I've never been an individual entity.
Sixty trillion cells!
I'm a living collection
staggering zigzag along.
Sixty trillion cells! All drunk.

A Friend

Hey! With the clay you dug out
I fashioned a Buddha.
It rained.
The Buddha turned back into clay.

Clear skies after rain are pointless.

Ripples

Look! Do all the ripples move
because one ripple started to move?
No.
It's just that all the ripples move at once.
Everything's been askew from the start.

A Shooting Star

Wow! You recognized me.

A Moonless Night

No moon up
yet the two hundred miles
between you and me
shine bright all the night long.
That dog that'll die tomorrow
doesn't know it's going to die.
It's barking fiercely.

One hundred and eight poems because there are 108 beads on a Buddhist "rosary," and in the old learning 108 karmic bonds of passion and delusion.

Note: Several volumes of Ko Un's work are now available: Ten Thousand Lives, *translated by Brother Anthony of Taizé and Gary Gach (Green Integer);* Flower of the Moment, *translated by Brother Anthony of Taizé and Gary Gach (BOA Editions); and* The Three-Way Tavern, *translated by Claire Yoo and Richard Silverg (University of California Press).*

JANUARY 11

In Memoriam: Denise Levertov

Denise Levertov died just before Christmas, of cancer, in Seattle. She was seventy-four and one of the defining poets of her generation. Her passing, so soon after Allen Ginsberg, reminded me of some lines she wrote in the 1960s about William Carlos Williams and Ezra Pound:

> This is the year the old ones,
> the old great ones
> leave us alone on the road.
>
> The road leads to the sea.
> We have the words in our pockets,
> obscure directions. The old ones
>
> have taken away the light of their presence,
> we see it moving over a hill . . .

This comes from the 1964 volume, *O Taste and See* (New Directions). Here is the title poem from that book:

> *O Taste and See*
>
> The world is
> not with us enough.
> **O taste and see**

the subway Bible poster said,
meaning **The Lord,** meaning
if anything all that lives
to the imagination's tongue,

grief, mercy, language,
tangerine, weather, to
breathe them, bite,
savor, chew, swallow, transform

into our flesh our
deaths, crossing the street, plum, quince,
living in the orchard and being

hungry, and plucking
the fruit.

She will be missed, sorely. Almost all of her books are available from New Directions and should be in the bookstores, her essays on poetry as well as her poems.

I walked into a classroom once where she had been teaching at a summer writers' workshop and saw scrawled across the board in her hand these words: *Accuracy is always the gateway to mystery.* So I think she would not mind if I took this space to repair a mistake in a column of a few weeks ago, where Wallace Stevens's famous poem "The Snow Man" appeared with an incorrect first line. The poem begins:

One must have a mind of winter . . .

The poem ends with the line about seeing "nothing that is not there and the nothing that is." A small poem in Denise Levertov's last book, *Sands of the Well,* may have had this poem in mind:

Seeing the Unseen

Snow, large flakes,
whirling in midnight air,
unseen, coming to rest

on a fast-asleep, very small village
set among rocky fields: not one
lit square of wakeful window.

JANUARY 19

In Memoriam: William Matthews

Before Denise Levertov died in December, one of the gifted poets of my generation, William Matthews, died, at the age of fifty-six, of heart failure, in New York City on a November evening while he was getting ready to go with his lover to the opera. Bill had style—a learned, bitter, brilliant wit, an easy elegance that he liked to entangle and roughen. I think he always wanted to be a jazz musician and, often, he wrote like one. And he was attentive to moments of grace in the botched world. A friend once said of him that he had the most forgiving of unforgiving eyes. The last poem in his last book, *Time and Money* (Houghton Mifflin), was about opera and the world; his wicked wit is in it and the things he cared about in art:

A Night at the Opera

"The tenor's too fat," the beautiful young
woman complains, "and the soprano
dowdy and old." But what if Otello's
not black, if Rigoletto's hump lists,
if airy Gilda and her entourage
of flesh outweigh the cello section?

In fairy tales, the prince has a good heart,
and so as an outward and visible
sign of an inward, invisible grace,
his face is not creased, nor are his limbs gnarled.
Our tenor holds in his liver-spotted
hands the soprano's broad, burgeoning face.

Their combined age is ninety-seven; there's
spittle in both pinches of her mouth;
a vein in his temple twitches like a worm.
Their faces are a foot apart. His eyes
widen with fear as he climbs to the high
B-flat he'll have to hit and hold for five

dire seconds. And then they'll stay in their stalled
hug for as long as we applaud. Franco
Corelli once bit Birgit Nilsson's ear
in just such a command embrace because
he felt she'd upstaged him. Their costumes weigh
fifteen pounds apiece; they're poached in sweat

and smell like fermenting pigs; their voices rise
and twine not from beauty, nor from the lack
of it, but from the hope for accuracy
and passion, both. They have to hit the note
and the emotion, both, with the one poor
arrow of the voice. Beauty's for amateurs.

Bill Matthews published ten books of poems, and I'm told he finished another before his death. It helps to think that new book will be appearing and a collected poems after that. It will give us some time to absorb his passion and his accuracy, both.

JANUARY 25

Frank Bidart

Here is a poem that imagines Lady Bird Johnson contemplating with a kind of practical sadness the fact that she and her husband will never be loved as their predecessors were loved. In the poem Mrs. Johnson knows this because her mother died young, and she knows how her father's gaze rested on her, when it did. The poet tells the story as briefly as possible. It isn't a dire poem, but in its quiet way the territory it inhabits is implacable: in this life the heart is going to be injured.

Lady Bird

Neither an invalid aunt who had been asked to care for a sister's little girl, to fill the dead sister's place, nor the child herself

did, could: not in my Daddy's eyes—nor
should they;

   so when we followed that golden couple into the White House

I was aware that people look at
the living, and wish for the dead.

This comes from a new book, *Desire* (Farrar, Straus & Giroux) by Frank Bidart. He's one of our most powerful poets and in some ways one of the strangest. His poems are almost always intense; they deal with what's most irreparable and terrible in living. The figures in his poems are often transfigured by the painfulness of life, and they are not saved by it. Bidart isn't interested in the formulas of redemption. As in the great tragedies, the source of the light that shines from his poems is conscious suffering, no more but no less.

The strangeness of his work has to do with its bluntness, the often abstract language, and with the way he uses his sources. He likes to represent to us instances from his wide and curious reading of some of the most basic dilemmas of the human condition, refashioned in a stark, contemporary language. This poem must have come from a biography of Lady Bird Johnson. Another poem seems to be a recasting of a sonnet from Dante's fourteenth-century meditation on love, *La Vita Nuova*. In early Italian poetry "EROS" or "AMOR"—the name of the god is capitalized in the first printings of these poems—is a long way from our cute little Cupid. He is usually a young male figure, terrible in his beauty. In this poem Bidart does a harsh, almost ragged contemporary version of the classic Italian sonnet—two quatrains and two triple-rhymed three-line stanzas—to give us what seems to be a dream or an allegory of the awful and devouring power of love and its loss:

Love Incarnate

To all those driven berserk or humanized by love
this is offered, for I need help
deciphering my dream.
When we love our lord is LOVE.

When I recall that at the fourth hour
of the night, watched by shining stars,
LOVE at last became incarnate,
the memory is horror.

In his hands smiling LOVE held my burning
heart, and in his arms, the body whose greeting
pierces my soul, now wrapped in bloodred, sleeping.

He made him wake. He ordered him to eat
my heart. He ate my burning heart. He ate it
submissively, as if afraid, as LOVE wept.

All of Frank Bidart's earlier books have been gathered in a single vol-
ume, *In the Western Night,* also from Farrar, Straus & Giroux.

FEBRUARY I

A Polish Poet: Adam Zagajewski

One of my favorite contemporary poets is Adam Zagajewski, a Polish
poet who lives in Paris. Zagajewski was a member of the generation of
Polish writers who came of age during the Solidarity years. Two volumes
of translations of his poems have been published in English, *Tremor* and
Canvas, both from Farrar, Straus & Giroux, and two volumes of his essays,
Solidarity, Solitude (Ecco Press) and *Two Cities* (Farrar, Straus & Giroux),
imaginative and surprising books about politics and art. Lately, he has
been teaching half the year in Houston. And here, from his new book,
Mysticism for Beginners (Farrar, Straus & Giroux), is a poem that comes out

of that experience. It's a poem of the idling mind in that hour of dusk when consciousness flickers like a pilot light:

Houston, 6 P.M.

Europe already sleeps beneath a coarse plaid of borders
and ancient hatreds: France nestled
up to Germany, Bosnia in Serbia's arms,
Lobely Sicily in azure seas.

It's early evening here, the lamp is lit
and the dark sun swiftly fades.
I'm alone. I read a little, think a little,
listen to a little music.

I'm where there's friendship,
but no friends, where enchantment
grows without magic,
where the dead laugh.

I'm alone because Europe is sleeping. My love
sleeps in a tall house on the outskirts of Paris.
In Krakow and Paris my friends
wade in the same river of oblivion.

I read and think; in one poem
I found the phrase "There are blows so terrible…
Don't ask!" I don't. A helicopter
breaks the evening quiet.

Poetry calls us to a higher life,
but what's low is just as eloquent,
more plangent than Indo-European,
stronger than my books and records.

There are no nightingales or blackbirds here
with their sad, sweet cantilenas,

only the mockingbird who imitates
and mimics every living voice.

Poetry summons us to life, to courage
in the face of the growing shadow.
Can you gaze calmly at the Earth
like the perfect astronaut?

Out of harmless indolence, the Greece of books,
and the Jerusalem of memory there suddenly appears
the island of a poem, unpeopled;
some new Cook will discover it one day.

Europe is already sleeping. Night's animals,
mournful and rapacious,
move in for the kill.
Soon America will be sleeping, too.

The translator is Clare Cavanagh. It's a complicated poem—the exile at a loss in a place where he cannot feel roots, or rather like some seed beginning tentatively to send out roots; the acute sense of the violence of history, the oddness of the circadian rhythms of our lives in relation to that violence, the ordinariness of sleeping and waking. Zagajewski's sense of the power of art—of books, music, poetry—is never ironic. In his work Earth belongs to the shadow, poetry to courage and the light. But in this poem, anyway, poetry is an island, unpeopled, waiting to be discovered, and in the last stanza the night animals are moving in. A rather terrible lullaby.

There are perhaps a couple of details to gloss. The line "There are blows so terrible... Don't ask" comes from the great Peruvian poet César Vallejo who died in 1938. This comes from the first line of the title poem of his first book, *Los Heraldos Negros (The Black Messengers)*. It is a book and a poem very much worth looking up. And another detail: there are, of course, blackbirds in Texas, but not *Turdus merula,* the European blackbird, which is a species of thrush and has a very rich song.

Zagajewski's essays and poems are worth getting to know. Both can be radiant, sharply intelligent, suffused with an irony bred of Eastern Europe's encounter with history, but full also of unexpected joy. *Mysticism for Beginners* has these qualities, also a restless melancholy, as if, when history takes an encouraging turn, as it has in Poland, the despairing landscapes that we carry inside us and that the world keeps echoing with renewed violence and misery elsewhere become more clear.

Note: Adam Zagajewski continues to spend time in Houston, but he has moved to Krakow from Paris, and a volume of selected poems in translation has appeared, Without End, *and another collection of prose,* In Defense of Ardor *(both published by Farrar, Straus & Giroux).*

A Question of Decency: Walt Whitman

Walt Whitman's *Leaves of Grass* has been in the news again. Of course, if poetry is news that stays news, it should be. It is, after all, one of the great books in American literature, as wild, alive, and surprising now as on the day it first appeared, and it's also a profound argument for the idea that the spirit of sympathy for other people and their problems is the root spirit of American democracy. But this time around, because it was given as a gift by a president to a White House intern, it was described by one print journalist as "a favorite passed among lovers, specifically for one poem, 'Song of Myself,' with its intimations of oral sex in Canto 5." I've seen at least one television journalist ogle at the mention of the book's name. Walt Whitman might have been amused, if he had not had his own troubles with official Washington. Here, to put the matter in perspective, is the fifth section of "Song of Myself," the famous account of the ecstatic union of body and soul, and the way it returns us to the world, alive with attention:

> I believe in you my soul, the other I am must not abase itself to you,
> And you must not be abased to the other.
>
> Loafe with me on the grass, loose the stop from your throat,
> Not words, not music or rhyme I want, not custom or lecture,
>   not even the best,
> Only the lull I like, the hum of your valvèd voice.

I mind how once we lay such a transparent summer morning,
How you settled your head athwart my hips and gently turn'd over
    upon me,
And parted the shirt from by bosom-bone, and plunged your
    tongue to my bare-stript heart,
And reach'd till you felt my beard, and reach'd till you felt my feet.

Swiftly arose and spread around me the peace and knowledge that
    pass all the arguments of the earth,
And I know the hand of God is the promise of my own,
And I know the spirit of God is the brother of my own,
And that all the men born are also my brothers, and the women
    my sisters and lovers,
And that a kelson of the creation is love,
And limitless are leaves stiff and drooping in the fields,
And brown ants in the little wells beneath them,
And mossy scabs of the worm fence, heap'd stones, elder, mullein
    and poke-weed.

But let me stray from scandal a moment to gloss the poem. "Kelson" is a wonderful old term from nineteenth-century boatmaking. It means the bar of wood at the bottom of a boat that fastens the floor timbers to the keel: "The kelson of creation is love." "Worm fence" is another old American term. Here's a passage from an English traveler's book of 1796, describing the characteristic look of the American countryside: "They place split logs angular-wise on each other making what they call a "worm-fence" and which is raised about five feet high."

Walt Whitman came to Washington in 1863 to volunteer as a nurse with a commission from the YMCA. There were forty or fifty tent-hospitals in those days of the worst fighting of the Civil War, and rare breezes in the muggy summer were said to carry the moans of young men and the reek of gangrene across Capitol Hill. Whitman spent his days in the grim and overcrowded wards, ministering to young soldiers. It was at this time that he wrote these other well-known lines from *Leaves of Grass:*

Come sweet death! be persuaded O beautiful death!
In mercy come quickly.

He also visited Congress and listened to the proceedings: "Much gab, great fear of public opinion, plenty of low business talent, but no masterful man."

According to his biographer Justin Kaplan, he began to look for work when his money ran out, his health nearly broken by the long hours in the hospital. But Washington, you will be surprised to learn, was full of literary critics and keepers of the public morality. A friend went to the secretary of the Treasury, Salmon Chase, to ask about getting Whitman a clerk's position at the Treasury. He brought with him a letter from Ralph Waldo Emerson recommending Whitman as one of America's great writers. Chase turned down Whitman's application because he had written a "very bad book" and was "a decidedly disreputable person." However, Secretary Chase, who collected autographs, kept Emerson's letter of recommendation: "I have nothing of Emerson's in his handwriting, and I shall be glad to keep this."

Eventually Whitman got a position as a clerk at the Department of the Interior in the Office of Indian Affairs. He had hardly settled in when a new secretary, Senator James Harlan of Iowa, took over the department. Harlan was a militant Methodist. Also, according to Mark Twain, a "great Injun pacificator and land dealer." He fired Whitman immediately: "I will not have the author of that book in this department." And while he was at it, he fired everyone "whose conduct does not come within the rules of decorum and propriety prescribed by a Christian Civilization," including all the women in the department, since he regarded their presence as "injurious to . . . the morals of the men."

"The meanest feature of it all," the old poet remembered years later in Camden, "was not his dismissal of me, but his rooting around in my desk in the dead of night looking for evidence against me."

FEBRUARY 15

Stanley Plumly

Here's a poem of Washington, D.C., on a winter day. It's by Stanley Plumly, from his book *The Marriage in the Trees* (Ecco Press):

Farragut North

In the tunnel-light at the top of the station two or three
figures huddled under tarps built against the wind crossing
Connecticut at K. It'll be noon before they rise in their
Navajo blankets, trinkets, ski masks and gloves to start the
day, noon before the oil slicks of ice on the sidewalks thaw.—
In the forties, after the war, in the land of Uz, when
somebody came to the house for a handout, my mother'd give
him milk money or bread money as well as bread and milk.
To her each day was the thirties. The men at the door had the
hard-boiled faces of veterans, soldiers of the enemy. My
mother saw something in them, homelessness the condition
of some happiness, as if in the faces of these drifters could be
read pieces of parts of herself still missing: like the Indian
woman in Whitman's *Sleepers* who comes to his mother's door
looking for work where there is no work yet is set by the fire
and fed: so that for my mother, the first time she left, it
became a question of whom to identify with most, the
wanderer or the welcomer.—The stunted sycamores on K are
terminal, though they'll outlast the hairline fractures marbling
the gravestones of the buildings. Under the perfect pavement
of the sky the figures frozen in this landscape contemplate the
verities too fundamentally for city or country: their isolation
is complete, like the dead or gods. When I think of a day with
nothing in it, a string of such days, I think of the gray life of
buildings, of walking out of my life in a direction just
invented, or, since some of us survive within mental wards
of our own third worlds, I see myself disguised for constant
winter, withdrawn into the inability to act on the least impulse
save anger and hear myself in street-talk talking street-time.
—Such is the freedom of transformation, letting the deep
voice climb on its own: such is the shell of the body broken,
falling away like money's new clothes; such is my mother's
truant spirit, moving dead leaves with the wind among
shadows . . .

I can tell you what interests me about this poem technically. Poets in the sixteenth century used to describe a poem that shoulders out past the usual base of ten syllables as written in a "strong line." This poem seems to have a base of fourteen syllables; it gets longer than that, but no shorter, except in the second to last line. And it does what poems based on syllable count often do: it mostly ignores the line-end, sweeps right past it, ends the line raggedly on articles and prepositions. And this usually doesn't work very well with a long-lined poem; it tends to make the line itself as a musical measure disintegrate so that you get a feeling that you're reading chopped-up prose, unless the forward momentum of the sentences and the thought gathers you with it. Which, I think, in this poem they do.

Everyone projects their own dramas onto street people and probably projects different dramas at different times. I like the way this poem's long breath, impatient, impelled forward, doesn't have breathless urgency, which is the effect you'd most likely get from this technique. Instead it feels like the long breaths of hard walking in the cold. Plumly grew up in rural Ohio and Virginia and teaches now at the University of Maryland. He's long been admired as a poet and critic, and in both his poetry and criticism he's been interested in John Keats, has written a poetry that seemed American and Southern but could be gorgeous in the way of Keats. So there is something surprising for people who know his work in the toughness and force of this poem.

What moves and interests me about it though is what any reader would probably get from it whether they knew his work or took an interest in technique. The way the city's homeless in the winter set him to thinking about old American archetypes, his mother's kitchen-door kindness to strangers, tough strangers, as a habit of the Depression years, and the memory of the beautiful passage in Whitman about the Indian woman at his mother's door in rural nineteenth-century Long Island, these makeshift and homemade charities of another age. And then the reversal comes: that his mother was one of these wanderers. And then the question for all of us about whom we identify with in the sentimental (but practical enough) tableaus of charity. And then the end of the poem, which seems to me curiously adult and bitter with an uncomfortable mix of wistfulness and emptiness in it. And there's another darkness here, I suppose. This is, after all, the capitol city, the symbolic repository of an idea of freedom. Wanderer, welcomer, body broken, truant spirit, all of us with our private wounds and longings for transformation.

FEBRUARY 22

Sonia Sanchez

One of the nominees this year for the National Book Critics Circle Award in poetry is Sonia Sanchez's *Does Your House Have Lions?* (Beacon Press). It's a book-length narrative poem about a Southern black family come to New York in the 1960s. The speakers are a young brother who has plunged into the gay subculture of the city and into the civil rights movement and who ultimately dies of AIDS; a Southern father afraid for his children and guilty at his neglect of them; a sister who must come to terms with her anger and grief; ancestral voices that speak the story against the background of African American life. It's written in a series of intricately rhymed seven-line stanzas, each one a small song.

Here's the sister speaking of her seventeen-year-old brother, who is on the scene in Manhattan:

> and the bars. the glitter. the light
> discharging pain from his bygone anguish
> of young black boy scared of the night.
> sequestered on this new bank, he surveyed the fish
> sweet cargoes crowded with scales feverish
> with quick sales full sails of flesh
> searing the coastline of his acquiesce.

Here is the brother drawn out of the life of the bars by a new voice in the streets:

> came the summer of nineteen sixty
> harlem luxuriating in Malcolm's voice
> became Big Red beautiful became a city
> of magnificent Black Birds steel eyes moist

as he insinuated his words of sweet choice
while politicians complained about this racist
this alchemist. this strategist. this purist.

Here is the father who has not been there for his son:

i was a southern Negro man playing music
married to a high yellow woman who loved my unheard
face, who slept with me in nordic
beauty. i prisoner since my birth to fear
i unfashioned buried in an open grave
of mornings unclapped with constant sight
of masters fattened decked with my diminished light.

Here are the ancestral voices that end the poem:

have you prepared a place of honor for me?
have you recalled us from death?
where is the *mmenson* to state our history?
where are the griots the food my failed breath?
where is the morning path i crossed in good faith?
what terror slows your journey to this dawn?
have you prepared a place for us to mourn?

In a note Sanchez explains that a *mmenson* is an "orchestra of seven
elephant tusk horns used on state occasions to relate history." This is a
metaphor for her seven-line stanza, seven horn flourishes to tell the story
and preserve the memory.

MARCH I

Marie Howe

Marie Howe's new book, her second book of poems, is called *What the
Living Do* (Norton). Many of the poems deal with a beloved brother's
death from AIDS, but the book begins with poems of childhood and
adolescence. The boys' fort that the girls couldn't go into. The initiation

where boys tie up girls, and things start to get out of hand, and the one boy the girls might trust is afraid to say, "Stop it." The pajama parties where girls talk about boys and practice kissing. They're delicious poems, and they have the effect of making you understand how powerful the love between a brother and sister can be, and what it might mean to have your older brother and protector die before your eyes.

Howe's way with language is very spare. Many of the poems have a stripped-down, point-blank quality that gives them a certain radiance. Here's one:

The Last Time

The last time we had dinner together in a restaurant
with white tablecloths, he leaned forward

and took my two hands in his hands and said,
I'm going to die soon. I want you to know that.

And I said, I think I do know.
And he said, What surprises me is that you don't.

And I said, I do. And he said, What?
And I said, Know that you're going to die.

And he said, No, I mean know that you are.

Here's another:

The Promise

In the dream I had when he came back not sick
but whole, and wearing his winter coat,

he looked at me as though he couldn't speak, as if
there were a law against it, a membrane he couldn't break.

His silence was what he could not
not do, like our breathing in this world, like our living,

as we do, in time.
And I told him: I'm reading all this Buddhist stuff,

and listen, we don't die when we die. Death is an event,
a threshold we pass through. We go on and on

and into light forever.
And he looked down, and then back up at me. It was the look
   we'd pass

across the table when Dad was drunk again and dangerous,
the level look that wants to tell you something,

in a crowded room, something important, and can't.

MARCH 8

John Koethe

I've been reading an extraordinarily interesting book of poems, *Falling Water* (HarperPerennial) by John Koethe. It interests me so much because one of his subjects is the kind of psychic withdrawal from public life that many people who came of age in the 1960s underwent.

I hadn't really thought about that time for a while or my own experience of it. Think about the young Americans who grew up having the protected childhoods of the 1950s, threw themselves ardently into the civil rights movement and the peace movement, found their heroes in public figures like John and Robert Kennedy and Martin Luther King and Malcolm X, and saw them assassinated one by one, gunshots that rang through the decade. And there was more: the shots fired at Kent State by National Guardsmen in the wake of yet another escalation of the war, the inconclusive and belated American withdrawal from Vietnam, the investigation of burglaries sanctioned by a sitting president. These same young people found themselves a few years later in the middle of adult life in Ronald Reagan's America when the public style was conspicuous indulgence, the gap between rich and poor was growing, and the media heroes were millionaires like Donald Trump.

What happened to many of them was a retreat into private life, a kind of internal exile they only half-recognized themselves, and it's a story that hasn't been registered in our literature very well. Koethe's book is about disappointment in many forms. But I think one of the things he's trying to do is find a way to speak about this generational experience from the point of view of a writer. The language of the poems is calm, analytical, even abstract, and there is a dry anguish in it, an undertow of complex and baffled emotion. The quality of the language may have to do with the fact that he is a philosopher by profession. He's written a book about Ludwig Wittgenstein.

It doesn't make for easy poems, but reading him I felt the "shock of recognition" that lets you know you're in the presence of real writing. See what you think:

Morning in America

It gradually became a different country
After the reversal, dominated by a distant,
Universal voice whose favorite word was *never,*
Changing its air of quiet progress into one of
Rapidly collapsing possibilities, and making me,
Even here at home, a stranger. I felt its tones
Engaging me without expression, leaving me alone
And waiting in the vacuum of its public half-life,
Quietly confessing my emotions, taking in its cold
Midwinter atmosphere of violence and muted rage. I
Wanted to appropriate that anger, to convey it, not
In a declamatory mode, but in some vague and private
Language holding out, against the clear, inexorable
Disintegration of a nation, the claims of a renewed
Internal life, in these bleak months of the new year.
That was my way of ruling out everything discordant,
Everything dead, cruel, and soulless—by assiduously
Imagining the pages of some legendary volume marked
Forever, but without ever getting any closer. As I

Got older it began to seem more and more hopeless,
More and more detached—until it only spoke to me
Impersonally, like someone gradually retreating,
Not so much from his life as from its settings,
From the country he inhabits; as the darkness
Deepens in the weeks after the solstice.

What gets set against this in the book is a world older readers will recognize and younger readers have heard the legends of. For example, the first poem, "From the Porch," begins like this:

The stores were bright, and not too far from home.
The school was only a half a mile from downtown

A nice detail: the time before malls, shopping centers. That reassuring rhythm is the English pentameter, right out of Shakespeare and Longfellow. Later, he lets it swell a little to evoke that other time more fully:

                            . . . a small midwestern town
Some forty years ago, before the elm trees died.
September was a modern classroom and the latest cars,
That made a sort of futuristic dream, circa 1955.
The earth was still uncircled. You could set your course
On the day after tomorrow. And children fell asleep
To the lullaby of people murmuring softly in the kitchen,
While a breeze rustled the pages of *Life* magazine
And the wicker chairs stood empty on the screened-in porch.

MARCH 15

Sylvia Plath

The appearance of Ted Hughes's *Birthday Letters* has gotten so much attention in the press that even my local baker asked me about it the other morning when I stopped for coffee. "What's the deal?" he asked. My impulse was to lend him the book. I said that Ted Hughes was the

English poet laureate, a Yorkshireman, and that he wrote poems about the natural world in something like the spirit of D. H. Lawrence, including a mythic book about the darkness of just about everything called *Crow*—a crow-eat-crow book about the fierceness and terror of the world, and that thirty years ago he'd been married to a brilliant American poet, that it was a difficult marriage, that they were living in the country in Dorset on the west coast of England when the marriage blew up, that when Hughes left her for another woman they had a five-month-old baby and a toddler about three, that she moved to London and in the middle of the coldest winter of the century, feeling abandoned and enraged, she shut herself in the kitchen, taped the doors, and, just before the babysitter was to arrive, stuck her head in a gas oven and killed herself. I said that there had been earlier suicide attempts, that she'd written a novel about one of them, that her poems appeared after her death edited by her husband and made her famous, and that he was now years later supposedly telling his side of the story.

I felt like I was summarizing a soap opera, not sure which details were the relevant ones, the ones that would answer his question. So I found myself tailing off and said, "You know, what you should do first is read her poems," and the next morning I dropped off a copy of Sylvia Plath's *Ariel*.

Here is a poem from that time. It was written in October 1962, after Hughes had left and before she had moved from the cottage in Dorset. The person in the poem is imagined to be speaking to a baby, trying to put a baby to sleep. They are in candlelight, and the brass candlestick has on it a figure of Atlas, who seems to be lifting up the candle, and as she speaks the figure of Atlas becomes the figure, maybe, for the absent father, or maybe a figure for the woman herself, or for the effort of art. Atlas is holding up all the light there is. It's not like a soap opera; things stand for more than one thing, stand for opposite things at once. We're in the territory of poetry:

By Candlelight

This is winter, this is night, small love—
A sort of black horsehair,
A rough, dumb country stuff
Steeled with the sheen

Of what green stars can make it to our gate.
I hold you on my arm.
It is very late.
The dull bells tongue the hour.
The mirror floats us at one candle power.

This is the fluid in which we meet each other,
This haloey radiance that seems to breathe
And lets our shadows wither
Only to blow
Them huge again, violent giants on the wall.
One match scratch makes you real.
At first the candle will not bloom at all—
It snuffs its bud
To almost nothing, to a dull blue dud.

I hold my breath until you creak to life,
Balled hedgehog,
Small and cross. The yellow knife
Grows tall. You clutch your bars.
My singing makes you roar.
I rock you like a boat
Across the Indian carpet, the cold floor,
While the brass man
Kneels, back bent, as best he can

Hefting his white pillar with the light
That keeps the sky at bay,
The sack of black! It is everywhere, tight, tight!
He is yours, the little brassy Atlas—
Poor heirloom, all you have,
At his heels a pile of five brass cannonballs,
No child, no wife.
Five balls! Five bright brass balls!
To juggle with, my love, when the sky falls.

This version comes from Sylvia Plath's *Collected Poems,* published by HarperPerennial. The line I find myself thinking about is "One match scratch makes you real." Literally, it's about becoming visible in the mirror when the candle is lit. It's also probably a metaphor for conception, for the flare of sex. And the famous line of Shakespeare's Macbeth must hover around it: "Out, out, brief candle."

Next week, Ted Hughes.

MARCH 22

Ted Hughes

In 1972, nine years after the death of Sylvia Plath and one year after the woman he had left her for had killed both herself and her child, Ted Hughes published a book called *Crow.* I think it's a more interesting book than his *Birthday Letters,* which is now on best-seller lists because people are so curious about the Plath–Hughes marriage and about his life, which has looked to the world cursed or culpable, or both. Here are a couple of poems from that earlier book:

Crow's Nerve Fails

Crow, feeling his brain slip,
Finds his every feather the fossil of a murder.

Who murdered all these?
These living dead, that root in his nerves and his blood
Till he is visibly black?

How can he fly from his feathers?
And why have they homed on him?

Is he the archive of their accusations?
Or their ghostly purpose, their pining vengeance?
Or their unforgiven prisoner?

He cannot be forgiven.

His prison is the earth. Clothed in his conviction,
Trying to remember his crimes

Heavily he flies.

Lovesong

He loved her and she loved him
His kisses sucked out her whole past and future or tried to
He had no other appetite
She bit him she gnawed him she sucked
She wanted him complete inside her
Safe and sure forever and ever
Their little cries fluttered into the curtains

Her eyes wanted nothing to get away
Her looks nailed down his hands his wrists his elbows
He gripped her hard so that life
Should not drag her from that moment
He wanted all future to cease
He wanted to topple with his arms round her
Off that moment's brink and into nothing
Or everlasting or whatever there was
Her embrace was an immense press
To print him into her bones
His smiles were the garrets of a fairy palace
Where the real world would never come
Her smiles were spider bites
So he would lie still till she felt hungry
His words were occupying armies
Her laughs were an assassin's attempts
His looks were bullets daggers of revenge
His glances were ghosts in the corner with horrible secrets
His whispers were whips and jackboots
Her kisses were lawyers steadily writing

His caresses were the last hooks of a castaway
Her love-tricks were the grinding of locks
And their deep cries crawled over the floors
Like an animal dragging a great trap
His promises were the surgeon's gag
Her promises took the top off his skull
She would get a brooch made of it
His vows pulled out all her sinews
He showed her how to make a love-knot
Her vows put his eyes in formalin
At the back of her secret drawer
Their screams stuck in the wall

Their heads fell apart into sleep like the two halves
Of a lopped melon, but love is hard to stop

In their entwined sleep they exchanged arms and legs
In their dreams their brains took each other hostage

In the morning they wore each other's face

MARCH 29

Spring, and a New Translation of Horace

It's spring. And here's a chance to print a song of the season that comes from a very old, sun-lit, Mediterranean sanity. Also a chance to notice a remarkable new book.

One of the central poets to the history of lyric poetry in the European tradition is Quintus Horatius Flaccus, whom we know as Horace. He was born into the turmoil of Roman history when Rome was emerging as a world power. He fought, as a young man in those turbulent years, in the wars that followed the assassination of Julius Caesar, and wrote most of his poems in the age of Augustus.

With Catullus and Vergil and Ovid, he's one of the four great lyric poets of ancient Rome, studied and studied by English poets when all schoolchildren studied Latin and English poetry was finding its way. Indeed for English poets from Shakespeare's time to the end of the nineteenth century, he was the man. He spent most of his life in retirement—he practically invented the idea of "retirement" for European culture—on a modest Sabine farm in the country outside Rome. He wrote immensely civilized, poised, exquisitely polished, and apparently casual poems about the countryside and the Roman seasons, about not living in whatever the Augustan equivalents were for the corridors of power and the feeding frenzies of the media and the fevers of the deal.

His values were the gentleman farmer's ideals. Balance was what he admired, independence, privacy, friendship, a sensible prosperity, good wine, the fruits of the season. Republican rather than Empire in a Roman—and probably in an American—sense. All of the founding fathers of the American republic had learned their Latin by translating his poems as schoolboys, and many of their assumptions (including the assumption, much uneasier in the Americans, of a slave-owning economy) were Horace's assumptions. Thomas Jefferson's vision, though he thought it would take a revolution to get there, was, I think it's accurate to say, Horatian.

These are reasons to read Horace, but the deepest reason is pleasure. He's a beguiling poet. Reading him in stray moments for weeks on end is, I've been finding, like carrying around a particularly delicious and soothing dream-trace. "Soothing" isn't quite accurate for the complexity of Horace's mind, but it was the idea of him for the poets of the early twentieth century, which is why he fell out of favor and why he hasn't really had a good English translator—until now—in this century. But now there is one. David Ferry, a New England poet and a Wordsworth scholar, has published a complete translation of Horace's most famous work, *The Odes of Horace* (Farrar, Straus & Giroux), and it's wonderful to read, as if it were composed in the mind's own suave version of English Latin. The *Odes* have to be lived with—they'll make great summer reading of a mellow and reflective kind—and one sample won't convey that. But here's the flavor—cut to a spring day in Italy two thousand years ago where Horace's friend Lucius Sestius is worried about his place in society and about his love life:

To Sestius

Now the hard winter is breaking up with the welcome coming
    Of spring and the spring winds; some fishermen,
Under a sky that looks changed, are hauling their caulked boats
    Down to the water; in the winter stables the cattle
Are restless; so is the farmer sitting in front of his fire;
    They want to be outdoors in field or pasture;
The frost is gone from the meadow grass in the early mornings.
    Maybe, somewhere, the Nymphs and Graces are dancing,
Under the moon the goddess Venus and her dancers;
    Somewhere far in the depth of a cloudless sky
Vulcan is getting ready the storms of the coming summer.
    Now is the time to garland your shining hair
With myrtle or with the flowers the free-giving earth has given;
    Now is the right time to offer the kid or lamb
In sacrifice to Faunus in the firelit shadowy grove.

Revenant white-faced Death is walking not knowing whether
    He's going to knock at a rich man's door or a poor man's.
O good-looking fortunate Sestius, don't put your hope in the
    future;
    The night is falling; the shades are gathering around;
The walls of Pluto's shadowy house are closing you in.
    Those who will be lord of the feast? What will it matter,
What will it matter there, whether you feel in love with Lycidas,
    This or that girl with him, or he with her?

APRIL 5

Passover: Linda Pastan

Next Saturday is Passover. Here's a poem by Linda Pastan, from her new
book *Carnival Evening: New and Selected Poems 1968–1998* (Norton), a gath-
ering of thirty years' work. If there is a poet of the Washington, D.C.,
region in this generation, she is it—though she's more than that. This is an

early poem, from 1971; it's about Passover, it's also about being an American Jew, and it may be about slavery and the civil rights movement of those years and the Vietnam war, and about evolution as a kind of migration, and about poverty in America, and about being a mother. Look at the range of themes she draws together:

Passover

1.
I set my table with metaphor:
the curling parsely—green sign nailed to the doors
of God's underground; salt of the desert and eyes;
the roasted shank bone of a Paschal Lamb,
relic of sacrifice and bleating spring.
Down the long table, past fresh shoots of a root
they have been hacking at for centuries,
you hold up the unleavened bread—a baked scroll
whose wavy lines are indecipherable.

2.
The wise son and the wicked, the simple son
and the son who doesn't ask, are all my son
leaning tonight as it is written,
slouching his father calls it. His hair is long:
hippie hair, hassid hair, how strangely alike
they seem tonight. First Born, a live child cried
among the bulrushes, but the only root
you know stirs between your legs, ready
to spill its seed in gentile gardens.
And if the flowers be delicate and fair,
I only mind this one night of the year
when far beyond the lights of Jersey,
Jerusalem still beckons us, in tongues.

3.

What black-throated bird
in a warm country
sings spirituals,
sings spirituals
to Moses now?

4.

One exodus prefigures the next.
The glaciers fled before hot whips of air.
Waves bowed at God's gesture
for fugitive Israel to pass;
while fish, caught then behind windows
of water, remembered how their brothers once
pulled themselves painfully from the sea,
willing legs to grow
from slanted fins.
Now the blossoms pass from April's tree,
refugee raindrops mar the glass,
borders are transitory.
And the changeling gene, still seeking
stone sanctuary, moves on.

5.

Far from Egypt, I have sighted blood,
have heard the throaty mating of frogs.
My city knows vermin, animals loose in hallways,
boils, sickness, hail.
In the suburban gardens
seventeen-year locusts rise
from their heavy beds
in small explosions of sod.
Darkness of newsprint.
My son, my son.

I think the locust-frenzy of newsprint at the end of the poem is Viet-
nam, though it could be any war we read about in papers and send our
children into.

APRIL 12

Easter: Mary Karr

Mary Karr's poignant, tough-talking memoir of a Texas Gulf childhood, *The Liar's Club,* was on best-seller lists for sixty weeks. It's probably the best-loved, most widely read work of literary nonfiction in this decade. Her newest book, her third book of verse, is called *Viper Rum,* and it's published by New Directions. Here, for Easter, is one of the poems:

The Grand Miracle

Jesus wound up with his body nailed to a tree—
a torment he practically begged for,
or at least did nothing to stop. Pilate

watched the crowd go thumbs down
and weary, signed the order.
So centurions laid Jesus flat

on a long beam, arms run along the crosspiece.
In each palm a long spike was centered,
a stone chosen to drive it. (Skin

tears; the bones start to split.)
Once the cross got propped up,
the body hung heavy, a carcass—

in carne, the Latin poets say, in meat.
(—The breastbone a ship's prow . . .)
At the end the man cried out

as men cry. (Tears that fill the eyes
grow dark drop by drop: One
cries out.) On the third day,

the stone rolled back, to reveal
no corpse. History is rife
with such hoaxes. (Look at Herodotus.)

As to whether he multiplied
loaves and fishes, that's common enough.
Poke seed-corn in a hole and see if more corn

doesn't grow. Two fish in a pond
make more fishes. The altar of reason
supports such extravagance. (I don't even know

how electricity works, but put trust
in light switches.) And the prospect
of love cheers me up, as gospel.

That some creator might strap on
an animal mask to travel our path between birth
and ignominious death—now that

makes me less lonely. And the rising up
at the end into glory—the white circle of bread
on the meat of each tongue that God

might enter us. For 2000-near years
my tribe has lined up at various altars,
so dumbly I open this mouth for bread and song.

APRIL 19

An Irish Poet: Derek Mahon

Derek Mahon belongs to the same generation of Northern Irish poets
as Seamus Heaney. Like Heaney, he was born in Belfast and educated at
Trinity College in Dublin. I have been thinking about his poems in these
days when the world is holding its breath over the Belfast agreements,
waiting to see if more sectarian violence will bring them down. In some
of his poems Mahon speaks—with irony so deep it's hard to gauge—
about hope for the future, for a normal future, as if he were trying to cast
a spell. This one, for example:

Everything Is Going to Be All Right

How should I not be glad to contemplate
the clouds clearing beyond the dormer window
and a high tide reflected on the ceiling?
There will be dying, there will be dying,
but there is no need to go into that.
The poems flow from the hand unbidden
and the hidden source is the watchful heart.
The sun rises in spite of everything
and the far cities are beautiful and bright.
I lie here in a riot of sunlight
watching the day break and the clouds flying.
Everything is going to be all right.

One of his best-known poems is an elegy for another Northern poet of an earlier generation, Louis MacNeice. It was this poem that brought Derek Mahon to mind. I was thinking of the way he plays with the idea of "future tense":

In Carrowdore Churchyard

Your ashes will not stir, even on this high ground,
However the wind tugs, the headstones shake.
This plot is consecrated, for your sake,
To what lies in the future tense. You lie
Past tension now, and spring is coming round
Igniting flowers on the peninsula.

Your ashes will not fly, however the rough winds burst
Through the wild brambles and the reticent trees.
All we may ask of you we have; the rest
Is not for publication, will not be heard.
Maguire, I believe, suggested a blackbird
And over your grave a phrase from Euripides.

Which suits you down to the ground, like this churchyard
With its play of shadow, its humane perspective.

Locked in the winter's fist, these hills are hard
As nails, yet soft and feminine in their turn
When fingers open and the hedges burn.
This, you implied, is how we ought to live.

The ironical, loving crush of roses against snow,
Each fragile, solving ambiguity. So
From the pneumonia of the ditch, from the ague
Of the blind poet and the bombed-out town you bring
The all-clear to the empty holes of spring,
Rinsing the choked mud, keeping the colors new.

Derek Mahon's *Selected Poems* is published by Penguin Books.

APRIL 26

Audubon's Birthday: Birds by Robert Frost, W. C. Williams, and Robinson Jeffers

Here are three poems by twentieth-century American masters for the birthday—which is today—of John James Audubon:

The Oven Bird

There is a singer everyone has heard,
Loud, a mid-summer and a mid-wood bird,
Who makes the solid tree trunks sound again.
He says the leaves are old and that for flowers
Mid-summer is to spring as one to ten.
He says the early petal-fall is past
When pear and cherry bloom went down in showers
On sunny days a moment overcast;
And comes that other fall we name the fall,
He says the highway dust is over all.
The bird would cease and be as other birds
But that he knows in singing not to sing.

The question that he frames in all but words
Is what to make of a diminished thing.

—Robert Frost,
Collected Poems, Prose & Plays, Library of America

To Waken an Old Lady

Old age is
a flight of small
cheeping birds
skimming
bare trees
above a snow glaze.
Gaining and failing
they are buffeted
by a dark wind—
But what?
On harsh weedstalks
the flock has rested,
the snow
is covered with broken
seedhusks
and the wind tempered
by a shrill
piping of plenty.

—William Carlos Williams,
Collected Poems: Volume I 1909–1939, New Directions

Vulture

I had walked since dawn and lay down to rest on a bare hillside
Above the ocean. I saw through half-shut eyelids a vulture
    wheeling high up in heaven,

And presently it passed again, but lower and nearer, its orbit
   narrowing, I understood then
That I was under inspection. I lay death-still and heard the
   flight-feathers
Whistle above me and make their circle and come nearer.
I could see the naked red head between the great wings
Bear downward staring. I said, "My dear bird, we are wasting
   time here.
These old bones will still work; they are not for you." But how
   beautiful he looked, gliding down
On those great sails; how beautiful he looked, veering away in the
   sea-light over the precipice. I tell you solemnly
That I was sorry to have disappointed him. To be eaten by that
   beak and become part of him, to share those wings and
   those eyes—
What a sublime end of one's body, what an enskyment;
   what a life after death.

—Robinson Jeffers, *Selected Poems,* Vintage Books

MAY 3

In Memoriam: Octavio Paz

I was in San Miguel Allende in January when I heard that Octavio Paz
was gravely ill. My hotel room had a rooftop patio. When I walked out
onto it at dawn, six thousand feet up in the Sierra Madre, I looked out at
a late Renaissance dome, eighteenth-century church spires, laundry lines,
utility lines, black rooftop cats gazing with what seemed religious rever-
ence at the pigeons they could not quite reach, and in the distance at the
lines of low bare hills that formed the high shallow valley of San Miguel.
Overhead there was a flock of what must have been two hundred cormo-
rants flying silently and swiftly north. In the dawn light it looked as if the
white sky were full of broken black crosses, a kind of aerial, fast-moving
cemetery. It could have been an image from one of his poems.

He was not only Mexico's greatest poet. He was one of the most remarkable literary figures of this half century. His essays are at least as compelling as his poems and a good way for English readers to get to know him. Paz's great prose book is probably his stunning meditation on the nature of poetry, *The Bow and the Lyre,* and there are others: his book-length essay on Mexico and Mexican culture, *The Labyrinth of Solitude,* and his biographical study of Mexico's great poet of the Colonial Period, Sor Juana de la Cruz, and his essays on history and politics, *One Earth, Four or Five Worlds,* and his essays on Mexican art. Only Czeslaw Milosz among the poets of his generation has had the same depth and range.

But he was a poet first of all. The best volumes of his work in English are *Selected Poems* and *A Tree Within,* both published by New Directions. Here is one of his poems, gorgeous in Spanish, and you can almost hear the original in this translation from *Selected Poems:*

Wind and Water and Stone

The water hollowed the stone,
the wind dispersed the water,
the stone stopped the wind.
Water and wind and stone.

The wind sculpted the stone,
the stone is a cup of water,
the water runs off and is wind.
Stone and wind and water.

The wind sings in its turnings,
the water murmurs as it goes,
the motionless stone is quiet.
Wind and water and stone.

One is the other, and is neither:
among their empty names
they pass and disappear,
water and stone and wind.

MAY 10

Mother's Day: Dorianne Laux

Here, for Mother's Day, is a poem from *What We Carry* by Dorianne Laux (BOA Editions). I like the mother in this poem, rendered in the vivid, circumstantial style of contemporary autobiographical poetry. The gesture with which the poem ends intrigues me:

The Ebony Chickering

My mother cooked with lard she kept
in coffee cans beneath the kitchen sink.
Bean-colored linoleum ticked under her flats
as she wore a path from stove to countertop.
Eggs cracked against the lips of smooth
ceramic bowls she beat muffins in,
boxed cakes and cookie dough.
It was the afternoons she worked toward,
the smell of onions scrubbed from her hands,
when she would fold her flowered apron
and feed it through the sticky refrigerator
handle, adjust the spongy curlers on her head
and wrap a loud Hawaiian scarf into a tired knot
around them as she walked toward her piano,
the one thing my father had given her that she loved.
I can still see each gold letter engraved
on the polished lid she lifted and slid
into the piano's dark body, the hidden hammers
trembling like a muffled word,
the scribbled sheets, her rough hands poised
above the keys as she began her daily practice.
Words like *arpeggio* sparkled through my childhood,
her fingers sliding from the black bar of a sharp
to the white of a common note. "This is Bach,"
she would instruct us, the tale of his name hissing
like a cat. "And Chopin," she said, "was French,
like us," pointing to the sheet music. "Listen.

Don't let the letters fool you. It's best
to always trust your ear."
She played parts of fugues and lost concertos,
played hard as we kicked each other on the couch,
while the meat burned and the wet wash wrinkled
in the basket, played Beethoven as if she understood
the caged world of the deaf, his terrible music
pounding its way through the fence slats
and the screened doors of the cul-de-sac, the yards
where other mothers hung clothes on a wire, bent
to weeds, swept the driveways clean.
Those were the years she taught us how to make
quick easy meals, accept the embarrassment
of a messy house, safety pins and rick-rack
hanging from the hem of her dress.
But I knew the other kids didn't own words
like *fortissimo* and *mordant, treble clef*
and *trill,* or have a mother quite as elegant
as mine when she sat at her piano,
playing like she was famous,
so that when the Sparklets man arrived
to fill our water cooler every week
he would lean against the doorjamb and wait
for her to finish, glossy-eyed
as he listened, secretly touching the tips
of his fingers to the tips of her fingers
as he bowed, and she slipped him the check.

Dorianne Laux lives in Eugene, Oregon, where she teaches creative
writing.

MAY 17

Agha Shahid Ali

Agha Shahid Ali is a Kashmiri-born American poet who teaches in Amherst, Massachusetts. His newest book, *The Country Without a Post Office* (Norton), has as its main subject the violence in Kashmir that's gone on since 1990, mostly in the form of Muslim resistance to Hindu rule. Ali loves intricate poetic forms, and the book is full of them: *ghazals,* villanelles, *pantoums,* sonnets. It's a book of laments. Here is a poem that, because of its rhythms, has stuck in my mind ever since I read it. What the formal requirements of the ghazal are, you'll see as you read:

Ghazal

The only language of loss left in the world is Arabic—
These words were said to me in a language not Arabic.

Ancestors, you've left me a plot in the family graveyard—
Why must I look, in your eyes, for prayers in Arabic?

Majnoon, his clothes ripped, still weeps for Laila.
O, this is the madness of the desert, his crazy Arabic.

Who listens to Ishmael? Even now he cries out:
Abraham, throw away your knives, recite a psalm in Arabic.

From exile Mahmoud Darwish writes to the world:
You'll all pass between the fleeting words of Arabic.

The sky is stunned, it's become a ceiling of stone.
I tell you it must weep. So kneel, pray for rain in Arabic.

At an exhibition of miniatures, such delicate calligraphy:
Kashmiri paisleys tied into the golden hair of Arabic!

The Koran prophesied a fire of men and stones.
Well, it's all now come true, as it was said in the Arabic.

When Lorca died, they left the balconies open and saw:
his *qasidas* braided, on the horizon, into knots of Arabic.

Memory is no longer confused, it has a homeland—
Says Shammas: Territorialize each confusion in a graceful Arabic.

Where there were homes in Deir Yassein, you'll see dense forests—
That village was razed. There's no sign of Arabic.

I too, O Amichai, saw the dresses of beautiful women.
And everything else, just like you, in Death, Hebrew, and Arabic.

They ask me to tell them what *Shahid* means—
Listen: It means "The Beloved" in Persian, "witness" in Arabic.

This requires a gloss. But in a way the point is what Western read-
ers don't know about the Arabic tradition. So here is a partial gloss. The
ghazal, which originated in Persian and was written in Arabic all over the
Muslim world, is the Islamic equivalent of the sonnet. *Majnoon* and *Laila*
are—reader, look them up. *Ishmael,* in Muslim traditions, not Isaac, was
the son God demanded of Abraham as a sacrifice. *Mahmoud Darwish* is a
Palestinian poet. *Federico García Lorca,* the great Spanish poet executed
by Franco's fascists, wrote *qasidas,* old Spanish song forms derived from
Islam. *Anton Shammas* is a contemporary Palestinian novelist. *Deir Yessein*
is—reader, look it up. *Yehuda Amichai* is a contemporary Israeli poet.

This book is full of epigrams as haunting as the poems, especially now
when our country has undertaken, selectively, to be the world's peace-
keeper. One epigram comes from something a British chieftain said
about the Roman empire. It's quoted in Tacitus: "They make a desert and
they call it peace." Another comes from the Serbian-born American poet
Charles Simic: "No human being or group of people has the right to pass
a death sentence on a city."

*Note: Agha Shahid Ali died of brain cancer in December 2001 at the age of fifty-
two. He was a charming man, witty, sociable, a wonderful cook, and much loved
by his friends, one of whom reported on his state of mind when he was undergoing
chemotherapy. "Darling," he told her on the phone, "I've lost all my hair. If I say
so myself, I look very sexy." His last book was* Rooms Are Never Finished

(Norton, 2002). Readers will also want to look at Ravishing Disunities *(Gibbs M. Smith), a book he edited of ghazals in English, and at* The Rebel's Silhouette *(University of Massachusetts Press), his translations from Urdu of the twentieth-century Pakistani poet Faiz Ahmed Faiz.*

MAY 24

Margaret Atwood

Margaret Atwood is best known, of course, as a novelist. But she brings to her poetry the same sharp eye and stinging, ironic wit. Here's a poem from her new book, *Morning in the Burned House* (Houghton Mifflin). The book contains a moving sequence of elegies for her father, but this poem belongs to her satiric vein. It's for the boys, and the women who love them:

Romantic

Men and their mournful romanticisms
that can't get the dishes done—
that's freedom, that broken wineglass
in the cold fireplace.

When women wash underpants, it's a chore.
When men do it, an intriguing affliction.
How plangent, the damp socks flapping on the line,
how lost and single in the orphaning air . . .

She cherishes that sadness,
tells him to lie down on the grass,
closes each of his eyes with a finger,
applies her body like a poultice.

You poor thing, said the Australian woman
while he held our baby—
as if I had forced him to do it,

as if I had my high heel in his face.

Still, who's taken in?
Every time?
Us, and our empty hands, the hands
of starving nurses.

It's bullet holes we want to see in their skin,
scars, and the chance to touch them.

MAY 31

Memorial Day and Shakespeare

I try to see a few of Shakespeare's plays every summer and to read or reread the plays before I see them. Over the years I've seen a knockabout *As You Like It* in Golden Gate Park in San Francisco—it was foggy at noon for the first act, and everyone was shivering when the first actor appeared to say, "If music be the food of love, play on. Give me excess of it," and they had their shirts off in the summer heat by the middle of the play; a version of *The Tempest* on a beach in the Sierra Nevada Mountains, the sun going down and turning the patches of snow on the peaks in the distance to a pale rose—magic enough for the magic to come; and an *Anthony and Cleopatra*—*that* is a play for grown-ups—in an amphitheater in a redwood grove. And in the past few years I've taken to keeping one play by my bedside all summer.

A Midsummer Night's Dream, which I kept reading all of last summer, is an early play. The critics think it was written around the same time as *Romeo and Juliet,* and so the young Shakespeare wrote his tragedy that ought to have been a comedy (those teenagers should not have had to die for love) and the comedy that could only be a comedy almost in the same breath. They are both plays about the magical and delusory power of sexual longing and romantic love. *Midsummer Night* celebrates it, almost purely. And because it's an early play, it's written by the young poet who still loved showing off his gifts. The later Shakespeare cuts to the chase. The young Shakespeare likes to dazzle at the outset with the verbal equivalent of fancy camerawork. The play is contained by the marriage of two powerful adults, Theseus, Duke of Athens (who knows what the sixteenth-century English idea of eighth-century B.C. Athens was?) and Hippolyta, Queen of the Amazons. They lay out the basic problem of romantic drama, that it involves a woman and a man who desire each other. The rest of the play is going to be a wild excursion into what that means. Theseus and Hippolyta speak about their marriage in the opening lines, and they are married in the closing lines. Everything in between is the dream.

A reader who knows the plot opens the play and reads for pure pleasure:

Theseus: Now, fair Hippolyta, our nuptial hour
            Draws on apace. Four happy days bring in
            Another moon: but O, methinks how slow
            This old moon wanes! She lingers my desires
            Like to a step-dame or a dowager,
            Long withering out a young man's revenue.

Hippolyta: Four days will quickly steep themselves in night:
            Four nights will quickly dream away the time:
            And then the moon, like to a silver bow
            New-bent in heaven, shall behold the night
            Of our solemnities.

There is the pretty metaphor: "the moon, like to a silver bow new-bent in heaven." And the witty metaphor based on a contemporary social situation: "like to a step-dame." And there is the gorgeous expression of Theseus's impatience: "How slow this old moon wanes! She lingers my desire," with its curious and delicious way of using "linger" as a transitive verb. And then Theseus shakes off his impatience and turns to an attendant lord and tells him to "stir up Athenian youth to merriment," and in doing so he describes what is in store for Shakespeare's audience: "Awake the pert and nimble spirit of mirth."

Then comes on stage a father outraged that his young daughter has fallen in love and refuses to marry the man of his choice. And the play is under way. The principle is to do a tour of the magic and ridiculousness of human passions. The young lovers moon over each other blindly. The

oaf Bottom (maleness, here), through the intervention of fairies, gets bed-
ded down royally by Titania, the Queen of the Fairies, who conceives a
passion for him, also due to the intervention of the fairies, because he has
been given the head of an ass (femaleness, here)—which, thinking he is
beautiful, she curls the hair of. And then there are Pyramis and Thisbe, the
tragic lovers in the play the town bumpkins put on for the Duke. They
are a comic version of tragic lovers, separated by a wall that is given to
philosophical reflections on its wall-ness, and communicating through a
"chink" that seems to be a sexual pun.

Readers of the play remember Theseus's speech on the madness of love.
It is one of the set pieces of Shakespearean sentence:

> Theseus: Lovers and madmen have such seething brains,
> Such shaping fantasies, that apprehend
> More than cool reason ever comprehends.
> The lunatic, the lover, and the poet
> Are of imagination all compact.
> One sees more devils than vast hell can hold;
> That is the madman. The lover, all as frantic,
> Sees Helen's beauty in a brow of Egypt.
> The poet's eye, in a fine frenzy rolling,
> Doth glance from heaven to earth, from earth to heaven;
> And as imagination bodies forth
> The forms of things unknown, the poet's pen
> Turns them to shapes, and gives to airy nothing
> A local habitation and a name.

They also remember Bottom waking from his magical one-night stand.
Shakespeare gives us this in prose:

> Bottom: I have had a most rare vision. I have had a dream—
> past the wit of man to say what dream it was. Man
> is but an ass if he go about to expound this dream.
> Methought I was—there is no man can tell—what.
> Methought I was, and methought I had . . . but man
> is but a patched fool if he can offer to say what
> methought I had. The eye of man hath not heard,
> the ear of man hath not seen, man's hand is not

able to taste, his tongue to conceive, nor his heart to
report, what my dream was. I will get Peter Quince
to write a ballad of this dream: It shall be called
Bottom's Dream because it hath no bottom . . .

And no end of other silliness.

In Shakespeare's comedy, as generations of critics and scholars have
observed, magic wins and youth wins, and they are brought back into
the round of social life through marriage. Reading *Midsummer* in bits, I
noticed for the first time the strangeness in this play of the blessing at the
end. After all the confusion, "every Jack shall have Jill, naught shall go ill,"
as Robin Goodfellow puts it, but once all the weddings are over and the
lovers retired to their apartments, this is the final blessing that Oberon,
King of the Fairies, confers:

Oberon: Now until the break of day
            Through this house each fairy stray.
            To the best bride-bed will we:
            Which by us will bless-ed be:
            And the issue, there create,
            Ever shall be fortunate:
            So shall all the couples three
            Ever true in loving be:
            And the blots of Nature's hand
            Shall not in their issue stand.
            Never mole, hare-lip, nor scar,
            Nor mark prodigious, such as are
            Despis-ed in nativity,
            Shall upon their children be.
            With this field-dew consecrate,
            Every fairy take his gait,
            And each several chamber bless,
            Through this palace, with sweet peace . . .

That list of birth defects delivered into the consciousness of the audience
just as the play ends is very odd indeed. And, I think, pure Shakespeare: if
we are going to celebrate natural magic, let's have a glimpse of the other
kind of dream, of the horror of nature gone wrong.

Anyway, all this is by way of saying that summer is coming. There are plays in the park and quiet reading in late sunsets after dinner. Natural magic enough.

Summer and Baseball: Linda Gregerson

Here's a piece for baseball season. It comes from Linda Gregerson's *The Woman Who Died in Her Sleep* (Houghton Mifflin). This is Gregerson's second book; she lives in Ann Arbor, Michigan. Her subject this time is "the body in health, the body in sickness, / inscribing / its versatile logic till the least / of us must, willy-nilly, learn / to read." So this is for the versatile logic of the body:

Line Drive Caught by the Grace of God

Half of America doubtless has the whole
of the infield's peculiar heroics by heart,
this one's way with a fractured forearm,
that one with women and off-season brawls,

the ones who are down to business while their owner
goes to the press. You know them already, the quaint
tight pants, the heft
and repose and adroitness of men

who are kept for a while while they age
with the game. It's time
that parses the other fields too,
one time you squander, next time you hoard,

while around the diamond summer runs
its mortal stall, the torso that thickens,
the face that dismantles its uniform.
And sometimes pure felicity, the length

of a player suspended above the dirt
for a wholly deliberate, perfect catch
for nothing, for New York,
for a million-dollar contract which is nothing now,

for free, for the body
as it plays its deft decline and countless humbling,
deadly jokes, so the body
may once have flattered our purposes.

A man like you or me but for the moment's
delay and the grace of God. My neighbor
goes hungry when the Yankees lose,
his wife's too unhappy to cook,

but supper's a small enough price to pay,
he'd tell you himself, for odds
that make the weeks go by so personal,
so hand in glove.

JUNE 14

Encompassing Nature:
Sappho, Lady Komachi, and an Irish Bard

Hymns to the earth thirty-five-hundred years old, from the beginning of
Aryan culture on the Ganges plain. Pliny the Elder, a Roman naturalist
from the time of Christ, describing rumors from far to the East of a giant,
striped, man-eating cat, the tiger. A second-century Greek mathematician
and philosopher wondering at the perfect efficiency of the hexagon out of
which bees construct their honeycombs. The medieval astronomer Tycho
Brahe, who firmly believed that the heavens were eternal and unchange-
able, recording his witness of an impossible event, one that would change
western science forever: the birth of a new star. A Renaissance English-
man making a description of the teeming and completely unexpected life
seen through a microscope in a drop of water. Two hundred years later a

Quaker botanist from Philadelphia collecting plants in Florida and coming across a wide green river so thick with alligators he could have crossed it walking on their backs, the river a cauldron of their thrashing.

I have been reading a book of marvels, that is also a marvel of the book publishing trade. It's called *Encompassing Nature: A Sourcebook*. And it not only encompasses these moments in the history of human consciousness, but it makes them come alive in the words of the people who experienced them. It's edited by a classicist and professor of comparative literature at the University of California at Davis named Robert Torrance, the founder of a program there called Nature and Culture. The book, over twelve hundred pages long and beautifully produced, attempts to collect the whole history of the human response to the natural world—in science, philosophy, theology, poetry—from ancient Mesopotamia to the bewigged rationalists of eighteenth-century Europe, right up to the moment when the Romantic poets and philosophers discovered Nature. It's published by Counterpoint Press, costs twice the price of an ordinary hardbound book, and is a work of staggering erudition.

Impossible to represent what's in it just in the way of poetry, from the old Vedic hymns to Greek lyricists and Taoist sages, from the first contemplative poetry of Japan to Celtic bards to the songs from Shakespeare's plays. Here's a sample, for summer (translated by Diane Wolkstein and Samuel Noah Kramer), a song from ancient Iraq:

A song to Sumerian Inanna,
the earth goddess, thirty-five-hundred years old:

O Lady, your breast is your field.
Inanna, your breast is your field.
Your broad field pours out plants.
Your broad field pours out grain.
Water flows from on high for your servant.
Bread flows from on high for your servant.
Pour it out for me, Inanna.
I will drink all you offer.

From the fragments of Sappho, at the very beginning of European poetry:

Desire overwhelmed my heart
    like a whirlwind plummeting down upon mountain oaks

From the T'ang dynasty hermit poet who took the name of the mountain he lived on, Han Shan, or Cold Mountain (in the translation of Gary Snyder in his Beat Generation years):

In a tangle of cliffs I chose a place—
Bird-paths, but no trails for men.
What's beyond the yard?
White clouds clinging to vague rocks.

A *waka* (thirty-one syllables, five lines) from that astonishing contemplative tradition for thinking about nature and the human heart that emerged in eighth-century Japan, this one by Lady Komachi, translated by Arthur Waley:

The lustre of the flowers
Has faded and passed,
While on idle things
I have spent my body
In the world's long rains.

And this anonymous early Irish poem from the bardic tradition that sounds a little like Walt Whitman and a little like an old Vedic hymn; it's been given a title, "The Mystery." The translation is by Yeats's friend Douglas Hyde:

I am the wind which breathes upon the sea,
I am the wave of the ocean,
I am the murmur of the billows,
I am the ox of the seven combats,
I am the vulture upon the rocks,
I am a beam of the sun,
I am the fairest of plants,
I am a wild boar in valor,
I am a salmon in the water,
I am a lake in the plain,

I am a word of science,
I am the point of the lance of battle,
I am the God who created in the head the fire,
Who is it who throws the light into the meeting on the
    mountains?
Who announces the ages of the moon?
Who teaches the place where couches the sun?
(If not I)

It's worth calling to your attention the fact that this book would make
a great Father's Day gift.

JUNE 21

Father's Day: Cornelius Eady

Cornelius Eady is a New York City poet. Last year he published a small
book about his father's death. It's called *You Don't Miss Your Water*. The
title comes from a song lyric: "But when you left me, O how I cried. You
don't miss your water till the well runs dry." It's about a son's relation to a
difficult father at the time of his dying. Only about twenty pieces, a mix
of poems and short prose, written in the plainest language, the book also
became the basis for an off-Broadway theater piece. Here's a taste:

A Little Bit of Soap

One of the things my father never liked about me was my dark
skin. *You used to be so pretty* was the way he'd put it, and it was true,
there is proof, a baby picture of a curly-haired, just a hair's breadth
away from fair skinned child, me, my small fingers balled up into
a fist.

And then, as if some God shrugged and suddenly turned away
its gaze, something caved in, and I was dark, dark, and all that it
implied.

So what happened? My father always seemed to want me to
explain, what did this desertion mean? This skin that seemed

born to give up, this hair that crinkled to knots, this fairy tale–like transformation?

You used to look real good, my father, a man of slightly lighter hue, would say to me, his son, his changeling. *Maybe you ought to wash more.*

One Kind Favor

My father is close to death, and in his final hours, he begins his journey by asking anyone within earshot of his bed for a few things.

He asks to be allowed to go back home to Florida.

He asks to be able to cast off his dreary hospital gown, to be reunited to the shape of his own clothes.

He wants someone to fetch him his shoes, now useless for weeks, the impossible act of slipping them on, the slight miracle of bending and tying.

In his wishes, my mother arrives and sits at his bedside, or he changes it, and he walks back into his house, into the living room, his old chair.

He is so close to dreaming now, and his body lifts with the desire to fix things.

Paradiso

In Italy, a scholar is giving an after-dinner talk on her study of Dante and the many questions left unanswered about the afterlife.

For example, where does the shade of the body, the one true and indestructible rainbow vessel, go to wait for the end of time if the head goes one way at the moment of death, and the limbs another?

And I thought of my father, fired to dust in a plain urn, and all the answers I'd learned in church, how all the lost must rise, commuters home at last, from wherever fate has ditched them, with their dishonored ropes and blown equipment, up from the sea, the peat, the misjudged step, the angry fuselage, the air bright from ashes, as will and memory knit.

Will my father's glorified body be the one I'd grown up with, a stocky man, perhaps dressed in his one good suit?

Will he be the young boy I'll never know, Sonny Eady, who wanders off for months at a time, always returning with no accounting of his movements?

Will he be the groom my mother saw, or the shape of the man she claims visited her weeks after his funeral, appearing just to help my mother close this file on their lives, just to tell her *fare-thee-well, woman, I'll never see you no more?*

How can this be done? is one question the scholar is here to work on, and as she places our hands into Dante's, and night gathers in the mountains, I think that every hymn is a flare of longing, that the key to any heaven is language.

You Don't Miss Your Water is published by Henry Holt.

JUNE 28

Joseph Stroud and Larissa Szporluk

Here are two poems from new and especially interesting books. They also represent two very different styles in contemporary poetry that spring, I think, from different parts of European modernism. The first is from a very beautiful book by a West Coast poet, Joseph Stroud, *Below Cold Mountain* (Copper Canyon Press). It is a poem for solstice week:

Night in Day

The night never wants to end, to give itself over
to light. So it traps itself in things: obsidian, crows.
Even on summer solstice, the day of light's great
triumph, where fields of sunflowers guzzle in the sun—
we break open the watermelon and spit out
black seeds, bits of night glistening on the grass.

Stroud is about sixty. This poem belongs to a style that came of age when he was a young poet. It's been called "deep image" for its was with metaphor. The striking thing about it is its slow delivery, and perhaps the relation of

that to the plainness of the language. The tactic is to say it slowly and let
it sink in: to evoke out of summer the gold of sunflowers and the black of
watermelon seeds as if they belong to a cosmic drama. It's a way with meta-
phor that is a bit like Spanish-language poetry, Lorca or Pablo Neruda.

The second poem is by Larissa Szporluk, who lives in Ohio. *Dark Sky
Question,* her first book, was the 1997 winner of the Barnard New Poet's
Prize. It's published by Beacon Press. Her work is interior in a different way,
full of strange imagery, syntax as elusive as the logic of dreams, but quick in
its turning and surprises and in this way a bit like French surrealist poetry:

Sanctuary

Who loves the world? The sleeper does.
Where he is, the jungle is still large.
The things that sing, sing flight into his heart,
and sky, and sun, and sounds so glad
he thinks his mother was a bird,
but singing, warn him, as she didn't,
of the scourge to come, and feed him,
not as she did, warm against her plumes,
thistles, moths and worms,
but a hundred false beginnings
so the true one will be watered down,
will barely hurt him, scourge,
the true one, whose coming will ignite
like Babylon the great, in whose hold
he'll perish like a river in a cherished bed,
slowly turning pebbles, tossing mud
and weed, and fling himself
at last, like parrots leaving trees
for cages made of brass, too fresh and green,
too real once, to dream of real things.

Szporluk must be in her forties. The turnings in her poem come from
a style formed in the 1980s and early 90s. It's been called postmodernism,
also "the new difficulty." From Stroud I take the memory of an image: the
black seeds of our own death we spit out as we eat the melon of summer,
from Szporluk, sound first of all—"The things that sing, sing flight into

his heart"—and then the image, in which I am a parrot, in a brasss cage, dreaming of green trees.

It may be the poems simply reflect very different ways of experiencing and interpreting life. Stroud's poem suggests a world that's fairly straight-forward on the surface, but has a deep and disconcerting undertow. The world in Szporluk's poem is wildly out of control from the get-go. They manage each in their way to love a frightening world.

JULY 5

Independence Day: Ralph Waldo Emerson

In the June 11 *New York Review of Books* there's a very interesting essay by the historian Alexander Stille about the teaching of American history in our schools. It gives examples of the ways our national stories get told, the story, for example, of the momentous encounter at Lexington and Concord that began the American Revolution. Here is the account of it from the *Salem Gazette,* April 25, 1775: "The troops came in sight just before sunrise . . . the Commanding Officer accosted the militia in words to this effect: 'Disperse, you rebels, damn you, throw down your arms and disperse'; upon which the [American] troops huzzaed, and immediately one or two [British] officers discharged their pistols, which were instan-taneously followed by the firing of four or five soldiers, and then there seemed to be a general discharge from the whole body. Eight of our men were killed and nine wounded."

Here is the English version, from the *London Gazette,* June 10, 1775: "Six companies of light infantry . . . at Lexington found a body of the country people under arms, on a green close to the road. And upon the King's troops marching up to them, in order to inquire the reason of their being so assembled, they went off in great confusion. And several guns were fired upon the King's troops from behind a stone wall, and also from the meeting house and other houses . . . In consequence of this attack by the rebels, the troops returned the fire and killed several of them."

They read like today's newspapers: a skirmish between colonials and an occupying army, Israelis and Palestinians, Serbs and Albanians, Catholics and British soldiers in Belfast, each claiming the other shot first. By the beginning of the twentieth century, the story was being told like this by the popular historian John Fiske in his 1901 *The American Revolution:* "Colonel Smith then sent Major Pitcairn forward with six companies of light infantry to make all possible haste in securing the bridges over Concord River . . . When Pitcairn reached Lexington, just as the rising sun was casting long shadows across the village green, he found himself confronted by some fifty minute-men under command of Captain John Parker, a hardy veteran who, fifteen years before, had climbed the heights of Abraham by the side of Wolfe. 'Don't fire unless you are fired on,' said Parker; 'but if they want a war, it may well begin here.' 'Disperse, ye villians!' shouted Pitcairn. 'Damn you, why don't you disperse?' And as they stood motionless, he gave the order to fire. As the soldiers hesitated to obey, he discharged his own pistol and repeated the order, whereupon a deadly volley slew eight of the minute-men and wounded ten."

The most famous literary version of this moment is Ralph Waldo Emerson's "Concord Hymn." I heard President Clinton read it this spring at the White House during an evening celebrating American poetry. Emerson, who lived in Concord, wrote the poem—famous for one resonant line—sixty years after the event on the occasion of a monument being placed at the site. I'll give it here with its full title:

Hymn: Sung at the Completion of the Concord Monument, April 19, 1836

By the rude bridge that arched the flood,
    Their flag to April's breeze unfurled,
Here once the embattled farmers stood,
    And fired the shot heard round the world.

The foe long since in silence slept;
    Alike the conqueror silent sleeps;
And Time the ruined bridge has swept
    Down the dark stream which seaward creeps.

On this green bank, by this soft stream,
    We set to-day a votive stone;
That memory may their deed redeem,
    When, like our sires, our sons are gone.

Spirit, that made these heroes dare
To die, or leave their children free,
Bid Time and Nature gently spare
The shaft we raise to them and thee.

I guess this is how national memory is created. After the Concord monument, not so many years later, came the Gettysburg Battlefield Monument, consecrated by Lincoln's great speech. Then for World War I the Tomb of the Unknown Soldier. After World War II the country was in a mood to get back to work after the Depression, so we built infrastructure, Veterans Memorial bridges, and town halls and stadiums. Then the Vietnam Memorial. I can't think of any other poem about consecrating a national memory that has entered our national mythology in the way that Emerson's has. The one poem that comes to mind is Robert Lowell's "For the Union Dead," which is about a memorial in Boston to the black soldiers in the Civil War and to the New Englander who commanded them. It belongs to the tradition of holding us responsible for our ideals rather than to the idealizing tradition. I'll print it next.

JULY 12

Patriotism and Public Memory: Robert Lowell

We were talking about summer and patriotism and monuments. Robert Lowell's "For the Union Dead" is a poem about a bronze bas-relief memorializing a black infantry regiment that fought under the young Boston abolitionist, Robert Gould Shaw, in the Civil War. Their story was also told in the 1989 film *Glory*. The monument, which stands in Boston Common, was cast in bronze by the sculptor Augustus St. Gaudens. William James delivered the oration at its unveiling in 1897. Lowell's poem was written in 1960, at the height of the civil rights movement when the Southern Christian Leadership Conference and the Student Nonviolent Coordinating Committee had organized to take down apartheid in our southern states, and there were daily pictures on television of sheriffs turning fire hoses on marching black Americans and screaming mobs through which black school children had to pass to enter classrooms. Here's the poem:

For the Union Dead
"Relinquunt Omnia Servare Rem Publicam"

The old South Boston Aquarium stands
in a Sahara of snow now. Its broken windows are boarded.
The bronze weathervane cod has lost half its scales.
The airy tanks are dry.

Once my nose crawled like a snail on the glass;
my hand tingled
to burst the bubbles
drifting from the noses of the cowed, compliant fish.

My hand draws back. I often sigh still
for the dark downward and vegetating kingdom
of the fish and reptile. One morning last March,
I pressed against the new barbed and galvanized

fence on the Boston Common. Behind their cage,
yellow dinosaur steamshovels were grunting
as they cropped up tons of mush and grass
to gouge their underworld garage.

Parking spaces luxuriate like civic
sandpiles in the heart of Boston.
A girdle of orange, Puritan-pumpkin colored girders
braces the tingling Statehouse,

shaking over the excavations, as it faces Colonel Shaw
and his bell-cheeked Negro infantry
on St. Gaudens' shaking Civil War relief,
propped by a plank splint against the garage's earthquake.

Two months after marching through Boston,
half the regiment was dead;

at the dedication,
William James could almost hear the bronze Negroes breathe.

Their monument sticks like a fishbone
in the city's throat.
Its Colonel is as lean
as a compass-needle.

He has an angry, wrenlike vigilance,
a greyhound's gentle tautness;
he seems to wince at pleasure
and suffocate for privacy.

He is out of bounds now. He rejoices in man's lovely,
peculiar power to choose life and die—
when he leads his black soldiers to death,
he cannot bend his back.

On a thousand small town New England greens,
the old white churches hold their air
of sparse, sincere rebellion; frayed flags
quilt the graveyards of the Grand Army of the Republic.

The stone statues of the abstract Union Soldier
grow slimmer and younger each year—
wasp-waisted, they doze over muskets
and muse through their sideburns...

Shaw's father wanted no monument
except the ditch,
where his son's body was thrown
and lost with his "niggers."

The ditch is nearer.
There are no statues for the last war here;
on Boylston Street, a commercial photograph
shows Hiroshima boiling

over a Mosler Safe, the "Rock of Ages"
that survived the blast. Space is nearer.
When I crouch to my television set,
the drained faces of Negro school-children rise like balloons.

Colonel Shaw
is riding on his bubble,
he waits
for the blessèd break.

The Aquarium is gone. Everywhere,
giant finned cars nose forward like fish;
A savage servility
slides by on grease.

As you can see, the poem has several points of reference, and several historical layers. One is the 54th regiment itself and the soldiers who died in the war: Shaw and most of his troopers were killed in an engagement in South Carolina in 1863. There is the Boston culture of the late Victorian era that produced the monument. The Latin epigraph to the poem— "These gave all for the Republic"—is the inscription on the monument itself and the world of values it implies, and Lowell's lines echo the speech of William James. There is the Boston of Lowell's childhood in the 1920s and the present Boston of an urban renovation of the prosperous postwar, post-Hiroshima 1960s into which the national disgrace of segregation and the struggle to maintain it has erupted.

Helen Vendler, a Harvard professor, Boston Irish by birth, and an acute reader of poetry, sees in the poem a certain amount of mandarin snobbery. Lowell was related by marriage to Colonel Shaw, so for her this is a poem of a Boston Brahmin, heir to the New England of the Cabots and the Winslows and the Lowells, associating himself with the courage and idealism of the abolitionists and looking with disdain at the new Irish Catholic Boston of Jim Curley and the Kennedys. The poem certainly looks with some disgust on the present with its large-finned cars and dinosaur steam shovels, though I don't find Irish Catholic Boston in the poem.

Lowell died in 1977. He was, at the time "For the Union Dead" was written, probably the best-known, most widely admired poet in the country. His reputation seems to have faded a little since his death, perhaps because the reputations of poets seem to do that, perhaps because the poems were, like this one, so topical. But one of the great things in Lowell's poems for me is their subterranean strangeness. That's where much of the poetry is—in this case, the way in which the whole poem is seen as if from the perspective of a child looking into the world as if into the strangeness of an aquarium tank.

Note: My instructor on monuments and national memory is Kristin Ann Hass, Carried to the Wall: American Memory and the Vietnam Veterans Memorial *(University of California Press).*

JULY 19

Susan Wheeler

Postmodern poetry—experimental poetry—has been for the last fifteen years or so trying to figure out how to wriggle out of the sort of direct, personal poetry that the generation of Allen Ginsberg and Adrienne Rich made. Not necessarily because the younger poets didn't like it, but because they felt that work was being done and it was time to do something else. The project has gone in a lot of directions, but almost all of them have had in common an effort to subvert narrative, undermine the first person singular, and foreground the textures and surprises in language rather than the drama of content.

A rowdy and engaging instance is a second book from the New York City poet Susan Wheeler, *Smokes,* published by Four Way Books. To give you the flavor of it, here is a well-known poem from Robert Frost's first and much-loved book, *A Boy's Will,* published in 1915, and the poem by Wheeler that gives it a Monte-Pythonesque spin:

The Pasture

I'm going out to clean the pasture spring;
I'll only stop to rake the leaves away
(And wait to watch the water clear, I may):
I sha'n't be gone long.—You come too.

I'm going out to fetch the little calf
That's standing by the mother. It's so young,
It totters when she licks it with her tongue.
I sha'n't be gone long.—You come too.

That's Vermont in the tens of the century. Here is Manhattan in the nineties:

He or She That's Got the Limb, That Holds Me Out on It

The girls are drifting in their ponytails
and their pig iron boat. So much for Sunday.
The dodo birds are making a racket
to beat the band. You could have come too.

The girls wave and throw their garters
from their pig iron boat. Why is this charming?
Where they were nailed on their knees
the garters all rip. You were expected.

The youngest sees a Fury in a Sentra
in a cloud. This is her intimation and she balks.
The boat begins rocking from the scourge
of the sunset. The youngest starts the song.

Sometimes it seems that Wheeler is trying to marry the Talking Heads' *Stop Making Sense* to Victorian nonsense verse:

Shanked on the Red Bed

The perch was on the roof, and the puck was in the air.
The diffident were driving, and the daunted didn't care.
When I came out to search for you the lauded hit the breeze
On detonated packages the bard had built to please.

The century was breaking and the blame was on default,
The smallest mammal redolent of what was in the vault,
The screeches shrill, the ink-lines full of interbred regret—

When I walked out to look for you the toad had left his net.

The discourse flamed, the jurors sang, the lapdog strained its
    leash—
When I went forth to have you found the tenured took the beach
With dolloped hair and jangled nerves, without a jacking clue,
While all around the clacking sound of polished woodblocks blew.

When I went out to look for you the reductions had begun.
A demento took a shopgirl to a raisin dance for fun,
And for you, for me, for our quests ridiculous and chaste
The lead sky leered in every cloud its consummate distaste.

The mayors queued for mug shots while the banner rolled in wind
That beat at bolted windows and bore down upon the thin,
And everywhere warped deliverers got bellicose and brave,
When I walked out to find you in the reconstructed rave.

The envelopes were in the slots and paperweights were flung.
When I came down to seek you out the torrents had begun
To rip the pan from handle and horizons from their shore,
To rip around your heady heart looking there for more.

JULY 26

D. A. Powell

I'm not sure how to represent on this page the look of the poems in a
remarkable new book, a first book, by D. A. Powell, who is a young poet,
recently graduated from the Iowa Writers Workshop and living in San
Francisco. The book is called *Tea;* it's published by Wesleyan University
Press. "Tea" is gay slang for gossip. The book looks back across a young
man's introduction to life in the cut-loose years of gay liberation when
AIDS was still a rumor and all the disco songs equated, as Powell says,

"sex and death through an elaborate metaphor called 'Heaven.'" The poems are mostly short, but they're written in very long lines, usually with a cluster of three phrases to a line. The tone is open, associative, sassy; it studiously avoids, though it is full of deaths, whatever is grave and noble in the hindsight of elegy. Jumpy, full of energy, the book takes you there; it reads like a handheld camera. Here's an evocation of the bar scene:

[now the mirrored rooms seem comic. shattered light: I once
    entered the world through dryice fog]

    "this was the season disco finally died"
             —*Kevin Killian,* Bedrooms Have Windows

now the mirrored rooms seem comic. shattered light: I once
    entered the world through dryice fog
not quite fabulous. just young and dumb and full. come let me
    show you a sweep of constellations:

16, I was anybody's. favorite song: *dance into my life* [donna
    summer] and they did dance

17, first fake i.d. I liked *walk away* [donna summer] I ran with
    the big boys

18, by now I knew how to move. on top of the speakers. *give me
    a break* [vivien vee]

19, no one could touch me. donna summer found god. I didn't
    care. *state of independence*

20, the year I went through the windshield. sylvester sang *I want to
    be with you in heaven*

I said "you go" and "scared of you." I listened to pamala stanley *I
    don't want to talk about it*

To print the long lines, Wesleyan University Press made a book with long narrow pages and then bound it to look like it might be a Japanese book about the tea ceremony. It's a striking design and a moving, unexpected book of poems.

AUGUST 2

Arthur Sze

Arthur Sze was born in New York City and lives in Santa Fe, New Mexico. His first book, *The Willow Wind,* when it appeared in 1970 was one of the first books of poems ever published by an Asian American writer. His newest book, *The Redshifting Web: Poems 1970–1998* (Copper Canyon Press), looks back across his writing life. Sze writes very clear lines, quietly musical in the way that ordinary speech can be if it has a sense of measure. His recent poems seem dazzled and haunted by patterns that can't quite yield up their meaning—all the things going on in the continuum of a moment or all the parallels the mind finds in the formal shape of things. Here's an example from a sequence called "The String Diamond":

> Pin a mourning cloak to a board and observe
> brown in the wings spreading out to a series
>
> of blue circles along a cream-yellow outer band.
> A retired oceanographer remembers his father
>
> acted as a double agent during the Japanese occupation,
> but the Kuomintang general who promised a pardon
>
> was assassinated; his father was later sentenced
> as a collaborator to life in prison, where he died.
>
> Drinking snake blood and eating deer antler
> is no guarantee the mind will deepen and glow.

You notice three of the four corners of an intersection
are marked by gingko, horse chestnut, cluster

of pear trees, and wonder what the significance is.
Is the motion of a red-dye droplet descending

in clear water the ineluctable motion of a life?
The melting point of ice is a point of transparency,

as is a kiss, or a leaf beginning to redden,
or below a thunderhead lines of rain vanishing in air.

A "mourning cloak," I think it's clear from the context, is a kind of butterfly.

The Villanelle:
Theodore Roethke and Elizabeth Bishop

A reader from Maryland writes to ask where the villanelle came from. I looked it up: a very old Italian folk song form brought into medieval French poetry and then brought into English by poets at the end of the nineteenth century. It is based on an intricate rhyme scheme and a schematic repetition of key lines. The effect is mesmerizing; it makes of the music of the poem a kind of haunted waltz. It's easier to give examples than to describe it. Here are two of the best known villanelles in modern American poetry:

The Waking

I wake to sleep, and take my waking slow.
I feel my fate in what I cannot fear.
I learn by going where I have to go.

We think by feeling. What is there to know?
I hear my being dance from ear to ear.
I wake to sleep and take my waking slow.

Of those so close beside me, which are you?
God bless the Ground! I shall walk softly there,
And learn by going where I have to go.

Light takes the Tree; but who can tell us how?
The lowly worm climbs up a winding stair;
I wake to sleep and take my waking slow.

Great Nature has another thing to do
To you and me; so take the lively air,
And, lovely, learn by going where to go.

This shaking keeps me steady. I should know.
What falls away is always. And is near.
I wake to sleep, and take my waking slow.
I learn by going where I have to go.

—Theodore Roethke, *Collected Poems*, Doubleday

One Art

The art of losing isn't hard to master;
so many things seem filled with the intent
to be lost that their loss is no disaster.

Lose something every day. Accept the fluster
of lost door keys, the hour badly spent.
The art of losing isn't hard to master.

Then practice losing farther, losing faster:
places, and names, and where it was you meant
to travel. None of these will bring disaster.

I lost my mother's watch. And look! my last, or
next-to-last, of three loved houses went.
The art of losing isn't hard to master.

I lost two cities, lovely ones. And, vaster,
some realms I owned, two rivers, a continent.
I miss them, but it wasn't a disaster.

—Even losing you (the joking voice, a gesture
I love) I shan't have lied. It's evident
the art of losing's not too hard to master
though it may look like (*Write* it!) like disaster.

—Elizabeth Bishop, *The Complete Poems, 1927–1979,*
Farrar, Straus & Giroux

AUGUST 16

In Memoriam: Zbigniew Herbert

Zbigniew Herbert died a few weeks ago in Warsaw at the age of seventy-three. He is one of the most influential European poets of the last half century, and perhaps—even more than his great contemporaries Czeslaw Milosz and Wladislawa Symborska—the defining Polish poet of the postwar years.

It's hard to know how to talk about him, because he requires superlatives and he despised superlatives. He was born in Lvov in 1924. At fifteen, after the German invasion of Poland, he joined an underground military unit. For the ten years after the war when control of literature in the Polish Stalinist regime was most intense, he wrote his poems, as he said, "for the drawer." His first book appeared in 1956. His tactic, as Joseph Brodsky has said, was to turn down the temperature of language until it burned like an iron fence in winter. His verse is spare, supple, clear, ironic. At a time when the imagination was, as he wrote, "like stretcher bearers lost in the fog," this voice seemed especially sane, skeptical, and adamant. He was also a master of the prose poem. Here are some samples:

Objects

Inanimate objects are always correct and cannot, unfortunately, be reproached with anything. I have never observed a chair shift from one foot to another, or a bed rear on its hind legs. And tables, even when they are tired, will not dare to bend their knees. I suspect that objects do this from pedagogical consider-ations, to reprove us constantly for our instability.

The Wind and the Rose

Once in a garden there grew a rose. A wind fell in love with her. They were completely different, he—light and fair; she—immobile and heavy as blood.

There came a man in wooden clogs and with his thick hands he plucked the rose. The wind leapt after him, but the man slammed the door in his face.

—O that I might turn to stone—wept the unlucky one—I was able to go round the whole world, I was able to stay away for years at a time, but I knew that she was always there waiting.

The wind understood that, in order really to suffer, one has to be faithful.

Emperor

Once upon a time there was an Emperor. He had yellow eyes and a predatory jaw. He lived in a palace full of statuary and po-licemen. Alone. At night he would wake up and scream. Nobody loved him. Most of all he liked hunting game and terror. But he posed for photographs with children and flowers. When he died, nobody dared to remove his portraits. Take a look, perhaps you still have his mask at home

Episode in a Library

A blonde girl is bent over a poem. With a pencil sharp as a lance she transfers words onto a white sheet of paper and translates them into lines, accents, caesuras. The fallen poet's lament now looks like a salamander gnawed by ants.

When we carried him off under fire, I believed his still warm body would be resurrected in the word. Now I see words dying. I know that there is no limit to decay. What will remain after us are fragments of words scattered on the black earth. Accent signs over nothingness and ash.

To Extract Objects

To extract objects from their majestic silence takes either ploy or crime.

A door's icy surface can be unfrozen by a traitor's knock, a glass dropped on the floorboards shrieks like a wounded bird, and a house set aflame chatters in the loquacious language of fire, the language of a stifled epic about everything the bed, the chests, the curtains kept to themselves for so long.

Anything Rather Than an Angel

If after our death they want to transform us into a tiny withered flame that walks along the paths of winds—we have o rebel. What good is eternal leisure on the bosom of the air, in the shade of a yellow halo, amid the murmur of two-dimensional choirs?

One should enter rock, wood, water, the cracks of a gate. Better to be the creaking of floor than a shrill and transparent perfection.

The first volume of Herbert to appear in English was *Selected Poems,* translated by Czeslaw Milosz and Peter Dale Scott and published by Penguin Books in 1968. A second *Selected Poems* in the translation of John and Bogdana Carpenter appeared from Oxford University Press in 1977. Two later volumes of his poems, both in the very good translations of the Carpenters, *Mr. Cogito* and *Report from the Besieged City,* were published by Ecco Press, which also published two volumes of Herbert's prose, *Still Life wirh a Bridle,* essays on Dutch painting that are also a meditation on the world human beings make and inhabit, and *The Barbarian in the Garden,* a book of essays written in the 1950s about

Herbert's first encounter with western Europe that manages also, in the ruinous postwar years, to be a profound meditation on the ideas of history and civilization.

Note: A long awaited Complete Poems *has finally appeared in a brand new English translation by Alissa Valles from Ecco/HarperCollins. It includes the Milosz-Scott translations. The texts above are taken from that book.*

AUGUST 23

Something Old, Something New: Charlotte Mew

New anthologies of English poetry are not, normally, a reason to get excited, I know, even for someone like me who would be apt to pick them up with some interest and curiosity. But there is a new anthology of English verse that I am actually very excited by. It's the *New Penguin Book of English Verse,* edited by the poetry editor at Faber & Faber (T. S. Eliot's former job) Paul Keegan, and it is a book that, if you have any interest in reading poetry, you are going to want to own. It's unusual in two ways—first, it is organized not by author but by the year in which the poem was published; second, unlike most of the anthologies created for use in courses on English literature, this one reads through English poetry with a completely fresh eye. There are not only delicious poems I hadn't seen before from medieval manuscripts—I am going to modernize the spelling in this one from some time between 1300 and 1350—

> All night by the rose, the rose,
> All night by the rose I lay.
> Though I dare not steal the rose,
> I bore the flower away—

Here, from 1916, in the years of American modernism, next to poems by D. H. Lawrence and Ezra Pound and H.D., is a piece by Charlotte Mew:

A Quoi Bon Dire

Seventeen years ago you said
    Something that sounded like Good-bye;
    And everybody thinks that you are dead,
        But I.

So I, as I grow stiff and old,
    To this and that say Good-bye too;
    And everybody sees that I am old
        But you.

    And one fine morning in a sunny lane
Some boy and girl will meet and swear
    That nobody can love their way again
        While over there
You will have smiled, I shall have tossed your hair.

The next year T. S. Eliot's "Love Song of J. Alfred Prufrock" would appear and come in another and more surprising way at the subject of lived and unlived life. It's fascinating to see, as Keegan allows us to do, the poems we know in relation to some of the poems we seem to have forgotten.

AUGUST 30

Yusef Komunyakaa

Yusef Komunyakaa, born in Bogalusa, Louisiana, currently a professor at Princeton University, served in Vietnam where he was a reporter for *Stars and Stripes*. He wrote what is probably the best book of poems by an American about the Vietnam war, *Dien Cai Dau* (Wesleyan University Press), and subsequently received the Pulitzer Prize for his selected poems, *Neon Vernacular* (also Wesleyan). His newest book is as strong as the best of

his earlier work, and it has immense range. The poem that caught my eye
begins as an observation about style among the young in the nineties.

Woebegone

We pierce tongue
& eyebrow, foreskin
& nipple, as if threading wishes
on gutstring. Gold bead
& question mark hook
into loopholes & slip
through. We kiss
like tiny branding irons.
Loved ones guard words
of praise, & demigods mortgage
nighttime. Beneath bruised
glamor, we say, "I'll show
how much I love you by
how many scars I wear."
As we steal the last
drops of anger, what can we
inherit from Clarksdale's blue
tenements? Medieval & modern,
one martyr strokes another
till Torquemada rises.
We trade bouquets
of lousewort, not for the red
blooms & loud perfume,
but for the lovely spikes.

This comes from *Thieves of Paradise,* just out from Wesleyan. Not bad:
beginning with eyebrow rings and getting to Clarksdale, Torquemada, and
lousewort in one small fever of a poem about the way we live now.

SEPTEMBER 6

Labor Day: Gary Snyder

The heroic period of the American labor movement seems a long way off as the sports utility vehicles inch toward the beaches in the holiday traffic. So here's a reminder from Gary Snyder's *Myths & Texts,* one of the landmarks of the Beat Generation. The sequence of poems deals with Snyder's time working in logging camps and on Forest Service road crews in the 1950s in the Pacific Northwest when the stories of International Workers of the World organizers in the lumber camps were still a faint echo.

There are a lot of things I admire about the art of this poem, and there is something else about it that delights me. Snyder, fresh out of Reed College with a degree in anthropology and literature, was reading Ezra Pound, the favorite poet of the avant-garde in those days, and adapted something of the rhythms of Pound's *Cantos* here. This was also the time of the folk revival in New York, when Bob Dylan was electrifying the young (and the acoustic guitar) with versions of Woody Guthrie, who sang some of the IWW songs. This poem puts those two things together in the early vision of a young Northwest poet who would become the Thoreau of his generation. Funny in a way, given Pound's politics and his use of obscure Italian and Provençal history. It's as if Snyder said, Ezra, meet Woody. Woody, this is Ezra. Here's the poem:

> Felix Baran
> Hugo Gerlot
> Gustav Johnson
> John Looney
> Abraham Rabinowitz
> Shot down on the steamer Verona
> For the shingle-weavers of Everett
>   the Everett Massacre November 5, 1916

> Ed McCullough, a logger for thirty-five years
> Reduced by the advent of chainsaws
> To chopping off knots at the landing:
> "I don't have to take this kind of shit,
> Another twenty years

and I'll tell 'em to shove it"
(he was sixty-five then)
In 1934 they lived in shanties
At Hooverville, Sullivan's Gulch.
When the Portland-bound train came through
The trainmen tossed off coal.

"Thousands of boys shot and beat up
For wanting a good bed, good pay,
          decent food, in the woods—"
No one knew what it meant:
"Soldiers of Discontent."

This comes from *Myths & Texts,* published by New Directions.

SEPTEMBER 13

May Swenson

When Mark McGwire was taking his victory lap the other night, half
dancing and half jogging around the bases after hitting his sixty-second
home run of the season, my companion, who is exceptionally literate and
takes a philosophical interest in the bodies of baseball players, regarded
his strangely bulked-up torso and murmured, musingly, "When Body, my
good bright dog is dead . . ." She was quoting May Swenson, a wonderful
and not-very-well-known poet—she died in 1989 at the age of seventy-
five—in the quirky tradition of Emily Dickinson and Elizabeth Bishop.
Here is the poem:

Question

Body my house
my horse my hound
what will I do
when you are fallen

Where will I sleep
How will I ride
What will I hunt

Where can I go
without my mount
all eager and quick
How will I know
in thicket ahead
is danger or treasure
when Body my good
bright dog is dead

How will it be
to lie in the sky
without roof or door
and wind for an eye

With cloud for shift
how will I hide?

Swenson is a quiet figure in her generation of poets and an atypical one, an atypical and interesting sort of American, in fact. She was born in Logan, Utah, in 1919, of Swedish immigrant parents who had converted to Mormonism. She was the oldest of ten siblings, and her first language was Swedish. She graduated from Utah State in 1939 and worked for a while as a reporter in Utah before moving to New York, where she worked as a secretary, an editor, and occasionally taught poetry. She was gay, and agnostic, which separated her from her large family. Her early poems with their deft and quirky formal play were quite fashionable in the 1950s when, a young poet in Greenwich Village, she began to publish her work and win prizes. Later her poetry had become distinctly unfashionable, and she seemed not to mind, went her own way. She lived for much of the latter part of her life on Long Island, facing the sea, and her poems have a wakeful, solitary air. I notice that she is included in some anthologies of modern poetry and not in others, an indication that her reputation is a bit dim at the moment. Here's another poem:

Death, Great Smoothener

Death,
great smoothener,
maker of order,
arrester, unraveler, sifter and changer;
death, great hoarder;
student, stranger, drifter, traveler,
flyer and nester all caught at your border;
death,
great halter;
blackener and frightener,
reducer, dissolver
seizer and welder of younger with elder,
worker with sleeper,
death, great keeper,
of all that must alter;
death,
great heightener,
leaper, evolver,
great smoothener,
great whitener!

These come from *Nature: Poems Old and New,* published by Houghton Mifflin.

SEPTEMBER 20

Donald Justice

Many readers wrote to express their interest in and ask questions about the poetic form called the villanelle after I printed a couple of them last month. The haunted and magic quality of that kind of formal repetition in poems must have struck a chord. One reader suggested that I print a *pantoum.* The pantoum has a curious history. It's a Malaysian song form, and it was adapted by French poets in the nineteenth century (one of the more obscure fruits of the age of imperialism) and came into English from poets who imitated the French. The pantoum has a four-line stanza, and the second and fourth lines of each stanza become the first and third lines of the next stanza.

Here's one by Donald Justice, who grew up in Florida and taught for many years at the Iowa Writers Workshop. The poems in his *New and Selected Poems* (Knopf), about Florida, the Miami of another era, and about growing up in the depression years are especially memorable. Justice is widely admired and imitated by other poets; he's a brilliant craftsman who has experimented with a lot of forms, including the pantoum. So here's an American poet using a Malay-French-English form to get the feel of America in the 1930s. In the nineteenth century the repetitions in the form seemed designed to give the poems a dazed, slightly stoned effect. Here they do just the reverse. The diction of the poem, almost mockingly plain and generalized, and the repeated phrase, slightly altered, want to render a life lived small, lived quietly, and, in doing so, to make us feel the whole cry of unlived life underneath it.

Pantoum of the Great Depression

Our lives avoided tragedy
Simply by going on and on,
Without end and with little apparent meaning.
Oh, there were storms and small catastrophes.

Simply by going on and on
We managed. No need for the heroic.
Oh, there were storms and small catastrophes.
I don't remember all the particulars.

We managed. No need for the heroic.
There were the usual celebrations, the usual sorrows.
I don't remember all the particulars.
Across the fence, the neighbors were our chorus.

There were the usual celebrations, the usual sorrows.
Thank god no one said anything in verse.
The neighbors were our only chorus,
And if we suffered we kept quiet about it.

At no time did anyone say anything in verse.
It was the ordinary pities and fears consumed us,
And if we suffered, we kept quiet about it.
No audience would ever know our story.

It was the ordinary pities and fears consumed us.
We gathered on porches; the moon rose; we were poor.
What audience would ever know our story?
Beyond our windows shone the actual world.

We gathered on porches; the moon rose; we were poor.
And time went by, drawn by slow horses.
Somewhere beyond our windows shone the world.
The Great Depression had entered our souls like fog.

And time went by, drawn by slow horses.
We did not ourselves know what the end was.
The Great Depression had entered our souls like fog.
We had our flaws, perhaps a few private virtues.

But we did not ourselves know what the end was.
People like us simply go on.
We have our flaws, perhaps a few private virtues,
But it is by blind chance only that we escape tragedy.

And there is no plot in that; it is devoid of poetry.

SEPTEMBER 27

Presidents, Poets, and Shame: James Wright

Art has a way of taking the side of sinners. The outcast in us wants to understand the outcast. Not just Dostoevsky and Victor Hugo, either, with Raskolnikov and Jean Valjean and the relentless policemen who tracked them down. By the time Oliver Stone and Anthony Hopkins were through with Richard Nixon in the Shakespearean film about Watergate, even though Nixon had hired burglars to rifle a man's psychiatric files and paid hush money out of his political slush fund to buy their silence and felt sorry for himself that he got caught, I felt kinship with him by the time the movie was over. I know it's sentimental not to recognize that acts have consequences. But art is more interested in private suffering than public judgment. It's mostly not on the side of the old *Dragnet* serial that used to end each week with a stern announcement of the sentence the malefactor had received, as if that settled the matter.

So I've found myself thinking this week about the Ohio poet James Wright. Wright, who died in 1980, grew up in Martin's Ferry, Ohio, in the middle of the depression. He knew what hard times were like in a factory town in America in those years when his father worked for Atlas Glass and his friends' fathers worked for Wheeling Steel and boys lurked aimlessly along the banks and among the sinkholes of the polluted river whose name—Ohio—meant "beautiful" in the native language of the place.

One of Wright's themes as a political poet was that the need of Puritan America to subject everything to the light came from a prurient fear of its own darkness. In a poem about Eisenhower's visit to Franco in 1959, he wrote:

> The American hero must triumph over
> The forces of darkness.

American light for him was fear of the unconscious, and its form was love of judgment. It judged sin, it judged poverty, and it judged people's class and their color. In another poem called "In Terror of Hospital Bills," he wrote:

> It snows freely and freely hardens
> On the lawns of my hope, my secret
> Hounded and flayed. I wonder
> What words to beg money with.
>
> Pardon me, sir, could you?
> Which way is St. Paul?
> I thirst.
> I am a full-blooded Sioux Indian.

He thought there was a connection between our self-righteousness as a people and the cost of our health care and our callousness and our shame.

Mainly I have been thinking of him because I have been feeling a mix of shame and anger at the voyeurism of our culture (which is embodied at the moment in the person of Kenneth Starr). Wright was a countryman of an Ohio president, Warren Harding, and he wrote a piece about him. It's called "Two Poems about President Harding" and is too long to quote here in full. Here's a part of it:

> How many honey locusts have fallen,
> Pitched rootlong into the open graves of strip mines,
> Since the First World War ended
> And Wilson the gaunt deacon jogged sullenly
> Into silence?
> Tonight,
> The cancerous ghosts of old con men
> Shed their leaves.
> For a proud man,
> Lost between the turnpike near Cleveland
> And the chiropractors' signs looming among dead mulberry trees,
> There is no place to go
> But home.

It is part of Wright's love-hate relationship with Ohio that the autumn trees are "the cancerous ghosts of old con men." The Harding poem ends like this:

> —he was the snowfall
> Turned to white stallions standing still
> Under dark elm trees.
>
> He died in public. He claimed the secret right
> To be ashamed.

Wright's poems can be found in *Above the River: The Complete Poems,* published jointly by Farrar, Straus & Giroux and University Press of New England.

OCTOBER 4

Filipino Poetry: *Returning a Borrowed Tongue*

Island cultures, I found myself thinking one summer in Crete after a day of gazing at Greek temples, Byzantine monasteries, and Venetian fortresses, do what they have to do. Imperial piracies wash over them, leaving their architectural and linguistic residues. The Philippine archipelago is not different. The islands were inhabited twenty-two-thousand years ago. By the third century B.C., they were trading with China and Vietnam. Magellan arrived very late, in 1521. Fifty years later a Spanish sailor seized Manila from its Muslim potentate and the Spanish empire controlled the islands for three hundred years. The United States seized the Philippines in 1898 and then paid $20 million for it after the fact. I have a great uncle who served in the Philippine-American War from 1898 to 1902. He supervised impressed road-building crews outside Luzon and, in the 1960s, a very old man, he still liked to take his pipe out of his mouth and demonstrate his ability to say, "Hurry up, you son of a bitch," in Tagalog.

The beginnings of Filipino poetry in English came not long after the war. A *Filipino Students' Magazine* appeared at the University of California in Berkeley in 1905. Filipino literature in English is now almost a century old. Coffee House Press in Minneapolis has just published an anthology of contemporary Filipino and Filipino American Poetry, *Returning a Borrowed Tongue,* edited by Nick Carbo.

It's as lively and various a gathering of poems and poetic styles as you would find anywhere else in American poetry. Here's a poem about learning English. Well, the metaphor may be more complicated than that: it's about falling down and learning English. The author, Maria Luisa Aguilar-Carino won the Manila Critics' Circle Award in 1993; she's now a Fulbright Fellow in Chicago.

Familiar

Like someone newly dead
I'm mourned on my seventh
birthday. Nose and forehead stamped
with blood, I wander into the house
after a fall among spiked flower

beds, rousing the womenfolk
to keening.

Poultices of warm vinegar. Years,
rows of crooked teeth later,
my face becomes familiar.
Once frail, my limbs
have filled out from balls of fish
and sticky rice my aunts
fed me with their fingers.

They tell me I am not beautiful,
but that my eyes are clear.
I drink from a clay bowl:
a forest of green mussel
shells floats, opening
to reveal mother-
of-pearl insides.

In the evenings my ears fold
close, against the clatter of dishes,
the sing-song of voices
bordering the road. I murmur
these incantations, spell words
on blue-lined paper: *bizarre, irrevocable,*
reproach, syllable, steerage, ballast,
gesture—taking them with me to sleep
like furry animals, hiding them
in my mouth like pebbles
newly dug up from the moonlit
garden—taste of earth,
crushed bones, verbena, flared
nasturtiums.

    I especially liked that last image of the taste of language on the
tongue.

OCTOBER II

John Ashbery

One of the new fall books is John Ashbery's *Wakefulness* (Farrar, Straus & Giroux). There is also a new and very readable book about Ashbery and some of the other poets associated with him, like Frank O'Hara and Kenneth Koch, poets who went from Harvard to Manhattan after World War II and began to write in the bright years of abstract expressionist painting. The book is called *The Last Avant-garde: The Making of the New York School of Poets,* and the author, David Lehman, writes to be understood. It's a lively book about art and poetry at a formative moment in the development of postwar American culture. And it might help those who find Ashbery, often regarded as the most original poet of this half-century, difficult or hard to understand.

He can be maddening. The typical sound of his poems is that of a man mumbling to himself, so he disconcerts our idea of music. His expressions —like "we may never realize about our lives"—have sometimes the vagueness of the way we actually speak to ourselves, and the poems seem not so much to develop an idea as veer all over the place the way our untended thought processes do. This is his medium, and it takes some getting used to. The stance is of someone who never quite "gets used to" anything in the way that part of all of us never does. He seems strange, and it's only after a while that you sense his aim, to be profoundly ordinary, which is the opposite of the aim of most poetry. That is his strangeness. Well, not all of his strangeness. Like Wallace Stevens, whom he is like in certain ways, a poet of the mind's unhinged dailiness, a philosophical comedian, he is also a contriver of metaphors you can't quite get your head around. In this poem, for example, what does he mean by "the friend who came at midnight and wanted to replace us with a song"?

Ashbery has many imitators among the young. Every time I print one of their poems I get a number of outraged letters from my always interesting readers that say in effect, "You think *that's* poetry? No wonder no one reads it." My response, I guess, is always something like this: you do not have to like it. That's why there are at any one moment different kinds of art. But if you are going to read a writer or look at a painter, what you owe them is looking long enough to see what they're doing. And, especially if you don't like what they're doing, the moment when you actually get it—which always comes as an intuition, a slipping into the other's skin, rather than as a clear thought—you've learned something.

Try this one. I think it's a rather amazing poem. It begins where Ashbery often begins. Mumbling to himself, thinking against the grain. A valedictory speaker seems to be droning on. The restless auditor is starting to have fantasies of the pointlessness of life, of how it ends in some surreal and stupid way. The vague form this thought takes is of "a man with a dog" who "comes to shoot us." The listener, though, discovers he has his own set of formulas, "everything has its own reward," for example, which he records with a not-entirely, or not only, self-mocking irony. Then we come to the friend. But I don't want to explain the poem to death. That's what the "valedictorian" in all of us wants to do:

The Friend at Midnight

Keeping in mind that all things break,
the valedictorian urged his future plans on us:
Don't give up. It's too soon. Things break. Yes, they fail
or they are anchored up ahead, but no one can see that far.
As he was speaking, the sun set. The grove grew silent. There
are more of us taking ourselves seriously now than ever,
one thought. We may never realize about our lives
till it's too late, and a man with a dog comes to shoot us.
I like to think though that everything is its own reward,
that liars such as we were made to last forever,
and each morning has a special chime of its own.

Thus we were pitted against the friend who came at midnight
and wanted to replace us with a song. We resisted furiously:
There was too much food on his table, the night was too black,
while all around us shrinking bands of outsiders
entered into negotiations with the darkness. It
seems to omit us, his reasoning, or in the well of time
we may be overdrawn, and cosmetics come to put a good face
    on us,
asking, why this magic wind, so many angles
against the river's prism and the burnt blue sky?
To which one answers, nothing is adrift

for long. Perhaps we will be overtaken
even in our happiness, and waves of passion drown us.
Now, wasn't that easy? A moment's breath and everyone
has gone outside to ponder the matter further.
Outside, children toboggan endlessly.

OCTOBER 18

Sterling Brown

This coming weekend at the Library of Congress a group of distinguished poets and critics will be gathering to honor the work of Sterling Brown, who was born in Washington, D.C., grew up in the vicinity of 11th and R Streets, and wrote one of the classic books of American poetry in this century, *Southern Road,* published in 1932.

Brown's father, who came into the world a slave in eastern Tennessee, was a professor of Religion at Howard University. His son went north to college—a B.A. from Williams College, an M.A. from Harvard—and then headed south to teach literature at some of the black schools that were founded during reconstruction—Virginia Seminary and College near Roanoke, Lincoln University in Missouri, and Fisk University in Tennessee. It was a time—the years of lynchings and share-cropping servitude and Klan intimidation—when African Americans were migrating out of the south in great numbers, so Brown's was a reverse migration. And *Southern Road* was the result of that experience.

It's a remarkable book and not as well known as it should be. Partly it's a record of the people Brown met and the music he heard: street corner blues singers and preachers, the gossip and oratory of Southern churches, the talk of men who had spent time on work gangs and prison gangs, in the cotton fields and hill fields of hardscrabble farms. His head was full of the poetry of his time—Thomas Hardy and E. A. Robinson and Robert Frost—and he listened to the language of that world and made poems out of it that are as powerful, in their way, and as indelible as the photographs of Walker Evans.

Here's the title poem from the book. It's a chain-gang song, the voice of an older man steadying a younger one and telling him his story. And weaving through it you hear one of the things that West African music brought to North America, the physical sounds of work embedded in the song—the up-from-the-gut *hunh* of physical labor, steel against stone, playing through the blues-like field chant like some final truth of bodily misery and bodily release.

Southern Road

Swing dat hammer—hunh—
Steady, bo';
Swing dat hammer—hunh—
Steady, bo';
Ain't no rush, bebby,
Long ways to go.

Burner tore his—hunh—
Black heart away;
Burner tore his—hunh—
Black heart away;
Got me life, bebby,
An' a day.

Gal's on Fifth Street—hunh—
Son done gone;
Gal's on Fifth Street—hunh—
Son done gone;
Wife's in de ward, bebby,
Babe's not bo'n.

My ole man died—hunh—
Cussin' me;
My ole man died—hunh—
Cussin' me;
Ole lady rocks, bebby,
Huh misery.

Doubleshackled—hunh—
Guard behin';

Doubleshackled—hunh—
Guard behin';
Ball an' chain, bebby,
On my min'.

White man tells me—hunh—
Damn yo' soul;
White man tells me—hunh—
Damn yo' soul;
Got no need, bebby,
To be tole.

Chain gang nevah—hunh—
Let me go;
Chain gang nevah—hunh—
Let me go;
Po' los' boy, bebby,
Evahmo'...

It's an exquisite act of listening and rendering, terrible in what it tells us and by now too familiar. I can see why people didn't get it at that time. If you just glance through it, it could look like another slightly quaint revival of folk poetry. You could miss the intelligence and exactness and anger and fatality in the writing. When *Southern Road* appeared at the tail end of the publishing boom that got called the "Harlem Renaissance," critics didn't know what to make of it. The Negro, as Langston Hughes dryly noted, was no longer in fashion. And I think people were faintly embarrassed by Brown's use of dialect. It seemed old-fashioned. The sound readers wanted to hear, if they wanted to hear anything at all, had the new jazz-and-blues-inflected sound of Harlem. So two of the great books of the period that looked at life in the South, Brown's book and Zora Neale Hurston's *Their Eyes Were Watching God*, seemed to disappear without a trace. Now both books are finding their place as essential American works, and this weekend in his native city, Sterling Brown is going to get some of the attention and admiration he's long deserved.

OCTOBER 25

Robert Bly

It has idly crossed my mind that, in human societies, fall has traditionally been the time of scapegoat rituals. But I reminded myself that the release of the Starr Report materials and the grand jury video were timed to do as much damage as possible before the November elections and not to clear the fields of the lingering and resentful spirits of the earth we have plowed and harvested in the months of the growing cycle. Halloween is our way of buying off the ghouls of autumn, whatever Congress is up to.

Here, anyway, is a poem of the fall with its sense-quickening feel of life and death. It comes from a pleasant and very readable new anthology, *Wild Song: Poems of the Natural World,* edited by John Daniel and published by University of Georgia Press. This one is by Robert Bly:

A Private Fall

Motes of haydust rise and fall
with slow and grave steps,
like servants who dance in the yard
because some prince has been born.

What has been born? The winter.
Then the Egyptians were right.
Everything wants a chance to die,
to begin in the clear fall air.

Each leaf sinks and goes down
when we least expect it.
We glance toward the window for some
thing has caught our eye.

It's possible autumn is a tomb
out of which a child is born.
We feel a secret joy
and we tell no one!

Robert Bly's newest book is *Morning Poems* (HarperFlamingo). It is a record of a project he undertook of writing a poem every morning, as his friend William Stafford had done. The project may have been a self-administered cure for the traumatic distraction, for a poet, of having written a best-seller. Bly's *Iron John* and the subsequent parody of its ideas in various television shows had made him the kind of public figure it's not very helpful for a poet to be. He seems to have responded by staying in bed and writing poems, which was, I think, a very admirable solution. And the poems, even the darkest of them, have a fresh playfulness. You can feel the way his imagination has been cut loose by the practice.

I ran into him on a fall morning a couple of years ago. He was chuckling to himself, looking both pleased and a little bewildered. I asked him what was on his mind, and he explained that on that morning he'd had a conversation with a mouse about sleeping curled up versus sleeping stretched out, and had written a poem about it, which he recited to me on the spot. I was amused to see that it had become the final poem in *Morning Poems:*

A Conversation with a Mouse

One day a mouse called to me from his curly nest:
"How do you sleep? I love curliness."

"Well, I like to be stretched out. I like my bones to be
All lined up. I like to see my toes way off over there."

"I suppose that's one way," the mouse said, "but I don't like it.
The planets don't act that way, nor the Milky Way."

What could I say? You know you're near the end
Of the century when a sleepy mouse brings in the Milky Way.

NOVEMBER I

Chase Twichell

Chase Twichell lives in the Adirondacks. In the last ten years she's published three very different and very strong books. The first, *Perdido,* was about desire and sexuality and dream. The second, *The Ghost of Eden,* came as a surprise, an angry clear-headed book about the destruction of the earth, as if she'd shaken off dream and desire and taken a hard look at the way things were. The newest book, *The Snow Watcher* (Ontario Review Press), has just arrived in bookstores, and it's a surprise again. Its setting is in her territory, the beautiful Keene Valley not too far from Lake Champlain, and the subject, or the background of her subjects, is her work as a student of Zen Buddhism. I recommend the new book, but if you go to poetry partly for a taste of the movement of the inner life, I recommend you read all three of them. They track the inner movements of one life with an unexpected freshness.

Reading the poems in *The Snow Watcher* is like breathing cold air. Organized as a kind of narrative of her apprenticeship in Zen meditation, they are full of sharp observation, both of the world and herself, unsentimental poems, with a sinewy intellectual toughness, and, as the book progresses, they open out into a stark, sometimes bewildered clarity. Here are a couple of them.

The Innocent One

The watcher guarded the innocent one,
that was their relationship.
When the innocent one was in danger,

had angered the mother or the father
maybe, walked out on some thin ice

on purpose (for the sharp defining edges
of it) and suddenly needed a rescue,
the watcher would be the rescuer.

That allowed the innocent one to grow up
reckless: she was always stabbing herself

in the heart to see what each new kind of love
felt like. Then her savior the watcher
would heal her wound by explaining everything.

We're a very solid couple, the two of us.
We've grown up into a fine double person.

Weightless, Like a River

I heard of a teacher and went to him.
In the monastery I studied his words
and the way he moved his body.

He seemed weightless, like a river,
both in his words and in his body.

Dawn zazen, the windows'
river light . . . I heard
his bare feet on the wood floor.

All the slow fish of ignorance
turned toward the sound.

The Verge

Inside language there was always
an inkling,
a dark vein branching,

bird-tracks in river sand spelling out
the fact of themselves,

asking me to come toward them
and scratch among them with a stick
all the secrets I could no longer keep,

until my words were nothing
but lovely anarchic bird-prints themselves.

I think that's the verge right there,
where the two languages
intertwine, twigs and thorns,

words telling secrets
to no one but river and rain.

NOVEMBER 8

A Canadian Poet: Roo Borson

The Toronto poet Roo Borson was born in California but has lived her
adult life in Canada and publishes her books there. They are not eas-
ily available in American bookstores, though she's become one of the
best-known Canadian poets of her generation. She's a clear writer, clear-
minded with a dark and musical imagination. I look forward to each of
her books. Her latest, *Intent, or The Weight of the World,* is published by
McClelland and Stewart in Toronto. Ask your local bookstore to order it.

Autumn

One night goes on longer than the rest, never so long,
whiled away. Then dawn.
Goodbye, insects. Hollow casings on the windowsill,
a dainty leg among the spice jars.
Goodbye, marigolds, the earth will not wait for you.
Trains hurtle by at the edge of cities,
the taste of bourbon, a mouthful of leaves.
Above everyone's dining-table a chandelier burns.
Now the luxurious old wine can be uncorked,
the slicing of meat and bread, uncorked,
and in the black panes life goes on.

And here's one, a quick notation for the end of daylight savings:

2 A.M.

2 A.M., and the clocks have been turned
one hour backwards. Summer's gone,
like rage or pleasure, the
possum we caught rolling,
drunk on garbage,
over the fence one morning,

and now the rain:
a glimpse, sometimes,
as of a second chance—
not fully fallen into sleep,
to be awakened.

NOVEMBER 15

A Portuguese Poet: Fernando Pessoa

When José Saramago won the Nobel Prize for Literature this fall, his name drew a blank from most of the literary folk I know. He is the first Portuguese Nobel laureate, and it mostly reminded poets of the fact that a Portuguese poet, who should have received the prize in his lifetime, didn't. Fernando Pessoa (1888–1935) is one of the great originals of modern European poetry and Portugal's premier modernist. He is also a strange and original writer. Other modernists—Yeats, Pound, Eliot—invented masks through which to speak occasionally, from Michael Robartes to Hugh Selywn Mauberly to J. Alfred Prufock. Pessoa invented whole poets. In fact, his work consists of the collected works of at least four very different poets, all invented by him. He called these alter egos his "heteronyms." There is Alberto Caeiro, the Master, a country gentleman without much formal education. And Alvaro de Campos, a naval engineer by profession, who began his poetic career as a futurist. And Ricardo Reis, a doctor and a classicist, with an attachment to the odes of Horace. There were others, including a reclusive man named Fernando Pessoa. All of the poets were about the same height and build, though of very different temperaments, and occasionally they wrote about each other.

There is no way, therefore, to represent Pessoa in a single poem, but one has to choose. So here is the beginning of a poem by the master, Alberto Caeiro. It dates from the 1920s:

> I've never kept sheep,
> But it's as if I did.
> My soul is like a shepherd.
> It knows the wind and sun,
> And walks hand in hand with the Seasons
> Looking at what passes.
> All the peace of Nature without people
> Sits down at my side.
> But I get sad like a sunset
> In our imagination
> When the cold drifts over the plain
> And we feel the night come in
> Like a butterfly through a window.
>
> Yet my sadness is a comfort
> For it is natural and right
> And is what should fill the soul
> Whenever it thinks it exists
> And doesn't notice the hands picking flowers.
>
> Like a sound of sheep bells
> Beyond the curve in the road
> My thoughts are content.
> My only regret is that I know they're content,
> Since if I did not know it
> They would be content and happy
> Instead of sadly content.
>
> Thinking is a discomfort, like walking in the rain
> When the wind kicks up and it seems to rain harder.

I have no ambitions and no desires.
To be a poet is not my ambition,
It's my way of being alone.

This translation comes from a new book, *Fernando Pessoa & Co.: Selected Poems,* translated by Richard Zenith and published by Grove Press. Also available and recently reissued by City Lights is the translation through which most English readers have gotten to know Pessoa's work, *Poems of Fernando Pessoa,* translated by Edwin Honig and Susan M. Brown. There is not much overlap—thanks to the generosity of Mr. Zenith—between the two books. So—though either would make a good introduction to his work—readers who want to get a sense of the size of Pessoa's startling work will want to acquire both.

NOVEMBER 22

Thanksgiving:
Harriet Maxwell Converse and Iroquois Song

Harriet Maxwell Converse was born on the western frontier of New York in 1836. Another of those remarkable and almost forgotten literary women of the American nineteenth century, she was a poet and an essayist who in the 1880s began to teach herself the culture of the Indians of New York State. She recorded the following prayer at a three-day Green Corn Festival on the Cattaraugus Reservation in September 1890. Her *Myths and Legends of the New York State Iroquois* was published after her death in 1908.

The Thanksgivings

We who are here present thank the Great Spirit that we are here to
    praise Him.
We thank Him that He has created men and women, and ordered
    that these beings shall always be living to populate the earth.
We thank Him for making the earth and giving these beings its
    products to live on.

We thank Him for the water that comes out of the earth and runs
on our lands.

We thank Him for all the animals on the earth.

We thank Him for certain timbers that grow and have fluids
coming from them for us all.

We thank Him for the shadows of the trees that grow shadows for
our shelter.

We thank Him for the beings that come from the west, the
thunder and lightning that water the earth.

We thank Him for the light which we call our oldest brother, the
sun that works for our good.

We thank Him for all the fruits that grow on the trees and vines.

We thank Him for his goodness in making the forests, and thank all
the trees.

We thank Him for the darkness that gives us rest, and for the kind
Being of the darkness that gives us light, the moon.

We thank Him for the bright spots in the skies that give us signs,
the stars.

We give Him thanks for our supporters, who have charge of our
harvests.

We give Him thanks that the voice of the Great Spirit can still be
heard through the words of Ga-ne-o-di-o.

We thank the Great Spirit that we have the privilege of this
pleasant occasion.

We give thanks for the persons who can sing the Great Spirit's
music, and hope they will be privileged to continue in His faith.

We thank the Great Spirit for all the persons who perform the
ceremonies on this occasion.

Converse supplies a couple of notes on the text. The "fluids" refer to
the sap of the maple. The "supporters" are "three sisters of great beauty,
who delight to dwell in the companionship of each other as the spiritual
guardians of the corn, the beans, and the squash . . . These guardians are
clothed in the leaves of their respective plants, and, though invisible, are
faithful and vigilant." "Ga-ne-o-di-o," or "Handsome Lake," was a Seneca
prophet of the Revolutionary War years. He lived into the nineteenth
century.

This translation could probably be improved upon. The "products" of the earth, and the "fluid" of the maple, and the "bright spots" of the stars are a little wooden. The moon in Iroquois song is often described as the grandmother, and the three "supporters," corn, beans, and squash, are the Three Sisters. But it is a tricky matter to rewrite these translations to conform with contemporary taste, without a personal or scholarly knowledge of the language. There are two more recent translations of thanksgiving songs available in English in Jerome Rothenberg's *Shaking the Pumpkin: Traditional Poetry of the Indian North Americas* (Anchor) and Brian Swann's *Coming to Light: Contemporary Translations of the Native Literature of North America* (Vintage). You will find an account of the life of Handsome Lake in Anthony Wallace's *The Death and Rebirth of the Seneca* (Knopf).

But for now: thanks to the maple sap, and to our older brother the sun, and to grandmother moon, and to the three sisters, and the stars that give us signs, and to the earth and the forests and the rivers and lakes, and all the animals of the earth. Have a good holiday.

NOVEMBER 29

A Swedish Poet: Tomas Tranströmer

I was just in Shanghai, which is undergoing a remarkable transformation. Across the river from the Bund, the old commercial district, which looks like a prosperous quayside in any European city of the Imperialist age, the city is a forest of cranes, and Pudong, a whole new city of postmodern glass and steel, is being thrown up. A friend had said to me that you could read the recent history of China in the faces on the street, as if you were surveying archaeological strata. And it was true. The elderly, remembering the time when Shanghai was the European banking city in Asia, would regard you with interest, might even approach you just to see if they could remember their English and practice it a little. The middle generations had endured famine; they had survived the Red Guard years, when the appearance of bourgeoisie tendencies could get you in trouble. They went by in an impassive stream, and if by chance they met your eye, they looked away quickly. The young looked like the young anywhere. They strolled, bantered with each other, chattered on cell phones, and regarded strangers with mild, good-natured curiosity.

The main experience of Shanghai, though, like the main experience of New York, is the sheer mass of people on the teeming streets. It reminded me, immediately, of a poem about those same streets written a couple of decades ago by the Swedish poet Tomas Tranströmer. Tranströmer is, by general consensus, one of the great living European poets. His work is characterized by a mix of precision, startling metaphors, and a piercing inwardness. He has some of the spiritual intensity and seriousness we associate with Scandinavian artists of an older generation, like Ingmar Bergman. So when I got home, I was very curious to see the poem again. Here is a northern Protestant sensibility, fascinated by the discrepancies between the outer world of public life and the inner world of feeling, meditating on the scene I had been visiting. I was amused to see that the poem did not, as I remembered, begin with the shock of the crowd. It began with a butterfly in the park. Here is the poem in the English translation of Samuel Charters:

Streets in Shanghai

I.
Many in the park are reading the white butterfly.
I love that cabbage butterfly as if it were a corner of truth itself!

At dawn the running crowds set our silent planet going.
Then the park fills with people. For each one eight faces polished
    like jade, for all situations, to avoid mistakes.
For each one also the invisible face that reflects "something you
    don't talk about."
Something that emerges in tired moments and is as pungent
    as a sip of Viper schnapps, with its long, scaly aftertaste.
The carp in the pond are always moving, they swim while they're
    sleeping, they are an example for the faithful: always in motion.

II.
Now it's noon. The washing flutters in the gray sea wind high
    above the cyclists who come in tight shoals. Notice the
    labyrinths to the sides!

I am surrounded by written characters I can't interpret. I am
   illiterate through and through.
But I have paid what I'm supposed to and I have receipts for
   everything. I have gathered so many unreadable receipts.
I am an old tree with withered leaves that hang on and can't
   fall to earth.

And a gust from the sea rustles all these receipts.

III.
At dawn the trudging crowds set our silent planet going.
We're all on board the street, it's as crowded as the deck of a ferry.
Where are we going? Are there enough teacups? We can consider
   ourselves fortunate for getting on this street in time!
It's a thousand years before the birth of claustrophobia.

Behind each one walking here hovers a cross that wants to catch
   up to us, pass us, join us.
Something that wants to sneak up on us from behind and cover
   our eyes and whisper, "Guess who?"
We look happy out in the sun, while we bleed to death from
   wounds we know nothing about.

Rereading these final lines also surprised me. Is it a Christian cross? The
metaphorical cross that we, each of us, have to bear of our own forms of
private suffering? Tranströmer is always interested in the individual soul,
not the public face. "We visited their home, which was well-appointed,"
one of his poems goes, "Where is the slum?" But a Christian metaphor
in this context—given the entangled history of missionary activity and
Western imperialism? It seems unlikely. This is one of those cases where
we are brought up against the limits of translation. One wants to know
what that "cross" is in Swedish and what its resonances are.

DECEMBER 6

Czeslaw Milosz: The Poet as a Road-side Dog

Here's a gift for the holidays.

For years now it's been a part of my routine to meet a morning or afternoon a week with Czeslaw Milosz and work for a couple of hours at making English language versions of his poems. Milosz is well into his eighties and not only keeps writing but keeps inventing. The last project we worked on is a book mostly of short prose pieces: aphorisms, anecdotes, musings, observations, thoughts on the wing. He called the book *Road-side Dog*. Which I suppose is a way of summing up his sense of his life. The first piece in the book reaches back to his youth in Lithuania early in the century and explains the title.

Road-side Dog

I went on a journey in order to acquaint myself with my province, in a two-horse wagon with a lot of fodder and a tin bucket rattling in the back. The bucket was required for the horses to drink from. I traveled through a country of hills and pine groves that gave way to woodlands, where swirls of smoke hovered over the roofs of houses, as if they were on fire, for they were chimneyless cabins; I crossed districts of fields and lakes. It was so interesting to be moving, to give the horses their rein, and wait until, in the next valley, a village slowly appeared, or a park with the white spot of a manor house in it. And always we were barked at by a dog, assiduous in its duty. That was the beginning of the century; this is its end. I have been thinking not only of the people who lived there once but also of the generations of dogs accompanying them in their everyday bustle, and one night—I don't know where it came from—in a pre-dawn sleep, that funny and tender phrase composed itself: a road-side dog.

One of my favorite pieces in the book was a musing on youth and age, time and eternity; it was initiated by a notice in the London *Times* that Christopher Milne, the son of A. A. Milne, who immortalized him in the person of Christopher Robin, had died at the age of seventy-five. The piece is written in the voice of Winnie-the-Pooh.

Christopher Robin

I must think suddenly of matters too difficult for a bear of little brain. I have never asked myself what lies beyond the place where we live, I and Rabbit, Piglet and Eeyore, with our friend Christopher Robin. That is, we continued to live here, and nothing changed, and I just ate my little something. Only Christopher Robin left for a moment.

Owl says that immediately beyond our garden Time begins, and that it is an awfully deep well. If you fall in it, you go down and down, very quickly, and no one knows what happens to you next. I was a bit worried about Christopher Robin falling in, but he came back and then I asked him about the well. "Old bear," he answered. "I was in it and I was falling and I was changing as I fell. My legs became long, I was a big person, I wore trousers down to the ground, I had a gray beard, then I grew old, hunched, and I walked with a cane, and then I died. It was probably just a dream, it was quite unreal. The only real thing was you, old bear, and our shared fun. Now I won't go anywhere, even if I'm called for an afternoon snack."

A few others to give you the flavor:

Learning

To believe you are magnificent. And gradually to discover that you are not magnificent. Enough labor for one human life.

O!

O objects of my desire, for whose sake I was able to practice asceticism, to be ardent, heroic, what pity I feel any time I think of your lips and hands and breasts and bellies consigned to bitter earth!

From My Dentist's Window

Extraordinary. A house. Tall. Surrounded by air. It stands. In the middle of a blue sky.

Road-side Dog is published by Farrar, Straus & Giroux.

DECEMBER 13

Israeli Poems on War and Peace: Yehuda Amichai

Eyes are on the Middle East again as we enter the holiday season. I have been browsing in a book called *After the First Rain: Israeli Poems on War and Peace* (Dryad Press), edited by Moshe Dor and Barbara Goldberg and translated by a number of eminent American poets. It begins with a foreword by Shimon Peres, who recalls in movingly spare and evocative language the ideals and the assassination of his friend Yitzhak Rabin. The poems, of course, speak about the tragedy of war and the longing for peace.

Great poetry doesn't necessarily get made out of important subjects. But this is an urgent subject, and the poems address it eloquently. War-weariness, piercing sadness, hope. One of the most eloquent is "Seven Laments for the War Dead" by Yehuda Amichai. Here is a section of it:

> Is all of this
> sorrow? I don't know.
> I stood in the cemetery dressed in
> the camouflage clothes of a living man: brown pants
> and a shirt yellow as the sun.
>
> Cemeteries are cheap; they don't ask for much.
> Even the wastebaskets are small, made for holding
> tissue paper
> that wrapped flowers from the store.
> Cemeteries are a polite and disciplined thing.
> "I shall never forget you," in French

on a little ceramic plaque.
I don't know who it is that won't ever forget:
he's more anonymous than the one who died.

Is all of this sorrow? I guess so.
"May ye find consolation in the building
of the homeland." But how long
can you go on building the homeland
and not fall behind in the terrible
three-sided race
between consolation and building and death?

Yes, all of this is sorrow. But leave
a little love burning always
like the small bulb in the room of a sleeping baby
that gives him a bit of security and quiet love
though he doesn't know what the light is
or where it comes from.

This translation from the Hebrew is by Chana Bloch.

DECEMBER 20

Christmas: Mark Doty

For Christmas week I ought to be able to find a poem that rings
out like Handel's *Messiah*. What I found was a poem that describes how
Handel's *Messiah* rings out. It's by Mark Doty, from his recent book *Sweet
Machine* (HarperCollins). It's too long to quote all of it here. It begins by
describing burning clouds, "torn and sun-shot swaddlings," over a Meth-
odist church where the Choral Society is preparing a performance:

Silence in the hall,
anticipatory, as if we're all
about to open a gift we're not sure
we'll like;

how could they
compete with sunset's burnished
oratorio? Thoughts which vanish
    when the violins begin.

Who'd have thought
they'd be so good? *Every valley,*
proclaims the solo tenor,
    (a sleek blonde

I've seen somewhere before
—the liquor store?) *shall be exalted,*
and in his handsome mouth the word
    is lifted and opened

into more syllables
than he could count, central *ah*
dilated in a baroque melisma,
    liquified; the pour

of voice seems
to *make* the unplaned landscape
the text predicts the Lord
    will heighten and tame.

This music
demonstrates what it claims:
glory shall be revealed. If art's
    acceptable evidence,

musn't what lies
behind the world be at least
as beautiful as the human voice?
    The tenors lack confidence,

and the soloists,
half of them anyway, don't
have the strength to found
    the mighty kingdoms

    these passages propose
—but the chorus, all together,
equals my burning clouds,
    and seems itself to burn,

    commingled powers
deeded to a larger, centering claim.
These aren't anyone we know;
    choiring dissolves

    familiarity in an up-
pouring rush which will not
rest, will not, for a moment,
    be still.

    Aren't we enlarged
by the scale of what we're able
to desire? Everything,
    the choir insists,

    might flame;
inside these wrappings
burns another, brighter life,
    quickened, now,

    by song: hear how
it cascades, in overlapping,
lapidary waves of praise? Still time.
    Still time to change.

I had to look up "melisma." It means, in Gregorian chant, "a passage sung to one syllable of text." So now I have a word for those sweet waterfalls made out of a single vowel sound in old carols. There is even, according to my dictionary, an adjectival form. So here's hoping your holidays are melismatic.

DECEMBER 27

A Poem for the End of a Thousand Years: W. H. Auden

We are about to enter the last year of the century and—I was going to write—of a millennium, but who, in fact, has any sense of the year 999, or for that matter 1132 or 1412? This last century has been more than enough for us to try to take in. So I found myself thinking about an appropriate valediction to this last extraordinarily violent hundred years. Sixty years ago this January, on the eve of the Second World War, the Irish poet William Butler Yeats died. A younger English poet, W. H. Auden, wrote an elegy for him. It's become a very famous poem. A winter like this one. The tenth year of an economic depression. Hitler's military, having annexed Austria and the Sudetenland, is drawing up plans for the conquest of Europe. And an Irish poet dies:

> *In Memory of W. B. Yeats*
> *(d. Jan 1939)*
>
> I.
> He disappeared in the dead of winter:
> The brooks were frozen, the airports almost deserted,
> And snow disfigured the public statues;
> The mercury sank in the mouth of the dying day.
> What instruments we have agree
> The day of his death was a dark cold day.
>
> Far from his illness
> The wolves ran on through the evergreen forests,

The peasant river was untempted by the fashionable quays;
By mourning tongues
The death of the poet was kept from his poems.

But for him it was his last afternoon as himself,
An afternoon of nurses and rumours;
The provinces of his body revolted,
The squares of his mind were empty,
Silence invaded the suburbs,
The current of his feeling failed; he became his admirers.

Now he is scattered among a hundred cities
And wholly given over to unfamiliar affections
To find his happiness in another kind of wood
And be punished under a foreign code of conscience.
The words of a dead man
Are modified in the guts of the living.

But in the importance and noise of to-morrow
When the brokers are roaring like beasts on the floor of the
    Bourse,
And the poor have the sufferings to which they are fairly
    accustomed,
And each in the cell of himself is almost convinced of his freedom,
A few thousand will think of this day
As one thinks of a day when one did something slightly unusual.

What instruments we have agree
The day of his death was a dark cold day.

II.
You were silly like us; your gift survived it all:
The parish of rich women, physical decay,
Yourself. Mad Ireland hurt you into poetry.
Now Ireland has her madness and her weather still,
For poetry makes nothing happen: it survives
In the valley of its making where executives
Would never want to tamper, flows on south

From ranches of isolation and the busy griefs,
Raw towns that we believe and die in; it survives,
A way of happening, a mouth.

III.
Earth, receive an honoured guest:
William Yeats is laid to rest.
Let the Irish vessel lie
Emptied of its poetry.

In the nightmare of the dark
All the dogs of Europe bark,
And the living nations wait,
Each sequestered in its hate;

Intellectual disgrace
Stares from every human face,
And the seas of pity lie
Locked and frozen in each eye.

Follow, poet, follow right
To the bottom of the night,
With your unconstraining voice
Still persuade us to rejoice;

With the farming of a verse
Make a vineyard of the curse,
Sing of human unsuccess
In a rapture of distress;

In the deserts of the heart
Let the healing fountains start,
In the prison of his days
Teach the free man how to praise.

The Bourse is the name of the French stock exchange.
Happy New Year.

A Scottish Poet for New Year's Day: George Mackay Brown

For the New Year and for the winter season, I turned to the Scottish poet George Mackay Brown. I discovered Brown's work only after his death in 1995 when I came across his *Selected Poems 1954–1992* (University of Iowa Press). When I thought about finding a poem for the first snows of the new year, something new and ancient and alive with wonder and with stinging cold, I turned to the book of his I ordered from an English publisher, *Following a Lark* (John Murray). Published in the last year of his life, it is as good as I remembered him to be, and I found exactly what I was looking for.

Brown was born on the Orkney Islands in the far north of Scotland in 1921 and lived in that remote place all his life, leaving it only to go to the University in Edinburgh. He wrote poems and plays and novels about his place, its history and lore, creating a body of work, as Seamus Heaney has said, that "has added uniquely and steadfastly to the riches of poetry in English." He's a wonderful poet, not to be missed. And it's possible to miss him; he has not registered with the makers of canons. You will not find his poems in any of the university anthologies of twentieth-century poetry I consulted. Here's a poem from *Following a Lark:*

A Boy in a Snow Shower

Said the first snowflake
No, I'm not a shilling,
I go quicker than a white butterfly in summer.

Said the second snowflake
Be patient, boy.
Seize me, I'm a drop of water on the end of your finger.

The third snowflake said,
A star?
No, I've drifted down out of that big blue-black cloud.

And the fourth snowflake,
Ah good, the road
Is hard as flint, it tolls like iron under your boots.

And the fifth snowflake,
Go inside, boy,
Fetch your scarf, a bonnet, the sledge.

The sixth snowflake sang,
I'm a city of sixes,
Crystal hexagons, a hushed sextet.

And the trillionth snowflake,
All ends with me—
I and my brother Fire, we end all.

JANUARY 10

In Memoriam: Margaret Walker

Margaret Walker Alexander died in December at the age of eighty-three.
A poet and novelist, black woman, minister's daughter, and an educator,
she was born in Birmingham, Alabama, grew up in New Orleans, and
went on to Northwestern University and the University of Iowa in the
difficult years of the Depression. Her first book, *For My People,* won the
Yale Younger Poet's award in 1942. Here, in her memory, is the title poem
from that book:

For My People

For my people everywhere singing their slave songs repeatedly:
their dirges and their ditties and their blues and jubilees, pray-
ing their prayers nightly to an unknown god, bending their
knees humbly to an unseen power;

For my people lending their strength to the years, to the gone
years and the now years and the maybe years, washing ironing
cooking scrubbing sewing mending hoeing plowing digging
planting pruning patching dragging along never gaining never
reaping never knowing and never understanding;

For my playmates in the clay and dust and sand of Alabama back-
yards playing baptizing and preaching and doctor and jail and
soldier and school and mama and cooking and playhouse and
concert and store and hair and Miss Choomby and company;

For the cramped bewildered years we went to school to learn
to know the reasons why and the answers to and the people
who and the places where and the days when, in memory of
the bitter hours when we discovered we were black and poor
and small and different and nobody cared and nobody won-
dered and nobody understood;

For the boys and girls who grew in spite of these things to
be man and woman, to laugh and dance and sing and play
and drink their wine and religion and success, to marry their
playmates and bear children and then die of consumption and
anemia and lynching;

For my people thronging 47th Street in Chicago and Lenox
Avenue in New York and Rampart Street in New Orleans, lost
disinherited dispossessed and happy people filling the cabarets
and taverns and other people's pockets needing bread and shoes
and milk and land and money and something—something all
our own;

For my people walking blindly spreading joy, losing time being lazy, sleeping when hungry, shouting when burdened, drinking when hopeless, tied and shackled and tangled among ourselves by the unseen creatures who tower over us omnisciently and laugh;

For my people blundering and groping and floundering in the dark of churches and schools and clubs and societies, associations and councils and committees and conventions, distressed and disturbed and deceived and devoured by money-hungry glory-craving leeches, preyed on by facile force of state and fad and novelty, by false prophet and holy believer;

For my people standing staring trying to fashion a better way from confusion, from hypocrisy and misunderstanding, trying to fashion a world that will hold all the people, all the faces, all the adams and eves and their countless generations;

Let a new earth rise. Let another world be born. Let a bloody peace be written in the sky. Let a second generation full of courage issue forth; let a people loving freedom come to growth. Let a beauty full of healing and a strength of final clenching be the pulsing in our spirits and our blood. Let the martial songs be written, let the dirges disappear. Let a race of men now rise and take control.

The poem was written in 1937 when she was twenty-two years old, and it became, a quarter of a century later, a kind of anthem of the civil rights movement. One of the things that's moving to me about it is the way that the young poet has found her voice in the Midwestern poetry of the period, especially Carl Sandburg's. Another is its feel for the lives of black people in the middle of the Depression and the way it gathers up the language and the anger and the idealism of the American radicals of the 1930s. Also the way the last lines of the poem use the language of progressives of the 1930s to call the generation of the 1950s and 1960s into being.

When Margaret Walker graduated from Northwestern in 1935 at the age of nineteen, she found work as a newspaper reporter and a social worker and joined the Federal Writers Project, where she met other Chicago writers like Gwendolyn Brooks, Nelson Algren, and Richard Wright. It was in those years and among this amazing collection of writers that the poem was written. "For My People" was published in *Poetry,* which was, of course, a Chicago magazine. Walker left Chicago in 1939 to get a master's degree in creative writing at the Iowa Writer's Workshop. It was her Iowa master's thesis that became her first, prize-winning book. She left Iowa in 1941 to teach at several small colleges in the South. She married in 1943 (and produced three of her four children in the next five years). In 1949 she took a job at Jackson State College in Jackson, Mississippi, and she taught there for thirty years, interrupted in the early 1960s by a return to Iowa, where she got a doctorate and worked on her long novel of black experience in the Civil War, *Jubilee,* which was published to wide admiration in 1968. She returned to poetry in her later years. She also wrote a biographical memoir of her friendship with Richard Wright and created the Institute for the Study of Black Life at Jackson State. In so many ways an exemplary life.

Her poems are collected in *This Is My Century: New and Selected Poems,* University of Georgia Press.

JANUARY 17

In Memoriam: Janet Lewis

Janet Lewis died in December at the age of ninety-nine. She is best known as a novelist, and she was a writer's writer. Her reputation rests on three short historical novels, *The Wife of Martin Guerre, The Trial of Soren Qvist,* and *The Ghost of Monsieur Scarron.* I don't know how many times over the years I've heard writers, making their lists of great neglected books of the twentieth century, begin talking with excitement about *The Wife of Martin Guerre.* Often enough. She has, in that way, always gotten her due. And there are also signs of a public revival of her reputation. There was a long essay about her recently by Larry McMurtry in the *New York Review of Books* and the obituary in the *New York Times* described *Martin Guerre* as the twentieth century's "Billy Budd" and placed her in the company of Melville and Stendahl.

She was also a poet and the wife of a poet. She was born in Chicago at the beginning of the century, went to high school in Oak Grove with Ernest Hemingway, majored in French at the University of Chicago,

and went to Paris. Tuberculosis made her a Westerner. She contracted
it in 1921 and spent the next five years at a sanitarium in Santa Fe. Her
earliest poems are imagist evocations of the Ojibway culture of northern
Michigan. Imagism—Ezra Pound's 1910 movement to modernize Ameri-
can poetry—was launched in Chicago's *Poetry* magazine, and the teens of
the century were also the period when Frances Densmore's now-classic
translations of Chippewa and Teton Sioux songs began to appear in the
ethnological and literary journals, so those influences might be what was
expected of an advanced young poet coming of age in 1920. But she had
her own way with them. Look, for example, at this early poem, "Like
Summer Hay." Part of its art is that she does not tell the reader until the
last word in the poem *what* is like summer hay:

Like Summer Hay

Like summer hay it falls
Over the marshes, over
The cranberry flats,
Places where
      the wild deer lay.

Now the deer leave tracks
Down the pine hollow; petals
Laid two by two, brown
Against the snow.

While she was in Santa Fe she began a correspondence with the soon-
to-be-famous poet and critic Yvor Winters, whom she had met in Chi-
cago. They married, and she followed him to California, where she settled
into a domestic life, raised her children, wrote her novels and her poems
(and short stories and five opera librettos), and left public literary life to
her husband, who achieved his notoriety as the fiercest and most com-
bative of the New Critics. I took a course from her husband but met
her only years later, an elderly woman of almost astonishing serenity and
presence whom I found myself sitting next to at some literary dinner to
raise money for environmental causes. What I remember of it is a lesson
in language. I thought that her eyes were as alert as some predatory bird's,
and during dinner someone else at the table described another person

as having "bird-like eyes." Janet Lewis folded her hands in her lap and smiled. "Oh, yes. Bird-like. That's what they say of us old ones if they want to say that we're still alive, that we have eyes like birds."

Here is one of her later poems, written when she was in her seventies, to a friend whose child was dying of leukemia:

For the Father of Sandro Gulotta

When I called the children from play
Where the westering sun
Fell level between the leaves
      of olive and bay,
There, where the day lilies stand,
I paused
      to touch with a curious hand
The single blossom, furled,
That with morning had opened wide,
The long bud tinged
      with gold of an evening sky.

All day, and only one day,
It drank the sunlit air.
In one long day
All that it needed to do in this world
It did, and at evening precisely curled
The tender petals to shield
From wind, from dew,
The pollen-laden heart.
Sweet treasure gathered apart
From our grief, from our longing view,
Who shall say if the day was too brief,
For the flower, if time lacked?
Had it not, like the children, all Time
In their long, immortal day?

A selection of her poems can be found in *Poems Old and New,* published by Swallow Press/Ohio University Press, which is also the publisher of her prose.

JANUARY 24

Philip Larkin

Though it's a little early for Groundhog Day, this modest little ritual in the annual calendar has been on my mind, partly because of its hypothetical quality. This year the groundhog may come up to see if the impeachment trial is over yet, sniff the winter air for spring, and then crawl back down to her den, still smelling faintly of the late summer grasses she padded it with, and go back to sleep until the drone ends and the crocuses are up. My annual quest for a Groundhog's Day poem was made much easier this year by a helpful reader who sent along this poem by the English poet Philip Larkin.

Philip Larkin's poem is about a groundhog, which the English call a hedgehog, but not, of course, about our solar holiday. Nevertheless you can think of the end of the poem as a sudden piercing beam of hypothetical sunlight. Here it is:

The Mower

The mower stalled, twice; kneeling, I found
A hedgehog jammed up against the blades,
Killed. It had been in the long grass.

I had seen it before, and even fed it, once.
Now I had mauled its unobtrusive world
Unmendably. Burial was no help:

Next morning I got up and it did not.
The first day after a death, the new absence
Is always the same; we should be careful

Of each other, we should be kind
While there is still time.

This can be found in Larkin's *Collected Poems* (Farrar, Straus & Giroux).

JANUARY 31

A Spanish Poet: Rafael Alberti

The American Association of Literary Translators gives an award every year to the best book of literary translation into English, and the book they selected for 1998 is a remarkable one. Rafael Alberti is one of the group of poets—the others were Federico García Lorca, Jorge Guillén, and Vicente Aleixandre—who shaped modern Spanish poetry. Alberti is still alive at the age of ninety-eight, and what many regard as his best book, *A la Pintura*, a celebration in language of the art of painting, has been translated to stunning effect by Carolyn Tipton.

Some of the poems are about painters: Giotto, Botticelli, Titian, van Gogh, Monet. Some are about the elements of painting: the palette, the line, the brush, perspective. And some are about colors. Here are some sections from a poem called "Red":

1.
I am morning's first color,
day's last.

2.
I wrestle with the green in fruit; I win.

3.
With my brothers, I submitted to the rigors
—Giotto—of geometric rapture.

7.
I congeal when my being
solidifies in black.

12.
Indistinct in certain nudes,
diluted by the snow.

15.
Purple through glass:
goblets, bottles, tumblers
warm with wine.

16.
Come to me cadmium yellow: I want to be an orange,
a lustrous sphere amidst the green.

21.
In Goya, I'm diluted by the air.

24.
All the way down to the rose rose of Picasso.

33.
Think how I'm lost
in the tiniest violet.

To Painting: Poems by Rafael Alberti, translated by Carolyn L. Tipton, was published by Northwestern University Press. The Spanish text is printed on the opposite page, and the book contains sixteen color prints of some of the paintings Alberti writes about. If you are thinking toward Valentine's Day, this book would make a beautiful gift.

FEBRUARY 7

George Herbert

Love poems: they are mostly about desire, especially unfulfilled desire. Either about the absent lover, like this well-known and anonymous poem, so simple and memorable it has survived since the fifteenth century:

Western wind, when wilt thou blow?
The small rain down can rain.
Christ, if my love were in my arms
And I in my bed again!

Or about lost love, like this also well-known song lyric from the mid-twentieth century, whose author is also, for all practical purposes, anonymous:

Well, since my baby left me,
I found a new place to dwell.
It's down at the end of Lonely Street
At Heartbreak Hotel.

There is, of course, the breezy approach of this lyricist who is not anonymous at all:

So good-bye, dear, and amen.
Here's hoping we meet now and then.
Well, it was great fun,
It was just one of those things.

One way or another, as sung by Elvis Presley or written by Cole Porter, they are mostly about loss or absence. So when someone suggested I print a love poem, I thought that I would not look for a poem about wanting someone. Wanting someone, I said to myself, isn't the hard part, and love gets interesting after you've been through some hard parts. I didn't have a poem in mind when I started browsing anthologies, but I had an instinct. It was connected to my memory of a passage in Milan Kundera's *The Book of Laughter and Forgetting* where he says, of his heroine, that she traversed the memory of her dead husband's body as if she were an old geographer running his hands across a vellum map he had made in his youth of the known world. I picked up a book of seventeenth-century poetry because I thought John Donne might have what I want. And then my eyes fell unexpectedly on this poem. It's by the English priest, George Herbert. It's a religious poem, tender and surprising. It wasn't what I had in mind. It's a poem about love as a gift and a feast, and about the fact that it's really ourselves we have to overcome if we are going to get to it:

Love (III)

Love bade me welcome: yet my soul drew back,
    Guilty of dust and sin.
But quick-eyed Love, observing me grow slack
    From my first entrance in,
Drew nearer to me, sweetly questioning
    If I lacked any thing.

"A guest," I answered, "worthy to be here":
    Love said, "You shall be he."
"I, the unkind, ungrateful? Ah, my dear,
    I cannot look on thee."
Love took my hand, and smiling did reply,
    "Who made the eyes but I?"

"Truth, Lord: but I have marred them; let my shame
    Go where it doth deserve."
"And know you not," says Love, "who bore the blame?"
    "My dear, then I will serve."
"You must sit down," says Love, "and taste my meat."
    So I did sit and eat.

FEBRUARY 14

Valentine's Day: Kenneth Rexroth

Kenneth Rexroth was the poet of San Francisco in the 1940s and 1950s. He was there as an elder statesman of the maverick strain in American poetry when the Beat Generation assembled itself, and he gave it his blessing. He was one of the best literary essayists of his generation, and his translations of classical Chinese and Japanese poetry are still widely read. A gathering of his love poems was published recently by Copper Canyon Press, *Sacramental Acts: Love Poems,* edited by Sam Hamill and Elaine Laura Kleiner. Here's one of them:

Lute Music

The earth will be going on a long time
Before it finally freezes;
Men will be on it; they will take names,
Give their deeds reasons.
We will be here only
As chemical constituents—
A small franchise indeed.
Right now we have lives,
Corpuscles, ambitions, caresses,
Like everybody had once—
All the bright *neige d'antan* people,
"Blithe Helen, white Iope, and the rest,"
All the uneasy, remembered dead.

Here at the year's end, at the feast
Of birth, let us bring to each other
The gifts brought once west through deserts—
The precious metal of our mingled hair,
The frankincense of enraptured arms and legs,
The myrrh of desperate, invincible kisses—
Let us celebrate the daily
Recurrent nativity of love,
The endless epiphany of our fluent selves,
While the earth rolls away under us
Into unknown snows and summers,
Into untraveled spaces of the stars.

Rexroth was, for a while, a devout Anglican and a left labor radical, later an anarchist and a Buddhist. His poetry is always aware of the Christian calendar. Even after his Christianity seemed to have lapsed, or broadened, he thought of the liturgical year as a European heritage, both Mediterranean and Northern, of myths and stories and feast days that sanctified the year. This poem must have been written for Christmas, "the feast of birth," or for Twelfth Night, the feast of the Epiphany. *Neige d'antan* is a phrase from a famous ballad by the French medieval poet Jacques Villion: "the snows of yesteryear." And the line in quotation marks may be a scrap from the Greek anthology, which he also translated. I was struck by the fact that the poem was a variation on the old theme—not "Gather ye rosebuds while ye may," but "Be glad for your rosebuds while ye may." Snow and roses. It seemed the right imagery for Valentine's Day.

And here, for good measure, are a couple of his translations of very old Japanese poems, probably lyrics from the folk-song tradition:

> The first time I saw you
> Was last year in May,
> In May, bathing in a pool
> Crowded with iris.

> The nightingale on the flowering plum,
> The stag beneath the autumn maple,
> And you and me together in bed,
> Happy as two fish in the water.

FEBRUARY 21

An Irish Poet: Paul Muldoon

Irish haiku? Irish haiku in New Jersey? Paul Muldoon is an Irish poet of the next generation after Seamus Heaney. Every generation has to clear a space to make itself heard, and Muldoon's way to clear a space in a tradition that included William Butler Yeats, a visionary and urbane poet, and Patrick Kavanaugh, an earthy country poet, and Seamus Heaney, who some have said is a perfect fusion of the two impulses, was to write a different poetry altogether: witty, cosmopolitan, playful, and postmodern. Lately Muldoon has been teaching at Princeton University, and his latest book, *Hay* (Farrar, Straus & Giroux), contains a sequence of haiku, mostly set in New Jersey. Muldoon's way with the form is to observe the syllable count—five syllables, seven syllables, five syllables—and to rhyme the first and last line. Here's a taste:

1.
The door of the shed
open-shuts with the clangor
of red against red.

2.
A muddle of mice.
Their shit looks like caraway
but smells like allspice.

5.
A stone at its core,
this snowball's the porcelain
knob on winter's door.

8.
Snow up to my shanks.
I glance back. The path I've hacked
is a white turf bank.

That one is definitely a poem of the Irishman in North America. If you've seen those cut black banks of peat in the Irish countryside, you'll recognize how the piled snow resembles it.

11.
Pennons in pine woods
where the white-tailed stag and doe
until just now stood.

I like this. Pennons are flags, those small banners of royalty or war; they resemble the flash of white tail you see when a deer suddenly starts and disappears.

12.
For most of a week
we've lived on a pot of broth
made from a pig's cheek.

19.
A mare's long white face.
A blazed tree marking a trail
we'll never retrace.

21.
Jean stoops to the tap
set into a maple's groin
for the rising sap.

This may have a double meaning, but I leave it to you.

22.
The Canada geese
straighten a pantyhose seam,
press a trouser crease.

And so through the year. He ends with the maple tree again:

90.
The maple's great cask
that once held so much in store
now yields a hip flask.

FEBRUARY 28

Ben Jonson

The young Shakespeare in *Shakespeare in Love,* a friend remarked as we
were walking out of the movie theater, was so handsome and so charm-
ingly inept that he didn't need to write soulful sonnets to get the girl.
There was a trace of rue in his voice. Not all of the tribe, whom a later
king of England, less literary than Elizabeth, called "ink-stained wretches,"
are so blessed. Shakespeare's friend and fellow playwright Ben Jonson,
for example, is one of the most elegant poets in the English language, a
master not only of biting stage satires like *Volpone* but of the smooth and

graceful courtly lyric, but he was not notably handsome. This is probably his best-known lyric:

Song: To Celia

Drink to me only with thine eyes,
    And I will pledge with mine;
Or leave a kiss but in the cup,
    And I'll not look for wine.
The thirst that from the soul doth rise,
    Doth ask a drink divine:
But might I of Jove's nectar sup,
    I would not change for thine.
I sent thee late a rosy wreath,
    Not so much honoring thee,
As giving it a hope, that there
    It could not withered be.
But thou thereon did'st only breathe,
    And sent'st it back to me;
Since when it grows, and smells, I swear,
    Not of itself, but thee.

Notice that she sent the wreath back. The poem may not have worked either. Jonson was a hulk of a man. One of my favorite poems of his is the one, written in middle age, in which he grumbles to himself about the failure of his poems to overcome what he seems to have regarded as his less than preposessing appearance:

My Picture Left in Scotland

I now think, Love is rather deaf, than blind,
    For else it could not be,
      That she,
Whom I adore so much should so slight me,
    And cast my love behind:
I'm sure my language to her, was as sweet,
     And every close did meet
    In sentence, of as subtle feet,

As hath the youngest he,
That sits in shadow of Apollo's tree.

Oh, but my conscious fears,
That fly my thoughts between,
Tell me that she hath seen
My hundred of grey hairs,
Told seven-and-forty years,
Read so much waist, as she cannot embrace
My mountain belly, and my rocky face,
And all these through her eyes, have stopped her ears.

MARCH 7

Pattiann Rogers

I always seem to want it to be spring before winter is done with. I start counting it as spring, secretly, mentally, from about March 1 onward, which is not really cheating in Washington, where the budgeting process leads to an entirely creative attitude toward time, or in California, where I start counting in mid-February. But I have thought "spring" and gone out looking for evidence in various climates—on the edges of Lake Erie, along the Iowa River, and even in muddy iced-over fields in the Norfolk Broads in bitter March, and in a Mexican desert in December. I was musing on this fact of my character when I came across this poem by Pattiann Rogers from her book *Eating Bread and Honey*. It was published in 1997, and I'm just catching up with it. Ms. Rogers lives in Colorado. Her work has always appealed to me because she knows so much natural history, and knows it with such exuberance.

Opus from Space

Almost everything I know is glad
to be born—not only the desert orangetip,
on the twist flower or tansy, shaking
birth moisture from its wings, but also the naked

warbler nesting, head wavering toward sky,
and the honey possum, the pygmy possum,
blind, hairless thimbles of forward,
press and part.

Almost everything I've seen pushes
toward the place of that state as if there were
no knowing any other—the violent crack
and seed-propelling shot of the witch hazel pod,
the philosophy implicit in the inside out
seed-thrust of the wood sorrel. All hairy
saltcedar seeds are single-minded
in their grasping of wind and spinning
for luck toward birth by water.

And I'm fairly shocked to consider
all the bludgeonings and batterings going on
continually, the head-rammings, wing-furors,
and beak-crackings fighting for release
inside gelatinous shells, leather shells,
calcium shells or rough, horny shells. Legs
and shoulders, knees and elbows flail likewise
against their womb walls everywhere, in pine
forest niches, seepage banks and boggy
prairies, among savannah grasses, on woven
mats and perfumed linen sheets.

Mad zealots, every one, even before
beginning they are dark dust-congealings
of pure frenzy to come to light.

Almost everything I know rages to be born,
the obsession founding itself explicitly
in the coming bone harps and ladders,
the heart-thrusts, vessels and voices
of all those speeding with clear and total
fury toward this singular honor.

Eating Bread and Honey comes from Milkweed Editions.

An Italian Poet: Eugenio Montale

In 1948, in the desolation following the war and the collapse of fascism, Eugenio Montale, then fifty-two years old, wrote what is perhaps the most famous and best-loved Italian poem of the twentieth century. Montale has been for me one of those poets, like Boris Pasternak, whose greatness a reader of translations has had to take on faith. I didn't feel that I got from the poems whatever it was that made his elusive and somewhat astringent spirit so central to modern European poetry.

Someone said, in the nineteenth century, that one reads poetry to hear great souls talking to themselves. Montale, especially the elder Montale, would have curled his lip at such a description, but the sensation I'd gotten from reading him was something like that—the sense of a great and necessary spirit, a man, in fact, with a troubled, almost dry, asperity of spirit and a wounding richness of mind, addressing himself—"muttering to himself," he said—often enough without hope, but with a willful refusal to abandon hope. There seems something about him of T. S. Eliot in that way, but also something of the learned, symbol-ridden, passionate, and questing side of W. B. Yeats. Montale has remained for me, for years, a sensibility that I'd imagined rather than taken in, a presence from whom I'd sensed there was much to learn, something crucial to learn, but to whom I never felt I had access.

Now an extraordinarily generous new translation has appeared of almost all of Montale's poems from the time of his early youth through the war years from the American poet Jonathan Galassi. The book gives you the Italian on the facing page, so that if you don't know or don't have much confidence with the language, you can at least glimpse across the page and get a sense of the music of the original. And it is packed with notes. Galassi has lived with these poems, studied Montale's prose, his letters and notebooks, studied the Italian critics who have commented on the poems lovingly (and learnedly), and he's given his readers the benefit of his own long absorption.

Here is the poem of 1948. It's about an eel. Montale caught them as a boy in the stream below his house, and they were a murky gold color in the muddy water.

The Eel

The eel, siren
of cold seas, who leaves
the Baltic for our seas,
our estuaries, rivers, rising
deep beneath the downstream flood
from branch to branch, from twig to smaller twig,
ever more inward,
bent on the heart of rock,
infiltrating muddy
rills until one day
light glancing off the chestnuts
fires her flash
in stagnant pools,
in the ravines cascading down
the Apennine escarpments to Romagna;
eel, torch, whiplash,
arrow of Love on earth,
whom only our gullies
or desiccated Pyrenean brooks lead back
to Edens of generation;
green spirit seeking life
where only drought and desolation sting;
spark that says that everything begins
when everything seems charcoal,
buried stump;
brief rainbow, iris,
twin to the one your lashes frame
and you set shining virginal among
the sons of men, sunk in your mire—
can you fail to see her as a sister?

The eel's gold color is caught in light reflected from the chestnuts of Romagna: it is an image of a world come back to life, an image, by the end of the poem, of the light in a woman's, an almost mythical woman's, eyes.

Galassi provides five pages of closely printed notes on this poem. His notes don't feel, ever, like pedantry. They are a kind of braille for people who can't see through to the music of the original. It makes for a book to be lived with.

MARCH 21

Claudia Rankine

Here is a difficult poem. It's written, like a piece of music, in three movements, and is meant, I think, to be read slowly. If you are going to know what's going on in an art, sometimes you have to give yourself to new and demanding work. This piece comes from *The End of the Alphabet,* recently published (Grove Press), a second book by Claudia Rankine, an African American poet born in Jamaica who lives in New York.

So—an adventurous young poet, willing to be difficult: the poem begins in a restlessness of spirit that needs to describe its condition. It picks its way, phrase to phrase, like music. Reading it, you have to be willing to give the poet a little of the indefiniteness of the state of feeling she's trying to describe and work through. That's what gives the poem its intimacy of voice, the sense that you are overhearing language the self speaks to the self, underneath the "light piled on indisputable light" of our more organized daytime speaking, in which the obligation to be clear is like the obligation to be cheerful and keeps everyone's obscure unhappiness or strangeness its own secret.

The Quotidian

> What we live
> before the light is turned off
> is what prevents the light from being turned off.
> In the marrow, in the nerve, in nightgowned exhaustion,
> to secure the heart,
> hoping my intention whole, I leave nothing
> behind, drag nakedness to the brisker air of the garden.

What the sweeper has not swept gathers
to delay all my striving. But here I arrive
with the first stars: the flame in each
hanging like a trophy in the lull just before
the hours, those antagonists
that haunt and confiscate
what the hardware of slumber draws below.

*

Night sky,

all day the light,

responding without proof, vigorously
embraced blue,
lavender-sucking bees,
a stone spewing water to golden carp.

Light piled on indisputable light rekindled bits of garden
until bare-shouldered, coherent, each root, its stem,
each petal and leaf
regained its original name
just as your door opened and we had to go through.

Which is to know your returned darkness was born first
with all its knowledge—
routine in the settling down, little thumps
like someone knocking at the temple—arriving

within each soul growing old
begging, impatient
for those nights to end, wanting
never darkness—

its murmurous mirror:

*

its drained tongue

as dead driftwood soaking the vein
as these words float up
out of body

in a joke sharpened in or sharpening
each myopic minute
met

and now dirtied up, or far too beautiful
for this

and now desperate for
the never would or could
or at least had not meant to mean).   Pity the stirred.

So stormed out, as in exhausted, my eardrums left watching.
Each nerve, in the mood exhumed,
hissing, *go away,*

go away,   night sky, did we come this far together?

I am cold. And in this next breath,
the same waking,

the same hauling of debris. I am
here in the skin of . . . otherwise) shoveling out, dryly

MARCH 28

Gerard Manley Hopkins

Gerard Manley Hopkins, an English Jesuit priest of the Victorian era who
spent much of his adult life in Ireland, is one of the great religious poets
in the English language. He is also—a somewhat different thing—a poet

of enormous spiritual intensity. Here are two of his best known poems, one of them full of joy, the other full of terrible suffering. They are both sonnets—though they burst the seams of that form; he gave them no titles. You can find them in the Penguin edition of *The Poems of Gerard Manley Hopkins:*

[As kingfishers catch fire . . .]

As kingfishers catch fire, dragonflies dráw fláme;
As tumbled over rim in roundy wells
Stones ring; like each tucked string tells, each hung bell's
Bow swung finds tongue to fling out broad its name;
Each mortal thing does one thing and the same:
Deals out that being indoors each one dwells;
Selves—goes itself; *myself* it speaks and spells,
Crying, *Whát I do is me: for that I came.*

Í say móre: the just man justices;
Kéeps gráce: thát keeps all his goings graces;
Acts in God's eye what in God's eye he is—
Chríst. For Chríst plays in ten thousand places,
Lovely in limbs, and lovely in eyes not his
To the Father through the features of men's faces.

[I wake and feel the fell . . .]

I wake and feel the fell of dark, not day.
What hours, O what black hours we have spent
This night! what sights you, heart, saw; ways you went!
And more must, in yet longer light's delay.
With witness I speak this. But where I say
Hours I mean years, mean life. And my lament
Is cries countless, cries like dead letters sent
To dearest him that lives alas! away.

I am gall, I am heartburn. God's most deep decree
Bitter would have me taste: my taste was me;
Bones built in me, flesh filled, blood brimmed the curse.

Selfyeast of spirit a dull dough sours. I see
The lost are like this, and their scourge to be
As I am mine, their sweating selves; but worse.

I once heard someone describe spirituality as "the vertical longings of the soul." I liked the definition; it brought to mind a shaft of cathedral sunlight or the soaring lift of a classic spiritual. But I also didn't like it because the conventional idea of heaven is up above. Religion is always a collective enterprise—a religion is communal worship centered on shared ideas of the sacred. Spirituality is always more individual. It has to do with the individual soul's struggle with its own meaning; it can even take the form of resistance to religion. Hopkins was certainly a religious poet. He submitted his work to his spiritual superiors and was in that way a faithful servant of his church. But, as these poems show, his spirituality was his own; he struggled with meaning on his own terms. In the first poem the soul's longings find a place on earth, or, in a flash of delight, he wants them to; in the other poem, they can't. In both—and this is what makes him such a remarkable poet—he wrings language out to speak the being that dwells, as he says, "indoors each one" of us.

APRIL 4

Easter: Charles Wright

Here is a poem for Easter. It comes from Charles Wright's most recent book, *Appalachia* (Farrar, Straus & Giroux). It's the third and final volume in his trilogy of suites of meditative poems that began with *Chickamauga* and *Black Zodiac,* which received the Pulitzer Prize in 1997.

Wright lives in Charlottesville, Virginia. In this poem it's the year of the Hale-Bopp comet, end of winter, light is coming over the Blue Ridge, and the poet is thinking about writing and about the idea of resurrection. And he takes his title from a great, funny, rueful line in a Bob Dylan song:

"When You're Lost in Juarez, in the Rain, and It's Easter Time Too"

Like a grain of sand added to time,
Like an inch of air added to space,

                    or a half-inch,

We scribble our little sentences.
Some of them sound okay and some of them sound not so okay.
A grain and an inch, a grain and an inch and a half.

Sad word wands, desperate alphabet.

Still, there's no alternative
Since language fell from the sky.
Though mystics have always said that communication is
    languageless.
And maybe they're right—

                  the soul speaks and the soul receives.
Small room for rebuttal there . . .

Over the Blue Ridge, late March late light annunciatory
    and visitational.

Tonight the comet Hale-Bopp

                will ghost up on the dark page of the sky
By its secret juice and design from the full moon's heat.
Tonight, some miracle will happen somewhere, it always does.
Good Friday's a hard rain that won't fall,
Wild onion and clump grass, green on green.

Our mouths are incapable, white violets cover the earth.

    You can feel the airiness of his style in this poem, the lightness. Wright's whole book is suffused with light, also with this sadness and religious—I think that's the word—longing. Reading the third volume, I began to see how much it is a journal of a certain kind of longing. And I was surprised to see how much the three books as a sequence reminded me of a poem I hadn't read in years, Tennyson's *In Memoriam A.H.H.*, that Victorian poem of doubt and religious longing I'd read in college and once or twice since. Most of what I carried away from it was a single line about a dark night of the soul and a morning that reveals nothing:

On the bald street breaks the blank day.

There is a little sequence of poems that runs through Wright's books called "The Appalachian Book of the Dead." And a sequence in this book is called "Opus Posthumous." There is a feeling in these poems of a consciousness on the edge of getting rid of the world, sloughing it off, studying the light for some sign that the old hymns are true, that something is coming to carry us home. The desire for it in the book's last poem is like a longing for absolute beauty. The poem itself is beautiful, almost apocalyptic, and—for me—a little scary:

Opus Posthumous III

Mid-August meltdown, Assurbanipal in the west,
Scorched cloud-towers, crumbling thrones—
The ancients knew to expect a balance at the end of things,
The burning heart against the burning feather of truth.
                                             Sweet-mouthed,
Big ibis-eyed, in the maple's hieroglyphs, I write it down.

All my life I've looked for this slow light, this smallish light
Starting to seep, coppery blue,
                    out of the upper right-hand corner of things,
Down through the trees and off the back yard,
Rising and falling at the same time, now rising, now falling,
Inside the lapis lazuli of late afternoon.

Until the clouds stop, and hush.
Until the left hedge and the right hedge,
                            the insects and short dogs,
The back porch and barn swallows grain-out and disappear.
Until the bypass is blown with silence, until the grass grieves.
Until there is nothing else.

This makes a cycle: from the annunciatory light of early spring to the grand closures of a late summer sunset. So grand it wants the clouds to stop.

Wright was born in Tennessee. He's a Southern poet whose work has been, for a long time, inflected by his love of Italian poetry and by the rhythms of Ezra Pound, out of which he's made his own music. Some of his best poems come from moments when his imagination seems to be idling, letting his attention find its focus, letting the world seep in, waiting for a music to come up. Almost like someone plucking at a guitar, waiting for the melody to take him, to tell him who he is or where he is. Here's one more:

Deep Measure

Shank of the afternoon, wan weight-light,
Undercard of a short month,
                    February Sunday . . .
Wordlessness of the wrong world.
In the day's dark niche, the patron saint of What-Goes-Down
Shuffles her golden deck and deals,
                    one for you and one for me . . .

And that's it, a single number—we play what we get.
My hand says measure,
                    doves on the wire and the first bulb blades
Edging up through the mulch-mat,
Inside-out of the winter gum trees,
A cold harbor, cold stop and two-step, and here it comes,

Deep measure,
                    deep measure that runnels beneath the bone,
That sways our attitude and sets our lives to music;
Deep measure, down under and death-drawn:
Pilgrim, homeboy of false time,
Listen and set your foot down,
                    listen and step lightly.

APRIL 11

Richard Wright and Langston Hughes

A surprise: a book of haiku written in his last years by the fierce and original American novelist, Richard Wright. Wright changed American literature by writing books—*Native Son, Black Boy*—that did not aim, as much of African American writing up to his time had done, to honor and celebrate African American experience; he wrote instead about the fact that poverty, discrimination, and hopelessness are not necessarily a formula for producing virtuous citizens. He wrote, especially in *Native Son,* the novel that brought him to public attention and became an un-expected best-seller in 1940, about the consequences of racism with an angry exactness that took readers—black and white—by surprise.

After the success of *Native Son* Wright moved to France and bought a farm in Normandy. His life there was partly exile and partly expa-triation. He escaped the daily humiliations of living with American apartheid, made friends with French writers like Sartre and Camus, and followed from a distance the controversy that continued to swirl about his reputation in the United States. He'd been for a while a Com-munist, like many other young American writers of the thirties, and into the 1950s American intelligence agencies kept black radical expatriates under surveillance.

It was in this context that, during the last eighteen months of his life, Wright discovered haiku. From the summer of 1959 until his death in late 1960, he studied the form and wrote, according to his editor, 4,000 poems. And then, "sifting through them to see if they are any good," he wrote to a friend, he put together a collection, *Haiku: This Other World,* which has only now been published in its entirety by Arcade Publishing in New York.

What an outpouring! Wright's way with the form was to keep strictly to the syllable count of the Japanese tradition—five syllables, seven syl-lables, five syllables. Many of the poems seem to be imitating and trying out Japanese ideas, applying them to the French countryside or to the remembered rural Mississippi of his childhood. Others try to bring the form to urban themes. Others—the most original—reach into the pulse of his own life.

The first poem in the book suggests why the form was so useful to him. I can't quote it directly—the publisher required permissions fees much larger than the budget of this book allowed us to pay but you will get a sense of it if I tell you it describes the sensation of a man watching a red sun go down in the fall and feeling like it's taking his name with it. In the brevity and ambiguity of haiku, you don't know if this is a premonition of death and a reflection on human insignificance, or if it carries in it a feeling of liberation—momentary or not—from the burden of being who he was, as if working in this small form with its requirement of quiet attention, he has been lifted away for a moment from his writer's vita, his radical's dossier, the fury of a life of literary controversy, and been given permission to be, to look.

In one poem, making a comedy of this, he gives the spring rain "permission" to soak a bed of violets. In another he observes a dog smelling out the telegram in the wet trunk of a tree. Some of them look back on his own life and also seem to absorb into him his own mortality. Another haiku watches an autumn bonfire of fallen leaves grow "bigger and bigger," a commentary on aging, but also a pun on the name of the angry black man, Bigger Thomas, who was the protagonist of *Native Son*.

Mostly they are shot through with moments of small intense observation: a warm wind drying a strand of hair on a woman's forehead; something about the straight lines of black steel in the railroad tracks that seems to have *caused* the snow that's falling on them; a hitchhiker in spring rain—something untrustworthy about his posture—who's not going to get a ride; summer rain and lights from a hospital slowly going on and off. It is wonderful to watch a writer practicing attention, and inspiring to see Richard Wright, past the burden of his fame, past politics, racism, war, exile, determined in this way to have his life on earth and to continue to have his say. You will have to look up the poems yourself. The book is worth owning, for the poems themselves and for the light they cast on Richard Wright's last years.

I can print one of his poems, because it's in the public domain. A collaboration with his friend Langston Hughes, it is an experiment in literary adaptation of the blues. It was published in the radical journal *New Masses* in August 1939:

Red Clay Blues

I miss that red clay, Lawd, I
Need to feel it in my shoes.
Says, miss that red clay, Lawd, I
Need to feel it in my shoes.
I want to get to Georgia cause I
Got them red clay blues.

Pavement's hard on my feet, I'm
Tired o' this concrete street.
Pavement's hard on my feet, I'm
Tired o' this city street.
Goin' back to Georgia where
That red clay can't be beat.

I want to tramp in the red mud, Lawd, and
The red clay round my toes.
I want to wade in that red mud,
Feel that red clay suckin' at my toes.
I want my little farm back, and I
Don't care where the landlord goes.

I want to be in Georgia, when the
Big storm starts to blow.
Yes, I want to be in Georgia when that
Big storm starts to blow.
I want to see the landlords runnin' cause I
Wonder where they gonna go!

I got them red clay blues.

Pleasant to think of the two of them—Hughes was 37, Wright 31;
Hughes already a famous poet, Wright having just come to prominence
with the book of stories, *Uncle Tom's Children*—hammering this out to-
gether. They must have had fun with the rhymes in the second stanza,
when the feet get tired of the concrete street.

APRIL 18

Wang Ping

Coffee House Press in Minneapolis has just published a book, *Of Flesh and Spirit*, by Wang Ping, a Shanghai-born novelist, poet, and short-story writer, who has made her home in New York since 1985. She writes in English, and seems to have developed her idiom and some of the freshness and energy of her poems from the scene around the St. Mark's Poetry Project, which has been a kind of home for experimental writing in the city for the last twenty-five years.

Of Flesh and Spirit experiments with lyric forms, prose forms, mixes of prose and verse, as it meditates on heritage, immigration, memory, anger, women's lives, and the life of the city. Here's a sample, a prose piece in which the author recalls her grandmother:

Resurrection

Who said a soul can't cross the sea? Last night, you slipped through my door again (three Medicos plus a latch), like a raindrop drifting into a broken dream. You leaned on the red brick wall, unwinding the endless bandages on your feet.

Eighty years, all carved on your huge heels and toeless soles. Your lips squirmed with your last request: a banana and a black silk gown.

No need to apologize, Nainai, for your reproaches or spankings. I only remember your tears of joy for the first bite of ice cream on your 79th birthday. It was a Friday. We were standing outside a food store on the Nanjing Road when you suddenly said it was your birthday. And I said, "Oh, let's celebrate," and ran in to get you a chocolate ice cream brick.

Please do not look at me with those bleak eyes. Even father's filial piety couldn't stop mother's fury and keep you at home. The night I carried you to the ship for Qingdao, I dreamed of turning into surging waves to retrieve your fading steps. I didn't realize until then that my childhood had been a vine hanging over the precipice of your life.

Do not wave your bandages at me. My feet have grown as hard as white poplars in our native town. I'll make a pair of wings with them, to carry your soul into spring, into the forest and grass, into a world without memory. Be a bird, a bee, or even a fly. Just to live again, with joy.

APRIL 25

Michael Ondaatje

Michael Ondaatje, who was born in Sri Lanka and lives in Toronto, has not published a book of poems in some years. During that interval he's made his reputation as a novelist with *In the Skin of the Lion* and *The English Patient,* and one of the most brilliant and strange and readable of memoirs in this time of memoirs, *Running in the Family.* The new book of poems, *Handwriting* (Alfred Knopf), is a departure from his rowdy and unpredictable early poems. It's extremely beautiful, for one thing, and much of it is set in Sri Lanka.

Here's a poem:

House on a Red Cliff

There is no mirror in Mirissa

the sea is in the leaves
the waves are in the palms

old languages in the arms
of the casuarina pine
parampara

parampara, from
generation to generation

The flamboyant a grandfather planted
having lived through fire
lifts itself over the roof

unframed

the house an open net

where the night concentrates
on a breath
                on a step
a thing or gesture
we cannot be attached to

The long, the short, the difficult minutes
of night

where even in darkness
there is no horizon without a tree

just a boat's light in the leaves

Last footsteps before formlessness

Parampara is Sri Lankan. It means "from generation to generation." I
don't know where this place is (a family house, the sense of generations
that the grandfather's tree would suggest), or why exactly the poem begins
by telling us there is no mirror there. Perhaps because the sense of time, of
trees that are in water and water that is in trees, of a house open to the air,
makes a place where it becomes possible to let the mirrored ego go.

A lot of the poems in the book are about place and about the architec-
ture of human desire. Here is a short poem that takes up the theme:

The First Rule of Sinhalese Architecture

Never build three doors
in a straight line

A devil might rush
through them
deep into your house,
into your life

Another poem's atmosphere reminds me of the old, wrecked Italian villa in *The English Patient*. It ends by describing an ancient Ceylonese Buddhist monastery, which becomes, like the villa in the novel, the source of a meditation on the architecture of desire:

Step

The ceremonial funeral structure for a monk
made up of thambili palms, white cloth
is only a vessel, disintegrates

completely as his life.

The ending disappears,
replacing itself

with something abstract
as air, a view.

All we'll remember in the last hours
is an afternoon—a lazy lunch
then sleeping together.

Then the disarray of grief.

*

On the morning of a full moon
in a forest monastery
thirty women in white
meditate on the precepts of the day
until darkness.

They walk those abstract paths
their complete heart
their burning thought focused
on this step, then *this* step.

In the red brick dusk
of the Sacred Quadrangle,
among holy seven-storey ambitions
where the four Buddhas
of Polonnaruwa
face out to each horizon,
is a lotus pavilion.

Taller than a man
nine lotus stalks of stone
stand solitary in the grass,
pillars that once supported
the floor of another level.

(The sensuous stalk
the sacred flower)

How physical yearning
became permanent.
How desire became devotional
so it held up your house,
your lover's house, the house of your god.

And though it is no longer there,
the pillars once let you step
to a higher room
where there was worship, lighter air.

MAY 2

Forrest Gander

Forrest Gander is a Southern poet of a relatively rare kind, a restlessly experimental writer. *Science and Steepleflower* (New Directions) is his fourth book and, as good as some of the earlier ones are—*Lynchburg, Deeds of Utmost Kindness*—it is perhaps his best yet.

   Be ready for a ride. The sentences often don't make sequential sense. He uses expressions from geology like "agnostoid lithofacies." It is a strange melange of pungent, physical detail, scraps of geological and evolutionary science, oddly erotic images, and almost surreally exact bits of description: a poet moving through words, through time, in a way that seems at once precise and hallucinatory.

Field Guide to Southern Virginia

True as the circumference
to its center. Woodscreek Grocery,
Rockbridge County. Twin boys
peer from the front window, cheeks
bulging with fireballs. Sandplum trees
flower in clusters by the levee. She
makes a knot on the inside knob
and ties my arms up
against the door. Williamsburg green.
With a touch as faint as a watermark.
Tracing cephalon, pygidium, glabella.

*

Swayback, through freshly cut stalks,
stalks the yellow cat. Can you smell
where analyses end, the orchard
oriole begins? Slap her breasts lightly
to see them quiver. Delighting in this.
Desiccation cracks, and plant debris
throughout the interval. In the Black-

water River, fishnets float
from a tupelo's spongy root
chopped into corks. There may be sprawling
precursors, descendent clades there are none.

*

The gambit declined was less
promising. So the flock of crows
slaughtered all sixty lambs. Toward the east, red
and yellow colors prevail.
Praying at the graveside,
holding forth the palm of his hand
as symbol of God's book.
For the entirety of the Ordovician.
With termites, Mrs. Elsinore explained,
as with the afterlife, remember:
there are two sides to the floor. A verb
for inserting and retrieving
green olives with the tongue. From
the scissure of your thighs.

*

In addition, the trilobites
were tectonically deformed. Snap-on
tools glinting from magenta
loosestrife, the air sultry
with creosote and cicadas.
You made me to lie down in a peri-Gondwanan back-arc basin.
Roses of wave ripples and gutter casts.
Your sex hidden by goat's beard.
Laminations in the sediment. All
preserved as internal molds
in a soft lilac shale.

*

Egrets picketing the spines of cattle in fields edged
with common tansy. Flowers my father gathered
for my mother to chew. To induce abortion. A common,
cosmopolitan agnostoid lithofacies naked in the foothills. I love
the character of your intelligence, its cast as well as pitch.
Border wide without marginal spines. At high angles
to the inferred shoreline.

*

It is the thin flute of the clavicles, each rain-pit
above them. The hypothesis of flexural loading. Aureoles
pink as steepleflower. One particular day, four hundred
million years ago, the mud stiffened
and held the strokes of waves. Orbital motion.
Raking leaves from the raspberries, you
uncover a nest of spring salamanders.

MAY 9

A Serbian Poet: Vasko Popa

Because, as I write this, American pilots are bombing the city of Belgrade,
I've been remembering a sunny fall day in the mid-1980s, when I walked
with friends through a park in the center of that city to an elegant old
apartment building on the park's edge where Serbia's best known poet,
Vasko Popa, lived. The neighborhood reminded me a little of Gramercy
Park in New York, though it was not in such good repair and it had had
a different history. There were still splinterings of bullet holes in some of
the old brownstones from what must have been machine gun fire in the
Second World War.

Popa belonged to the group of Eastern European poets—Zbigniew
Herbert in Poland, Miroslave Holub in Czechoslovakia—who went
through that war in their late adolescence and afterward wrote the poetry
that many of us turned to to understand what a poetry with a personal
acquaintance with historical and political disaster was like. I remember

that he seemed a radiantly healthy man with sad eyes, that we walked back through the park to a beautiful old restaurant full of gleaming mahogany, that the first course was a shot of cold Slivowitz—the transparent Serb plum brandy—and a plate full of raw, unpeeled sweet peppers, red and yellow and orange, which we ate like fruit. He did not speak much English, but my friends spoke both Serbian and English and Popa was fluent in French, so the conversation proceeded—much of it gossip about poets and poetry—in cheerful and polyglot high spirits in a mixture of the three languages that probably no one person at the table followed entirely.

Popa's poetry, especially the work of the 1970s, is steeped in Serbian history and national mythology and draws its style, or so I thought, from French surrealism. It seemed to me then a striking combination of tribal memory and modernist method. In these poems Belgrade is "the White City," Kosovo is "the Blackbird's Field," the Serbian people are the wolf's children, and St. Sava, the patron saint of the Serbs, is the wolf-shepherd, and the wolf's children are everywhere beset by enemies. Here, for example, are a few lines from a poem called "The Wolf Land":

> My son I see our land crucified
> Between four grindstones
> On which the wolf is sharpening his teeth

This was originally published in 1978 by Persea and is now available in *Collected Poems of Vasko Popa,* translated by Anne Pennington and Francis R. Jones (Anvil Press, 2001). I read it then as a dream journey through a violent past. I had no notion how active that past was, or could be made to seem. The sequence ends with the poet's return to Belgrade and with poems to the city and its river. Here they are:

Great Lord Danube

> O great Lord Danube
> In your veins flows
> The blood of the white town
>
> If you love it get up a moment
> From your bed of love
> Ride on your biggest carp

Pierce the leaden clouds
And visit your heavenly birthplace

Bring a gift to the white town
Fruits and birds and flowers of paradise

Bring too the stone which can be eaten
And a little air
Of which men do not die

The bell-towers will bow down to you
And the streets prostrate themselves before you
O great Lord Danube

Belgrade

White bone among the clouds

You arise out of your pyre
Out of your ploughed-up barrows
Out of your scattered ashes

You arise out of your disappearance

The sun keeps you
In its golden reliquary
High above the yapping of centuries

And bears you to the marriage
Of the fourth river of Paradise
With the thirty-sixth river of Earth

White bone among clouds
Bone of our bones

When I walked back to my hotel, it was almost four o'clock and the
streets were full of people, just walking; it was teeming with them, fam-
ilies, old women holding hands, young women holding hands, young

soldiers in pairs with loosely locked arms, old men talking and smoking. It was a custom, my friends said, all over Yugoslavia, and told me the Serbian word for it, something like "promenade." In the afternoons, if the weather was fine, the whole town turned out on the streets and strolled and visited and stopped at cafes for coffee or brandy.

MAY 16

Adrienne Rich

I was looking for a poem about spring, about the soft, almost-summer weather of mid-May, but it really wasn't what I was hungry for. The news has been so full of violence, and the violence—in Kosovo, in a high school in Colorado where two children had shot and killed their classmates—has been so dismaying that I found my mind wandering as I looked through old and new books for a lyric that called up the season. I needed to read something with more salt in it and more darkness. And the book that I found was Adrienne Rich's new volume, *Midnight Salvage* (W. W. Norton). Rich is one of our most distinguished poets—this is, by my count, her sixteenth book of poems—and one of the things that distinguishes her art is a restless need to confront difficulty, a refusal to be easily appeased.

I don't completely understand the poem that follows. I get the outline of it. Someone is walking up a hillside. It's probably fall: there's ground mist and the sun's tongue is "licking leaf upon leaf into stricken fluid." And the speaker comes across what she describes as a "shattered head," a skull, perhaps, such as one finds in the woods, a deer or a raccoon, but the description suggests a human head; in fact, it begins to feel as if it is the speaker's own head, imagined as the place that spring is going to come from: "tendrils soaked into matted compost." The lines that particularly moved me were:

> You can walk by such a place, the earth is made of them
> where the stretched tissue of a field or woods is humid
>   with beloved matter

The stanza continues in this way:

> the soothseekers have withdrawn
> you feel no ghost, only a sporic chorus
> when that place utters its worn sigh
>   *let us have peace*

I can think of poets who would end there, but Rich is not a poet to reconcile us, or herself, with the idea of death and regeneration. That is the quality of her mind for which I felt, this week, particularly grateful. In the poem the unappeased skull answers back. Here is the whole poem:

Shattered Head

A life hauls itself uphill
    through hoar-mist steaming
the sun's tongue licking
    leaf upon leaf into stricken liquid
When? When? cry the soothseekers
    but time is a bloodshot eye
seeing its last of beauty its own
    foreclosure
                            a bloodshot mind
finding itself unspeakable
    What is the last thought?
Now I will let you know?
    or, *Now I know?*
(porridge of skull-splinters, brain tissue
    mouth and throat membrane, cranial fluid)

Shattered head on the breast
    of a wooded hill
laid down there endlessly so
    tendrils soaked into matted compost
become a root
    torqued over the faint springhead
groin whence illegible
    matter leaches: worm-borings, spurts of silt

volumes of sporic changes
  hair long blown into far follicles
blasted into a chosen place

Revenge on the head (genitals, breast, untouched)
  revenge on the mouth
packed with its inarticulate confessions
  revenge on the eyes
green-gray and restless
  revenge on the big and searching lips
                    the tender tongue
revenge on the sensual, on the nose the
  carrier of history
revenge on the life devoured
in another incineration

You can walk by such a place, the earth is made of them
          where the stretched tissue of a field or woods is humid
      with beloved matter
the soothseekers have withdrawn
you feel no ghost, only a sporic chorus
when that place utters its worn sigh
  let us have peace

And the shattered head answers back
  I believed I was loved, I believed I loved,
  who did this to us?

MAY 23

Malena Mörling

Standing on the Metro, watching other people standing on the Metro, their faces, their body language, the tunnels flashing by, brightly lit stops full of posters advertising the glamour above ground—I recalled an old poet telling me once that he thought train travel had changed human consciousness forever. He was old enough to remember the shock of it, in Europe in the 1910s—plush coupes, and landscapes blurring past like a lesson in impressionist painting, and the bell they rang after every third stop to announce that the dining car was open.

Trains, he said, and big cities, the massive rhythm of crowds in big cities, had shown up at the same time in Western consciousness in the poetry of Charles Baudelaire in Paris and Walt Whitman in New York. Another American poet, George Oppen, described the awareness that grew on people in cities as "the fact of being numerous." And it taught us something about the solitariness of individual consciousness, and time speeding up or collapsing, and the mystery of other people with other lives, as if it were a sort of Buddhist allegory of the transience of things and the wonder of ourselves, of our single, instantaneous awareness.

I thought of this reading a first book, *Ocean Avenue,* by a new young poet, Malena Mörling, which captures these feelings in a very pure way. Mörling was born in Stockholm and lives in New York, so there is also something else in her poems that belongs to the twentieth-century business of crossing borders, cultures:

We Are Here

The train departs at dusk from New York
the neon signs begin to bleed their letters
the light goes into buildings
that pass like so much else that I notice
and forget and don't notice and remember
like specific places where litter ends up
and the last patches of snow
and the iron that rusts slowly
while millions of people are in a hurry.

There is no place to rush to or rush from
eternity is everywhere at once
in the instant the nail polish dries
on my mother's fingers
and my father does a card-trick
in front of the mirror

and I try to write on a train
in another country crossing a bridge
over the military green water
of the river to the Bronx and over the freeway
past Swingline Staplers and the Bronx Casket Co.
now that nothing is old or new
now that these words only resemble
the meaning of these words.

Here is another:

You Look Outside

You look outside.
Already it is five o'clock.
The world is disappearing.
Across the city, yellow leaves are dropping
from the trees—
lamps going out slowly—
In the Diamond district,
store owners undress
the windows. They unclasp necklaces
from the headless mannequins.
You look outside.
Already it is evening.
On the table, the books lie open
to where you stopped reading
about the Magellanic clouds.
The sky is violet against the iron railing.
In the river, cars drift
upside down with their lights on.

Maybe this consciousness also has to do with commercial culture—that linebreak on "store owners undress / the windows"—and the way our tired awareness wants to peel itself away from the continual sense of the world as theater, as a nervously hyped-up and faintly unreal show. In some of the poems this sense of things is touched by a visionary hunger:

When I Was Living Near the Ocean

When I was living near the ocean,
once or twice, suddenly
when I did not expect it,
when I was thinking about other things,
I looked up

and in the sunlight
through the green wigs of the trees
I saw the ocean.
But it was not the water,
it was something altogether different
that I could not name.

Ocean Avenue received the New Issues Poetry Prize from New Issues Press of Western Michigan University.

MAY 30

Memorial Day: Jaime Sabines

In March of this year, the most popular—"beloved" is the over-worked but accurate word in this case—of Mexican poets died at the age of seventy-two. Jaime Sabines was born in 1926 in the state of Chiapas, the son of a Lebanese immigrant father and a Mexican mother. He studied medicine and gave it up to write poetry, though he also had a public life. For six years in the mid-1970s, he served in the federal legislature. I think it's safe to say that we've never had such a congressman. In later years, I've been told, when he read his poems in public, the audience could chant them word for word. Here, in the translation of W. S. Merwin, is one of his best-known poems:

The Lovers

The lovers say nothing.
Love is the finest of silences,
the one that trembles most and is the hardest to bear.
The lovers are looking for something.
The lovers are the ones who abandon,
the ones who change, who forget.
Their hearts tell them that they will never find.
They don't find, they're looking.

The lovers wander around like crazy people
because they're alone, alone,
surrendering, giving themselves to each moment,
crying because they don't save love.
They worry about love. The lovers
live for the day, it's the best they can do, it's all they know.
They're going away all the time,
all the time, going somewhere else.
They hope,
not for anything in particular, they just hope.
They know that whatever it is they will not find it.
Love is the perpetual deferment,
always the next step, the other, the other.
The lovers are the insatiable ones,
the ones who must always, fortunately, be alone.

The lovers are the serpents in the story.
They have snakes instead of arms.
The veins in their necks swell
like snakes too, suffocating them.
The lovers can't sleep
because if they do the worms eat them.

They open their eyes in the dark
and terror falls into them.

They find scorpions under the sheet
and their beds float as though on a lake.

The lovers are crazy, only crazy
with no God and no devil.

The lovers come out of their caves
trembling, starving,
chasing phantoms.
They laugh at those who know all about it,
who love forever, truly,
at those who believe in love as an inexhaustible lamp.

The lovers play at picking up water,
tattooing smoke, at staying where they are.
They play the long sad game of love.
None of them will give up.
The lovers are ashamed to reach any agreement.

Empty, but empty from one rib to another,
death ferments them behind the eyes,
and on they go, they weep toward morning
in the trains, and the roosters wake into sorrow.

Sometimes a scent of newborn earth reaches them,
of women sleeping with a hand on their sex, contented,
of gentle streams, and kitchens.

The lovers start singing between their lips
a song that is not learned.
And they go on crying, crying
for beautiful life.

No translation can catch very well the music of the Spanish rhymes.
Try saying the last lines, even if you don't know the language. The *v* pro-
nounced as nearly *b,* the double *ll* as *y:*

Los amorosos se ponen a cantar entre labios
una canción no aprendida.
Y se van lloranado, lloranado
la hermosa vida.

His poems can be found in a beautiful bilingual edition, *Pieces of Shadow: Collected Poems of Jaime Sabines,* translated by W. S. Merwin, from Papeles Privados in Mexico City. If it's not in your bookstore, it's distributed in this country by Marsilio Publishers in New York.

JUNE 6

The Poetics of Travel: Elizabeth Bishop

Packing for summer travel, readers may want to think about bringing along the collected poems of Elizabeth Bishop, an inveterate traveler who was especially good at interrogating the usefulness of traveling at all. Here is a famous example, a poem that spends quite a lot of its time describing a songbird in a bamboo cage seen hanging above a broken pump in a gas station.

Bishop is a poet who can describe waterfalls as "mile-long, shiny, tear-stains" and make the architecture of a birdcage as interesting as any cathedral in a guidebook. And there are depths in her wryness and oblique humor:

Questions of Travel

There are too many waterfalls here; the crowded streams
hurry too rapidly down to the sea,
and the pressure of so many clouds on the mountaintops
makes them spill over the sides in soft slow-motion,
turning to waterfalls under our very eyes.
—For if those streaks, those mile-long, shiny, tearstains,
aren't waterfalls yet,
in a quick age or so, as ages go here,
they probably will be.
But if the streams and clouds keep traveling, traveling,

the mountains look like the hulls of capsized ships,
slime-hung and barnacled.

Think of the long trip home.
Should we have stayed at home and thought of here?
Where should we be today?
Is it right to be watching strangers in a play
in this strangest of theaters?
What childishness is it that while there's a breath of life
in our bodies, we are determined to rush
to see the sun the other way around?
The tiniest green hummingbird in the world?
To stare at some inexplicable old stonework,
inexplicable and impenetrable,
at any view,
instantly seen and always, always delightful?
Oh, must we dream our dreams
and have them, too?
And have we room
for one more folded sunset, still quite warm?

But surely it would have been a pity
not to have seen the trees along this road,
really exaggerated in their beauty,
not to have seen them gesturing
like noble pantomimists, robed in pink.
—Not to have had to stop for gas and heard
the sad, two-noted, wooden tune
of disparate wooden clogs
carelessly clacking over
a grease-stained filling-station floor.
(In another country the clogs would all be tested.
Each pair there would have identical pitch.)
—A pity not to have heard
the other, less primitive music of the fat brown bird
who sings above the broken gasoline pump
in a bamboo church of Jesuit baroque:

three towers, five silver crosses.
—Yes a pity not to have pondered,
blurr'dly and inconclusively,
on what connection can exist for centuries
between the crudest wooden footwear
and, careful and finicky,
the whittled fantasy of wooden cages.
—Never to have studied history in
the weak calligraphy of songbirds' cages.
—And never to have had to listen to rain
so much like politicians' speeches:
two hours of unrelenting oratory
and then a sudden golden silence
in which the traveler takes a notebook, writes:

"Is it lack of imagination that makes us come
to imagined places, not just stay at home?
Or could Pascal have been not entirely right
about just sitting quietly in one's room?

Continent, city, country, society:
the choice is never wide and never free.
And here, or there . . . No. Should we have stayed at home,
wherever that may be?"

This comes from Elizabeth Bishop, *The Complete Poems 1927–1979* (Farrar, Straus & Giroux).

JUNE 13

Paul Beatty

I recently saw on TV Bud Abbott and Lou Costello's famous baseball-and-language routine, "Who's On First," and it reminded me of a witty and appealing book of poems I'd read a while ago that had something to

say on the subject. This is from Paul Beatty's *Joker Joker Deuce,* published
in the Penguin Poets series:

Why That Abbott and Costello Vaudeville Mess
Never Worked with Black People

who's on first?
I don't know, your mama

Here's another:

Quote Unquote

i am telling you white people . . .
are evil

> how can you say that
> your own mother is white

then dont you think
i should know
what im talking about

Beatty was born in Los Angeles. In the poem "At Ease," too long to
quote in its entirety, the poet is in New York, considering the possibility
of fusing the rhythms of Allen Ginsberg and Thelonius Monk into some
grand new rainbow-hued aesthetic:

i admit theres an urge
to merge ginsbergs
ice age incantations
with some inspired spitfire monk vibes

> but no tai chi for me "g"
> nix on the tye dye

wont hindu my blues nor

> tofu my soulfood

im gonna be
   the bulemic bohemian

               eatin up my people
               then purgin their regurgitated words
               on the page
                         and the poems
                      become self made
            little icarus birds

    immaculately hatched
from the multicultural nest eggs
of the east village and west l.a.
             born to sing lyric segues
      while caged
whats the latin
    scientific
        slave name
for pretty peacocks
   whose feathers span the flesh spectrum
          but are stuck on with wax

it looks nice
but can it fly

Joker Joker Deuce is published by Penguin Books.

JUNE 20

Father's Day: Li-Young Lee

Here is a poem by Li-Young Lee, from his first book, *Rose* (BOA Editions.) Lee lives in Chicago and is the author of two widely admired books of poetry and a memoir. He was born in Jakarta, Indonesia, in 1957, of Chinese parents. The following year his father was arrested by the government of President Sukarno and spent a year as a political prisoner. The family fled Indonesia when the father was released, traveling from Hong

Kong to Macau to Japan, and in 1964, when Lee was seven, they settled
in the United States. Here is a poem about his father:

The Gift

To pull the metal splinter from my palm
my father recited a story in a low voice.
I watched his lovely face and not the blade.
Before the story ended, he'd removed
the iron sliver I thought I'd die from.

I can't remember the tale,
but hear his voice still, a well
of dark water, a prayer.
And I recall his hands,
two measures of tenderness
he laid against my face,
the flames of discipline
he raised above my head.

Had you entered that afternoon
you would have thought you saw a man
planting something in a boy's palm,
a silver tear, a tiny flame.
Had you followed that boy
you would have arrived here,
where I bend over my wife's right hand.

Look how I shave her thumbnail down
so carefully she feels no pain.
Watch as I lift the splinter out.
I was seven when my father
took my hand like this,
and I did not hold that shard
between my fingers and think,

Metal that will bury me,
christen it Little Assassin,
Ore Going Deep for My Heart.
And I did not lift up my wound and cry,
Death visited here!
I did what a child does
when he's given something to keep.
I kissed my father.

"The Gift," read once, would seem to be a fairly straightforward poem about learning loving and nurturing behavior from a loving and nurturing father. It's very pleasing that way, but there's a lot in the poem that such a reading doesn't account for. And so it's a good example of how much difference the active participation of the reader makes. We have to notice that it's also written in such a way that it's about how time collapses. The story of the father and the son folds so seamlessly into the story of the husband and wife. And it's about something more complicated in the relation of father and son. The hands that touch the boy so tenderly are also the "flames of discipline" that were raised above the boy's head. And the metal sliver is a "flame," a tear and a flame, and the father seems to be planting it in the son. So the poem is about learning love and punishment from the same hands. And it's about the metal sliver as the knowledge of mortality. The son, in the course of things, will bury the father. He is the "Little Assassin" and that knowledge, it would seem, is what goes for the heart. It's complicated, in the way that poetic logic often is, because it can mean in contradictory ways at the same time. If the son is the little assassin, and the sliver is also the little assassin, and the sliver is experienced as the threat of death, then the son is his own death, planted in his palm by his father. This is dream logic, the logic of each individual's sense of fate, and it is subterranean, like the father's story, "a well of dark water, a prayer." So interesting: the love the boy learned from the father he gives to the wife, as a gift; all the rest, too complicated to say, in a physical act, he gives to the poem.

Poetry and Weddings: Benjamin Saenz

For the June of weddings here is a poem by Benjamin Alire Saenz, from his book *Dark and Perfect Angels,* published by Cinco Puntos Press in El Paso, Texas. Mr. Saenz, who teaches at the University of Texas in El Paso, grew up in New Mexico, studied theology here and in Europe, was ordained a priest, left the priesthood, became a writer, and married a woman he had known since his childhood in Las Cruces. He's also the author of a book of short stories, *Flowers for the Broken* (Broken Moon Press) and a novel, *Carry Me Like Water* (Hyperion). The poem reads like an epithalamium—a poem to bless a wedding—that must have been written for friends, one of the useful occupations of a poet, and a natural one perhaps for a poet who had been a priest:

The Wedding Feast at Cana

> *This, the first of his miracles, Jesus*
> *performed at Cana in Galilee, and manifested his glory.*
> *—John 2:11*

for Larry and Katy

A man and woman meet. They fall
in love. This has been written; this
has been read; this is an old story.

In the body   there is a place:
those who work will know this space,
will know it's hard and holy, will
know it wears away the heart. We may
curse it day and night; we may
speak of it, point to it, pray to it—
it will not be appeased.

Listen to your names:
their sounds are like
no other: whispers of the world
needing to know if there is joy.
Is there joy? Listen to the hunger
forever—that song will never cease.
The song is sad. *You*
will never be full. Stay. Listen
to the hunger. Do not turn
from that sound. You cannot
run from earth. *Naked*
you came from the dirt. Naked you must
return. Flesh is flesh and it is flesh
till death.
                    This day, words
like thirst, and flesh, and hunger
mean *marriage.* Water is turned
into wine. This is the day of miracles.
Take. Drink. The best has been
saved for the poor. Taste. This is the cup
of salvation. Be drunk. Touch. Make love
through the lonely night—but when you wake
remember: this wine is good and sweet
but you will thirst again.

The book of life is hard to write:
it is written with bone and blood;
it is written with hearts that labor
and labor, beat and beat until the walls
fall down. Begin. Write: in the kingdom
of the naked, working heart
shame is banished. A man and woman
meet—this is an old—*write it!*
Begin. Begin. Begin.

Independence Day: Rita Dove

It is the instinct of most poets, when asked to write a poem for a patriotic occasion, to retreat, rapidly. So it must have taken a particular kind of courage, or fatalism in the form of cheerful resolve, for Rita Dove to respond when she was asked, on the two-hundredth anniversary of the United States Capitol in 1993, to write a poem for the figure of Liberty atop the newly restored Capitol dome. The poem appeared in the *Congressional Record* at the time, and it has been reprinted in her new book of poems, *On the Bus with Rosa Parks* (Norton). The figure she imagined is something of a bag lady and something of a Christ figure and she won't go away. Here is the poem:

Lady Freedom Among Us

don't lower your eyes
or stare straight ahead to where
you think you ought to be going

don't mutter *oh no*
not another one
get a job   fly a kite
go bury a bone

with her oldfashioned sandals
with her leaden skirts
with her stained cheeks and whiskers and heaped up trinkets
she has risen among us in blunt reproach

she has fitted her hair under a hand-me-down cap
and spruced it up with feathers and stars
slung over one shoulder she bears
the rainbowed layers of charity and murmurs
all of you   even the least of you

don't cross to the other side of the square
don't think *another item to fit on a tourist's agenda*

consider her drenched gaze   her shining brow
she who has brought mercy back into the streets
and will not retire politely to the potter's field

having assumed the thick skin of this town
its gritted exhaust its sunscorch and blear
she rests in her weathered plumage
bigboned   resolute

don't think you can ever forget her
don't even try
she's not going to budge

no choice but to grant her space
crown her with sky
for she is one of the many
and she is each of us

JULY II

Fanny Howe

Here is a tough poem, brilliant, I think, and rewarding. But it takes some work. Fanny Howe is a novelist as well as a poet, and one of the most admired experimental writers of her generation. Her work requires the active participation of the reader, and this poem needs to be read once as a delirium, and then again as an interpretative puzzle. If it's hard, it's hard because it stays near the language and experience of what she calls "the psyche's pre-self." She wants us to experience the disorientation of psychic disturbance, of not knowing quite where we are. "After all," she writes, "we were swimming in emotion, not water."

The Advance of the Father

From raindrenched Homeland into a well: the upturned animal
was mine by law and outside the tunnel, him again!
Everywhere I turned the children ran between. "Loose dogs!"
he roared. I remember one sequence: a gulf in his thinking
meant swim as fast as you can. But it was winter and the water
was closed. The mouths of the children were sealed with ice.
After all, we were swimming in emotion, not water.

"Shut up! you Father!" I shouted over my shoulder. Racing,
but not spent, my mind went, "It isn't good that the human being
is all I have to go by . . . It isn't good that I know who I love
but not who I trust . . . It isn't good that I can run to a priest
but not to a plane . . . I lost my way exactly like this."

Inverted tunnel of the self.
Throat or genital search for the self.
Light that goes on in the self when the eyes are shut.
Uniformity impossible in the psyche's pre-self
like a day never spent, or how the unseen can make itself felt.

It was as if a boy was calling from the end of a long island.
Docks were vertical and warlike.
I would be on one side of my bed like a mother who can tell
she's a comfort because she's called Mother.
Still, we both would be able to see the edge of the problem.

It's true that the person is also a thing.
When you are running you know the texture. I was clawing
at the palm of one hand and brushing up my blues with the other.
A man who wore his boxers at night remarked that my daughter
was tired. He had nothing to do with anything.

Ahead was the one with magnified eyes and historical data to last.
Know-how and the hysteria to accomplish his whole life.
It was horrible what we would do for peace.
We told him the story of the suffering he made us feel
with the ingratiating stoop of those who came second in the world.

The very first lines are a puzzle. Read again and again, they begin to yield meaning. "From raindrenched Homeland into a well" may be a way of describing growing up, passing from the father's home into the psychological trap it inflicted. "[T]he upturned animal / was mine by law," suggests, first of all, a kitten or some other small animal tossed down a well. That body is "mine by law," which may mean that she is grown, of age, legally her own person (though a drowned person tossed into a well), and once she gets outside of the tunnel, which must also be a well, there he is again, the real or symbolic father we carry with us. What to do with "Everywhere I turned the children ran between"? The first sense is simply confusion. Maybe it is the confusion of this woman, now an adult, trying to attend both to her self—the "inverted tunnel of the self" she will call it in the third stanza, and then compare it—the tunnel, the well—to the throat and to the vagina, speech and sex through which we try to come to some expression or understanding of ourselves. If so, the man roaring "Loose dogs!" may be the father, as it seems, or it may be the husband, complaining about the chaos of the household and, implicitly, holding the wife responsible for it. Hence her panic: "I remember one sequence: a gulf in his thinking / meant swim as fast as you can." We are back in the imagery of drowning. There is almost the outline of the plot of a novel here. The woman raised by a father who disliked disorder, who felt that she had been killed by him as one throws an animal down a well to drown, has married a man like her father. It is her children who are running around. And everything is frozen: "The mouths of the children were sealed with ice." Or maybe I am making up more story than the poem requires. Maybe the children are simply a symbol of lively, ungovernable life—"Loose dogs!"—and the woman is always in a panic of winter, always afraid of it.

Given a reading like this—or something like this—the second stanza comes into focus. It's about dealing in adult life with the internalized father. "Shut up," she says to him. But he won't shut up, and, her mind racing, she totals up the damage. The lines "It isn't good that the human being / is all I have to go by" is particularly moving to me and strange. It's hard to paraphrase, though I feel that I've been there. Trapped in one's own habits and ways of thinking is sometimes to feel trapped in the human dimension itself. In a simple way, the lines say: I can't get past what I've learned to be. In a more complicated way, they imply that there might be something beyond "the human being." So the poem is about the longing for God (also so often seen as a father) or about some realm uncontaminated by our human projections. "It isn't good that I know who I love / but not who I trust" is the problem of learning love at a source from which you don't get much.

So that the third stanza is about the search for the self of the person who has lost her way. The last three lines of that stanza are not easy, but they can be made out. And so can the next two stanzas that try to describe the lostness and the self-division. The most puzzling lines are probably these:

> A man who wore his boxers at night remarked that my daughter
> was tired. He had nothing to do with anything.

They seem to come from nowhere. What are they about? My sense is that we are in the presence of Howe the novelist again, that this is extreme condensation. The man is in boxer shorts at night. That implies an intimate relationship. But he's "a man," not "the man." He could be the husband and father, but he's seen as an object. "It's true," she's written at the beginning of the stanza, "that the person is also a thing." But he could be a boyfriend. He could be trying to get the child out of the way by suggesting that she ought to go to bed. In either case, the speaker finds herself in a relationship that's meaningless. The last sentence is withering: "He had nothing to do with anything."

The poem seems to end with another portrait of the father, "the one with magnified eyes and historical data to last. / Know-how and the hysteria to accomplish his whole life." It seems to address the whole male world of activity and precedent. The middle line of the stanza sums up in a single sentence all the family lives based on fear of the father's anger, fear of conflict: "It was horrible what we would do for peace." And the poem ends with a recapitulation of this cringing stance, even when she tries to tell the father what he has done:

> We told him the story of the suffering he made us feel
> with the ingratiating stoop of those who came second in the world.

The poem appears in Howe's *One Crossed Out* from Graywolf Press.

Lee Ann Brown

Lee Ann Brown is among the wittiest and most inventive of younger American poets. Her new book, *Polyverse,* comes from the stylish Sun and Moon Press in their New American Poets series. Here is a flavor. First, one about the fact that poetry only goes so far:

Words

weren't enough for her.

She often made
high cat cries
and danced hard
on the blue carpet.

She lives in New York and pays attention. Here's something from public transit, a sort of urban disorientation haiku:

Subway Exchange

What time is it?
  A little after nine.
At night, right?

And she is given to small observations, wry, ordinary, to which she sometimes gives a little spin with her titles. Like this:

South of the Mind

Covered with lotion
I watch
TV

One of her poems is called "Definitions at 3:15"; it includes this:

Poetry

a condensed form
of food & time

and, my favorite, this (you may have noticed that all serious academics use
this word constantly of late):

Discourse

talking fancy
without much to
drink

This is, I guess, inspired doodling, something in the spirit of the late
New York poet Frank O'Hara. One of the things I like about Brown is
that she plays with the world, with her perceptions, and with language.
She's always giving it a second look. She's the editor of a small press called
Tender Buttons, named for a famous prose poem of Gertrude Stein. So
that is another influence. Some of her pieces look like not much, this one,
for example:

Cafeteria

Ice Tea
Cream corn
Fried okra
plus one meat

I don't know what she had in mind here. First of all, a pokerface evoca-
tion of the full awfulness of one kind of American noon. But the day after
reading it I drove by a sports arena with a banner hanging from it and
mentally readjusted the sign so that it said TRACK MEAT. This suggested
other possibilities: "I'll be down to meat you in a taxi honey" or "Meat
me in St. Louis, Louie." Conversely, I thought, butcher shops could help
redefine the principle interaction between humans and other animal spe-
cies by putting up a sign that said FRESH MEET. "One meat" seemed like it
might make a good slogan for some group. Animal rights activists? The

U.N.? Anyway, this cocking of the hat of language and wearing it a little askew can be playfully subversive and can freshen attention.

In one series of poems, Brown turns the method to the description of flowers. Here's a little summer garland:

Pansy

Showy, invisible
not concerned with cherry pit
Five sepals, four with black, one cherry dot
leaves mutate
Back hook hooded, capped
point thin vein mouth
monk's rigid tuning
to a hard yellow

"Monk's rigid tuning"? Maybe she means Gregorian chant—for the way the flower flares from its dark center to its bright petals.

Peony

moist white collapse
marilyn's red kiss tissue

soft drop all at table bunching tinged
range: mauve, magenta, white carnation blue
collar of ants populate taste parts
traditionally departing painfully from an idea

JULY 25

A Serbian Epic: *The Battle of Kosovo*

Throughout the nineteenth century scholars puzzled over the riddle of the composition of Homer's *Iliad* and *Odyssey*. It was clear that the poems derived from a tradition of oral recitation, but it seemed inconceivable that anyone could recite for so long and so coherently. The poems must have been examples of early written composition based on an older oral tradition. This led scholars into the field to study the few remaining traditions extant in Europe where old peasant singers of tales still carried on this ancient form of entertainment and folk memory. And the place to which they turned was Serbia, where they found old men and old women—in a couple of cases blind old women—could sing traditional poems and poem cycles even longer than Homer's epics. The riddle of the *Iliad* was solved in the series of songs sung in the hills of Bosnia and Herzegovina about the Battle of Kosovo. The classic book on the subject is Alfred B. Lord's *The Singer of Tales,* which was published in 1960.

There is a splendid translation of the Kosovo cycle, *The Battle of Kosovo,* a collaboration between the American poet John Matthias and the Serbian mathematician Vladeta Vučković. The songs were transcribed by Serbian scholars early in the nineteenth century. The singers were called *guslars,* and they played a one-stringed instrument called a *gusle.* The American poet Charles Simic was born in Serbia and heard a guslar perform when he was a child. He described the experience this way: "The sound of that one string is faint, rasping, screechy, tentative. The chanting that goes with it is toneless, monotonous, and unrelieved by vocal flourishes of any kind. The singer simply doesn't show off. There's nothing to do but pay close attention to the words which the guslar enunciates with great emphasis and clarity . . . After a while the poem and the archaic, other-worldly-sounding instrument began to get to me and everybody else. Our anonymous ancestor poet knew what he was doing. The stubborn drone combined with the sublime lyricism of the poem touched the rawest spot in our psyche. The old wounds were reopened."

The poems tell of the great battle on the plain of Kosovo between the Serbian prince Lazar and the forces of the Turkish invader under Sultan Murad in 1389. The poems teem with characters: Lazar himself, his rivals, his fellow warriors, his wife, the sisters and mothers of the fallen warriors. They feel to me a little like the Robin Hood ballads with their story of the fight for freedom and the doughty band of heroes. They must have been sung endlessly in the five hundred years of Ottoman rule before they were written down, and they were sung long after that. Rebecca West, in her classic travel book about Yugoslavia, *Black Lamb and Grey Falcon,* describes hearing old Serbian women in the countryside in the late 1930s recite the poems as if they were saying the Pater Noster while she

looked out across the plain: "Here is the image of failure, so vast that it fills
the eye as failure sometimes fills an individual life, an epoch."

Impossible to convey the sweep of the cycle in a short space, but here,
a story of Lazar, is one of its best-known episodes. John Matthias has
used the device of spacing to indicate the pauses, something like those in
Anglo-Saxon oral poetry, that mark the classic Serbian ten-syllable line:

The Downfall of the Kingdom of Serbia

Yes, and from Jerusalem,
        O from that holy place,
A great gray bird,
        a taloned falcon flew!
And in his beak
        he held a gentle swallow.
But wait! it's not
        a falcon, this gray bird,
It is a saint,
        Holy Saint Elijah:
And he bears with him
        no gentle swallow
But a letter
        from the Blessed Mother
He brings it
        to the Tsar at Kosovo
And places it
        upon his trembling knees.
And thus the letter itself
        peaks to the Tsar:

"Lazar! Lazar!
        Tsar of noble family,
Which kingdom is it
        that you long for most?
Will you choose
        a heavenly crown today?
Or will you choose
        an earthly crown?

If you choose the earth
>   then saddle horses,
Tighten girths—
>   have your knights put on
Their swords and make
>   a dawn attack against
The Turks: your enemy
>   will be destroyed.
But if you choose the skies
>   then build a church—
O not of stone
>   but out of silk and velvet—
Gather up your forces
>   take the bread and wine,
For all shall perish,
>   perish utterly,

And you, O Tsar,
>   shall perish with them."
And when the Tsar
>   has heard these holy words
He meditates,
>   thinks every kind of thought:
"O Dearest God,
>   what shall I do, and how?
Shall I choose the earth?
>   Shall I choose
The skies?
>   And if I choose the kingdom,
If I choose
>   an earthly kingdom now,

Earthly kingdoms
>   are such passing things—
A heavenly kingdom,
>   raging in the dark,
>   endures eternally.

And Lazarus chose heaven,
        not the earth,
And tailored there
        a church at Kosovo—
O not of stone
        but out of silk and velvet—
And he summoned there
        the Partriarch of Serbia,
Summoned there
        the lordly twelve high bishops:
And he gathered up his forces
        had them
Take with him
        the saving bread and wine.
As soon as Lazarus
        had given out
His orders,
        then across the level plain
Of Kosovo
        pour all the Turks.

The Battle of Kosovo is published by Ohio University Press.

AUGUST 1

Denise Levertov

When Denise Levertov died in Seattle in 1997, she left behind forty fin-
ished poems in a loose-leaf notebook. They have been edited by Paul
Lacey and printed in the order that she wrote them. This final book is
called *The Great Unknowing: Last Poems* and is published by her pub-
lisher of thirty years, New Directions. I've been reading her all my adult
life, so it is an odd thing going through these last poems, reading them
slowly, a few a night, that she must partly have known, and partly not have
known, were her last poems. Whatever she thought, her habits are what
you notice, the dailiness of her attention. She was a meticulous craftsman,

and you always feel in her poems the pulse of her method of work. These
last poems are not, I think, her best, though it's hard for me to judge. I'm
attached to her early work, the first few of her American books that were
the ones in which I discovered her, and to two of her latest books, *Evening
Train* and *Sands of the Well,* in which she returned to her earlier mode.
These poems belong to her good work, the kind she did when she sat
down to practice her craft. She knew she had cancer and that knowledge
seems not to have made her reach for any grand synthesis. She went about
her business as she had always done.

Here are a few of them. This one seems to begin with the weather of
the Northwest and then leaps back, perhaps, as it reaches for a metaphor,
to a memory of her English childhood:

Celebration

Brilliant, this day—a young virtuoso of a day.
Morning shadows cut by sharpest scissors,
deft hands. And every prodigy of green—
whether it's ferns or lichen or needles
or impatient points of buds on spindly bushes—
greener than ever before.
                              And the way the conifers
hold new cones to the light for blessing,
a festive rite, and sing the oceanic chant the wind
transcribes for them!
A day that shines in the cold
like a first-prize brass band swinging along the street
of a coal-dusty village, wholly at odds
with the claims of reasonable gloom.

And this small poem gathers into a small notation one of her persistent
themes: the brokenness of the world, its violence and injustice, and her
longing for wholeness, the longing that sent her back to her Christian
roots at the end of her life. It has no title:

Scraps of moon
bobbing discarded on broken water

but sky-moon
complete, transcending

all violation.

Here she seems to be talking to herself about the shape of a life:

Once Only

All which, because it was
flame and song and granted us
joy, we thought we'd do, be, revisit,
turns out to have been what it was
that *once,* only; every initiation
did not begin
a series, a build-up: the marvelous
   did happen in our lives, our stories
   are not drab with its absence: but don't
expect now to return for more. Whatever more
there will be will be
unique as those were unique. Try
to acknowledge the next
song in its body-halo of flames as utterly
present, as now or never.

And here is the final poem in the book. It must be the last one she
wrote:

Aware

When I opened the door
I found the vine leaves
speaking among themselves in abundant
whispers.
   My presence made them
hush their green breath,
embarrassed, the way
humans stand up, buttoning their jackets,

acting as if they were leaving anyway, as if
the conversation had ended
just before you arrived.
                                        I liked
the glimpse I had, though,
of their obscure
gestures. I liked the sound
of such private voices. Next time
I'll move like cautious sunlight, open
the door by fractions, eavesdrop
peacefully.

Eavesdrop peacefully: it's what she's given us to do.

AUGUST 8

Summer Shakespeare

Outdoor Shakespeare, that unlikely ritual of the American summer, can
be very magical. I saw a cheerful, knockabout production of *Two Gentle-
men from Verona* the other night. It was one of Shakespeare's first plays.
It was wonderful to watch it in that leisurely way, the air just cooling
after a day of simmering heat. The lights went out, the audience subsided
into attention, and then the lights went up again, and two actors, dressed
in those peculiar Elizabethan garments, came sauntering onto the stage,
the little world of the stage, which the young Shakespeare was, over the
course of the next twenty years, going to own utterly.

A little flourish of music and we came to the opening speech: he's
already learned the trick of beginning in the middle of things. One
gentleman, Valentine, is telling the other, Proteus, that he can't talk him
into staying home. And the spectator has nothing to do but sink into the
rhythms of the language:

Cease to persuade, my loving Proteus;
Home-keeping youth have ever homely wits.
Were't not affection chains thy tender days

To the sweet glances of thy honoured love,
I rather would entreat thy company
To see the wonders of the world abroad
Than, living dully sluggardized at home,
Wear out thy youth with shapeless idleness.
But since thou lov'st, love still, and thrive therein,
Even as I would when I to love begin.

We are to gather from this that the two are friends, that one is about to embark on travels to see the world, that the other is in love with someone and is staying home. I got it all, more or less. But I mainly felt that familiar, and always surprising, intense happiness at the seemingly effortless verbal brilliance and playfulness of his language: "Home-keeping youth have ever homely wits"; "affection chains thy tender days"; the completely wonderful, casually over-the-top "living dully sluggardized at home"; and the dead-on accuracy of "wear out thy youth with shapeless idleness."

We had been talking before the lights went down about the restlessness of college kids at home for the summer and remembering our own summers during college, not knowing quite what to do with ourselves, living in the family house, bored with our summer jobs, wildly restive. And there it was, in his language, described with perfect accuracy: "wear out thy youth with shapeless idleness." The play was probably written around 1592, which would have made him twenty-eight years old. It could very well have called to his mind his own experience of leaving Stratford for London. The self-possession in the writing seems breathtaking.

I somehow escaped ever taking a Shakespeare course in college. I'm sure there are studies of how he learned his craft—of the conventions of wit and verbal play that were already out there, the *shtick* that he had already learned, that he must have sucked up like a sponge from plays he had seen and that he could already depend on. But I haven't read those studies, and part of the pleasure of the play for me was guessing at how he proceeded. The next bit of the opening scene, verbal patter between Valentine and Proteus on the subject of love, also supremely skillful and effortless, is probably pure shtick:

Valentine: Love is your master, for he masters you;
             And he that is so yoked by a fool
             Methinks should not be chronicled for wise.

Proteus: Yet writers say, as in the sweetest bud
                The eating canker dwells, so doting love
                Inhabits in the finest wits of all.

Valentine: And writers say, as the most forward bud
                Is eaten by the canker ere it blow,
                Even so by love the young and tender wit
                Is turned to folly, blasting in the bud,
                Losing his verdure, even in the prime,
                And all the fair effects of future hope.
                But wherefore waste I time to counsel thee
                That art a votary to fond desire?

In the next bit, Valentine leaves, and Proteus, alone on the stage, makes a
little speech to the audience right out of Elizabethan love sonnets (which
Shakespeare was probably also writing at this time):

He after honour hunts, I after love:
He leaves his friends to dignify them more;
I leave myself, my friends and all for love.
Thou, Julia, thou hast metamorphosed me:
Made me neglect my studies, lose my time,
War with good counsel, set the world at naught;
Made wit with musing weak, heart sick with thought.

Another set piece, fluent—and with that delicious word "metamor-
phosed" in it—that the available writing style had probably told him how
to do. Then Valentine's servant Speed comes in, looking for him. Proteus
tells him that Valentine has already "shipped." The servant—you know
that the actor who plays the servant will be a featured comic actor—puns
on "shipped" and "sheep":

Twenty to one, then, he is shipped already,
And I have played the sheep in losing him.

Sheep jokes are in the offing. And where there are sheep jokes, there
will be jokes about horns. Adultery—especially men whose women slept
around on them—seems to have been a source of reliable hilarity to the

late sixteenth-century English. Such men were "cuckolds" and—why I don't know—cuckolds had "horns."

Proteus: Indeed, a sheep doth very often stray,
                And if the shepherd be awhile away.

Speed: You conclude that my master is a shepherd then, and
                I a sheep?

Proteus: I do.

Speed: Why then, my horns are his horns, whether I wake or
                sleep.

More shtick. I was thinking about being in love in college in the summertime. Also making mental notes to myself about the brilliant and easy way the play was unfolding. We had blankets for the later acts if it cooled off, a bottle of white wine. And the last of the sunset sent up a little flush above the outdoor stage.

AUGUST 15

Louise Glück

For the lucky, born into a geography not visited by war or political terror, the events in life that leave the soul scoured and disoriented are death and divorce. Divorce is a kind of death. Even for people glad to get out of relationships, the props of a life have to be remade, families, habits, houses, even towns. And it can leave a life stripped bare.

Not surprising that it is a subject for poetry, but it is surprising how little serious and sustained examination of the subject there has been in our poetry, given how common and how devastating the experience can be.

For the last ten years Louise Glück, one of the purest and most accomplished lyric poets now writing, has turned from the form of her early books, traditional collections of poems written over a period of time, to a series of book-length sequences. They are written in her characteristically spare and elegant style. They are books of individual poems, but they make a narrative sequence, and so they are able to explore a subject in many moods and from many points of view in a way that is reminiscent of the old sonnet sequences that explored all the phases of a love affair. The first one, *Ararat,* dealt with a family of three women in the aftermath of the death of a husband and father. The second one, the Pulitzer Prize–winning *The Wild Iris,* was a meditation on the turning of the year in a northern New England garden. The third, *Meadowlands,* based on the story of Ulysses and Penelope and Telemachus, was about a marriage coming apart. The newest one, published this year, is *Vita Nova* (Ecco Press). Its subject is that life after divorce. It begins from something like the place Emily Dickinson described so accurately:

> After great pain, a formal feeling comes—
> The Nerves sit ceremonious, like Tombs—

Here are a couple of the poems:

The Garment

My soul dried up.
Like a soul cast into a fire, but not completely,
not to annihilation. Parched,
it continued. Brittle,
not from solitude but from mistrust,
the aftermath of violence.

Spirit, invited to leave the body,
to stand exposed a moment,
trembling, as before
your presentation to the divine—
spirit lured out of solitude
by the promise of grace,
how will you ever again believe
the love of another being?

My soul withered and shrank.
The body became for it too large a garment.

And when hope was returned to me
it was another hope entirely.

Earthly Love

Conventions of the time
held them together.
It was a period
(very long) in which
the heart once given freely
was required, a formal gesture,
to forfeit liberty: a consecration
at once moving and hopelessly doomed.

As to ourselves:
fortunately we diverged
from these requirements,
as I reminded myself
when my life shattered.
So that what we had for so long
was, more or less,
voluntary, alive.
And only long afterward
did I begin to think otherwise.

We are all human—
we protect ourselves
as well as we can
even to the point of denying
clarity, the point
of self-deception. As in
the consecration to which I alluded.

And yet, within this deception,
true happiness occurred.

So that I believe I would
repeat these errors exactly.
Nor does it seem to me
crucial to know
whether or not such happiness
is built on illusion:
it has its own reality.
And in either case, it will end.

AUGUST 22

In Memoriam: Sherley Anne Williams

The novelist and poet Sherley Anne Williams died last month, of cancer
at the age of fifty-four. She is probably best known for her 1986 novel,
Dessa Rose. She also wrote children's books and a one-actor play, *Letters
from a New England Negro.* She began her writing life as a poet. She was
born in Bakersfield, California, the child of migrant farm workers; she
was orphaned at sixteen and survived, as her parents had done, picking
crops in the field. I was struck by something she was quoted as saying
in the *New York Times* obituary. She was talking about finding herself,
a young woman who had seemed to have no prospects, with the seem-
ingly limitless opportunities that she felt as a student at the state college
right in the middle of the Central Valley of California where she and her
parents had done back-breaking stoop labor in the fields. She discovered
in Sterling Brown and Langston Hughes the poetry of African Americans.
"I was just captivated by their language, their speech and their character
because I always liked the way black people talk. So I wanted to work in
that writing." There couldn't be a much better description of the enabling
power of a tradition.

Here's an example:

Straight Talk from Plain Women

Evangeline made her
own self over in

'65, say she
looked in the mirror
at her face saw it
was pretty (her legs
was always fine and
she'd interrupt a
dude's rap to say how
it was a common
characteristic
amongst our women

Did
the same thang with her
neck pointin to
its length, its class. And
we dug where she
was comin from specially
that pretty part, how
she carried herself
with style, said go'n girl
so be it

Evangeline made her
self over and who
eva else didn't see
We is her witness.

And here's another. It's about learning manners and another kind of tradition, the one that comes to children from listening:

You Were Never Miss Brown to Me

I.
We were not raised to look in
a grown person's mouth when they
spoke or to say ma'am or sir—
only the last was sometimes
thought fast even rude but daddy

dismissed this: it was yea and
nay in the Bible and this
was a New Day. He liked even
less honorary forms—Uncle,
Aunt, Big Mama—mama to
who? he would ask. Grown
people were Mr. and Miss
admitting one child in many
to the privilege of their
given names. We were raised to
make "Miss Daisy" an emblem
of kinship and of love; you
were never Miss Brown to me.

II.
I call you Miss in tribute
to the women of that time,
the mothers of friends, the friends
of my mother, mamma
herself, women of mystery
and wonder who traveled some
to get to that Project. In the
places of their childhoods, the
troubles they had getting grown,
the tales of men they told among
themselves as we sat unnoted
at their feet we saw some image
of a past and future self.
The world had loved them even
less than their men but this did
not keep them from scheming on
its favor. It was this that
made them grown and drew from our
unmannerly mouths "Miss"
before their first names.

I call
you Daisy and acknowledge

my place in this line: I am
the women of my childhood
just as I was the women of
my youth, one with these women
of silence who lived on the
cusp of their time and knew it;
who taught what it is to be grown.

These poems come from *Some One Sweet Angel Chile*, published in 1982. You will also find them in *The Garden Thrives: Twentieth-Century African-American Poetry*, edited by Clarence Major (HarperPerennial).

AUGUST 29

Naomi Shihab Nye

Here's a poem for the season from Naomi Shihab Nye. She's a Palestinian American poet who lives in San Antonio. This comes from her most recent book, *Fuel*, published by BOA Editions:

The Last Day of August

A man in a lawn chair
with a book on his lap

realizes pears are falling
from the tree right beside him.

Each makes a round,
full sound in the grass.

Perhaps the stem takes an hour
to loosen and let go.

This man who has recently written words
to his father forty years in the birthing:

I was always afraid of you.
When would you explode next?

has sudden reverence for the pears.
If a dark bruise rises,

if ants inhabit the juicy crack,
or the body remains firm, unscarred,

remains secret till tomorrow . . .
By then the letter to his father

may be lying open on a table.
We gather pears in baskets, sacks.

What will we do with everything
that has been given us? Ginger pears, pear pies,

fingers weighing flesh.
Which will be perfect under the skin?

It is hard not to love the pile of peelings
growing on the counter next to the knife.

Here is a poem about a condition that many Americans experience,
belonging to more than one cultural tradition. Nye's theory of how to
negotiate this state is contained in the last line of the poem:

Half-and-Half

You can't be, says a Palestinian Christian
on the first feast after Ramadan.
So, half-and-half and half-and-half.
He sells glass. He knows about broken bits,
chips. If you love Jesus you can't love
anyone else. Says he.

At his stall of blue pitchers on the Via Dolorosa
he's sweeping. The rubbed stones
feel holy. Dusting of powdered sugar
across faces of date-stuffed *mamool.*

This morning we lit the slim white candles
which bend over at the waist by noon.
For once the priests weren't fighting
in the church for the best spots to stand.
As a boy, my father listened to them fight.
This is partly why he prays in no language
but his own. Why I press my lips
to every exception.

A woman opens a window—here and here and here—
placing a vase of blue flowers
on an orange cloth. I follow her.
She is making a soup from what she had left
in the bowl, the shriveled garlic and bent bean.
She is leaving nothing out.

SEPTEMBER 5

Labor Day: William Blake and Debra Allbery

I have read (in E. P. Thompson's *The Making of the English Working Class*) that the first man who attempted to establish a labor union in England at the end of the eighteenth century was arrested, tried for sedition, found guilty, and drawn and quartered in a public square by having draft horses attached to each of his arms and legs, which pulled him apart. He was then disemboweled and his guts were burned. Then they hanged what was left of him. One gathers from this punishment that the propertied classes were slow to accept the idea of organized labor. I don't know what the first poems and ballads on the subject were. I do know that a poem by William Blake, written in the early years of the industrial revolution, became a kind of anthem of the labor movement in England in the nineteenth century. You may have read the poem in school. It goes like this:

And Did Those Feet

And did those feet in ancient time
Walk upon England's mountain green?
And was the holy Lamb of God
On England's pleasant pastures seen?

And did the Countenance Divine
Shine forth upon our clouded hills?
And was Jerusalem builded here
Among these dark Satanic Mills?

Bring me my Bow of burning gold:
Bring me my Arrows of desire:
Bring me my Spear: O clouds unfold!
Bring me my Chariot of fire!

I will not cease from Mental Fight,
Nor shall my Sword sleep in my hand,
Till we have seen Jerusalem
In England's green & pleasant Land.

This was written around 1804. Whether Blake, when he coined the phrase "Satanic Mills," actually had in mind the new factories that had sprung up in the English countryside is not known, but people interpreted it that way and interpreted the poem as a challenge to the established church and a call for a new social order based on social justice. That time seems remote on a hot Labor Day weekend when the labor struggles in the American industrial economy are mostly forgotten, and when many of the jobs have been exported to developing countries where working people have been undertaking the same struggle more or less out of sight of American consumers. We hardly notice that the holiday itself was conceived, uneasily, perhaps as a kind of wishful thinking, to commemorate the closing of old wounds.

Here's a poem for Labor Day about American work. It's by Debra

Allbery and comes from her book *Walking Distance,* published by University of Pittsburgh Press in 1991. I came across it in an interesting new anthology, *Generations: Poems between Fathers, Mothers, Daughters, Sons,* edited by Melanie Hart and James Loader, and published by Penguin Books. A much quieter thing than the Blake poem, it describes a daughter's summer of work in the plant where her father spent his life. Its ambition seems to be to make a record, to say what it was like:

Assembler

My twentieth summer I go to a job in Door Locks
at the Ford plant where my father has worked
for twenty years. Five in the morning
we'd stand tired in the glare and old heat
of the kitchen, my father fiddling with
the radio dial, looking for a clear station.

There weren't any women in my department.
At first the men would ask me to lift
what I couldn't, would speed up the turntable,
juggling the greasy washers and bolts,
winking at each other, grinning at me.
In the break room they would buy me coffee,
study my check to see if I got shorted.
They were glad I was in school and told me
to finish, they said I'd never regret it.
Once I got loaned to Air Conditioners,
worked three days in a special enclosure,
quiet and cool and my hands stayed clean.
Out the window I could see Door Locks,
the men taking salt pills, 110 degrees.

In rest rooms there were women sleeping
on orange vinyl couches, oven timers ticking
next to their heads.

At lunch I'd take the long walk to my father.
I'd see him from a distance, wearing safety glasses

like mine, and earphones, bright slivers of brass
in his hair—him standing alone in strange sulfur light
amidst machines the size of small buildings.
Every twenty minutes he worked a tumbler,
in between he read from his grocery bag of paperbacks.
He would pour us coffee from a hidden pot,
toast sandwiches on a furnace. We sat
on crates, shouting a few things and laughing
over the roar and banging of presses.

Mostly I remember the back-to-back heat waves,
coffee in paper cups that said Safety First,
my father and I hurrying away from the time clocks,
proud of each other. And my last day, moving shy past
their *Good Lucks,* out into 5:00, shading my eyes.

SEPTEMBER 12

One Thousand Years of Poetry in English: A Millennium Gathering

In the year 991 Viking ships raided the west coast of England. These
raids had become an annual occurrence. This one ended in a pitched
battle near the Blackwater River in the county of Essex. The headman of
the Essex fighters, named Brythnoth, was killed in the fight. The battle
was recorded in a poem, one of the last that survives in the old Anglo-
Saxon tongue, just as the millennium was turning. So here is the death of
Brythnoth, and here is what the English language looked like, in the East
Anglian dialect, a thousand years ago:

>   Tha Brythnoth braegd,   bill of scaethe,
>   brad and brun-ecog,   and on tha byrnan sloh.
>   To rarthe hine gelette lidmanna sum,
>   tha he thaes eorles   earm amierde.
>   Feoll tha to   foldan fealu-hilte swurd;
>   ne miahte he gehealdan   heardne mece,
>   waepnes wealdan . . .

Poems like this were composed in the head for oral performance by a singer, or scop, who accompanied himself on a stringed instrument, a sort of harp. They were written down as an afterthought in the new technology of writing that the Germanic tribes picked up from the Romans. The organizing principles for the singer-bards were four beats to the line, a two-part line, and a linkage made of alliteration. The four beats were said to be based on the same rhythm that was used by rowers in the long ships and they gave the singer's harp a measure to play against. Here's a translation from the late twentieth century by Michael Alexander, from his *Earliest English Poems* (Penguin):

> Brythnoth broke out brand from sheath,
> broad, bright-bladed, and on the breastplate struck;
> but one of the spoilers cut short the blow,
> his swing unstringing the Earl's sword-arm.
> He yielded to the ground the yellow-hilted sword,
> strengthless to hold the hard blade longer up
> or wield weapon . . .

In 1066 the Normans, Scandinavians from the north who had settled on the west coast of France and acquired the French tongue, invaded England, and the Anglo-Saxons acquired French-speaking rulers. Their influence was to change the English tongue over the next three hundred years and bring it closer to modern English. The poetry of the years 1000 to about 1300 is difficult to date exactly. It exists in a variety of manuscripts, written in a variety of dialects. One of the earliest scraps of medieval verse was written by a monk sometime in the 1100s who was angry at the Baron of Urs for chopping down some trees that he loved:

> Hatest the, Urss
> May God the cursse.

> [Hatest thee, Urs. May God thee curse.]

Scholars think "The Cuckoo Song," one of the earliest English lyrics of the coming of spring, was probably composed between 1240 and 1310, though some think it may have been written in the twelfth century. It was written down in a commonplace book kept over a number of years by the monks of Reading Abbey. Here's a piece of the first stanza:

> Sumer is i-cumen in—
> Lhude sing, cuccu!
> Groweth sed and bloweth med
> And springth the wude nu.
> Sing, cuccu!
>
> —Anonymous, circa 1200–1250

> [Summer is coming in—Loud sing, cuckoo! Grow seed and blow meadow and spring the woods new. Sing, cuckoo.]

Two of the most beautiful medieval lyrics are from the thirteenth century. This Christian poem is intricate with puns. The sun goes down and, at the Crucifixion, the Son goes down. The "tre" and the "wode" of the forest are also the wood of the Cross at Calvary. The poem is about the suffering of Christ's mother. The tone is exquisitely tender. Some scholars think it dates from the early thirteenth century. Others have guessed early fourteenth.

> Nou goth sonne under wode—
> Me reweth, Marie, thi faire rode.
> Nou goth sonne under tre—
> Me reweth, Marie, thi sone and the.
>
> —Anonymous, circa 1200–1230

> [Now goes sun under wood—I rue, Mary, thy fair face. Now goes sun under tree—I rue, Mary, thy son and thee.]

"Fowles in the frith" was written on one page of a manuscript of legal texts, noted down by some monk going about his labor, or we would not have it. Some scholars read it as a love poem—"the best of bone and blood" in the last line is the beloved whom the speaker is going crazy over; others read it as a Christian poem and cite a verse in Matthew's gospel; "Foxes have their holes, the birds their roosts, but the Son of Man has nowhere to lay his head."

Fowles in the frith,
The fisshes in the flood,
And I mon waxe wood:
Much sorwe I walke with
For beste of boon and blood.

—Anonymous, circa 1270

[Birds in the woods, fishes in the sea, and I am going mad: I walk
with much sorrow for the best of bone and blood.]

By the middle of the fourteenth century the idea of individual author-
ship had appeared, yielding the first great poets in the English language,
Geoffrey Chaucer and William Langland, and the unknown poet from
the northeast midlands who wrote *Pearl* and *Sir Gawain and the Green
Knight*. By now we have some of the best known lines in English poetry:

Whan that Aprille with his shoures sote
The droghte of Marche hath perced to the rote,
And bathe every veyne in swich licour,
Of which vertu engendred is the flour . . .

—Geoffrey Chaucer, *The Canterbury Tales*, 1386

[When April with his sweet showers the drought of March has
pierced to the root, and bathed every vine in such liquor, by which
is engendered the flower.]

Here is a sweet song from about 1486 that has the flavor of the French-
inflected poetry of the courts. It was written in the middle of the War of
the Roses, the brutal and seemingly endless struggle between two families
in England for political power, when the white rose of York and the red
rose of Lancaster gave rise to a number of poems, apparently love poems,
that played with the question of favorite flowers. This song was entitled
"The Roses Entwined":

"I love a floure of swete odour."
"Magerome gentill, or lavenduore?"
"Columbine, goldis of swete flavour?"

> "Nay, May, let be!
> Is non of them
> That lyketh me."

I love a sweet-smelling flower, the first singer says. The noble marjoram, or lavender? guesses the second. Columbine or marigolds? guesses the third. No, no, leave me alone, the first sings. I don't like any of them—and the song goes on with its political/erotic guessing game through several more stanzas.

The single most important event for poetry in this last thousand years was the invention of the printing press. It occurred about halfway through the millennium. One of its consequences was the gradual standardization of English—by the ruling classes, of course, who came to define the dialect of London and its surroundings as the model of correct speech. Another was the separation of the short lyric from song. Short poems were still called lyrics, but they were thought of increasingly as primarily written compositions—so the folk tradition of song and ballad, and the tradition of written poetry, read by a learned minority, parted ways.

The first printed book of poetry in English, *Tottels Miscellany,* contained a number of sonnets. Here is one of them by a gentleman from Kent named Thomas Wyatt. Wyatt was a courtier and diplomat and one of the first modern masters of the short poem. It's possible to say that modern English poetry begins with him. He picked up the sonnet while traveling in Italy and wrote this one, which is said to be about his interest in Henry VIII's wife, Ann Boleyn. (Being interested in Henry's wife was probably about as safe a state of mind as having a thing for Stalin's mistress.) The Latin in the poem *Noli me tangere* means "You musn't touch," and it was said to be placed on medallions that were hung around the necks of the King's favorite deer in the Royal Forest:

Whoso List to Hunt

Whoso list to hunt, I know where is an hind,   *list=likes, hind=deer*
    But as for me, alas I may no more:
The vain travail hath wearied me so sore
    I am of them that farthest cometh behind;
Yet may I by no means my wearied mind

Draw from the deer: but as she fleeth afore,
Fainting I follow. I leave off therefore,
  Since in a net I seek to hold the wind.
Who list her hunt, I put him out of doubt,
  As well as I may spend his time in vain:
And, graven in diamonds, in letters plain
  There is written her fair neck round about:
Noli me tangere, for Caesar's I am;
  And wild for to hold, though I seem tame.

—Thomas Wyatt, circa 1540

By the end of the century Elizabeth was queen, Shakespeare was writing for the theater, and poetry in English had exploded. By the middle of the seventeenth century it had spread, along with the English colonists, to North America. Here is a quick run through the last half of the millennium, starting with the brilliance of Elizabeth's time and just after:

Not marble, nor the gilded monuments
Of princes, shall outlive this powerful rhyme

—William Shakespeare, circa 1590

Go and catch a falling star,
  Get with child a mandrake root,
Tell me where all past years are,
  Or who cleft the Devil's foot

—John Donne, circa 1610

Display thy breasts, my Julia, there let me
Behold that circummortal purity

—Robert Herrick, 1648

This kind of erotic playfulness would give way in the seventeenth century to a profound religious and meditative poetry:

Batter my heart, three personed God; for You
As yet but knock, breathe, shine, and seek to mend.
That I may rise and stand, o'erthrow me, and bend
Your force to break, blow, burn, and make me new.

—John Donne, 1633

Lord, how can man preach thy eternal word?
    He is a brittle crazy glass;

—George Herbert, 1633

They are all gone into the world of light!
    And I alone sit lingering here.

—Henry Vaughn, 1650

It was this more earnest tone that passed into the North American colony
of Massachusetts, where the first book of poetry in English was published
by a woman. Here is the beginning of a poem to her husband:

If ever two were one, then surely we.
If ever man were loved by wife, then thee;

—Anne Bradstreet, Massachusetts Colony, 1678

The early eighteenth-century poets liked the regularity of the rhymed
couplet, and they had a much more social, observant eye. Here is the
author of *Gulliver's Travels* describing a London morning:

The small-coal man was heard with cadence deep,
Till drowned in shriller notes of chimney-sweep:
Duns at his lordship's gate began to meet;
And brickdust Moll had screamed through half the street.

—Jonathan Swift, 1709

The English religious sects that swarmed into North America in the eigh-
teenth century—Baptists, Methodists, Presbyterians, Quakers—brought

with them the language of the many hymns composed in those years, including this Christmas hymn from a great Methodist preacher:

> Hark the herald angels sing!
> "Glory to the newborn king!
> Peace on earth and mercy mild,
> God and sinner reconciled!"

—Charles Wesley, 1739

In Massachusetts, in the years of the American Revolution, the first book of poems to be published by an African American woman in what was to be the United States came from a young slave girl living in Boston:

> Some view our sable race with scornful eye,
> "Their colour is a diabolic die."
> Remember, *Christians, Negros,* black as *Cain,*
> May be refin'd and join th' angelic train.

—Phyllis Wheatley, a slave, Massachusetts Colony, 1773

And in England, in the wake of the American and French revolutions, a new romantic poetry burst into life. Often it borrowed the language and forms of the hymns and gave them a new, defiant content:

> What is it men in women do require?
> The lineaments of Gratified Desire.
> What is it women do in men require?
> The lineaments of Gratified Desire.

—William Blake, circa 1800

Or dreamed of ideal beauty:

> "Beauty is truth, truth beauty,"—that is all
> Ye know on earth, and all ye need to know.

—John Keats, 1819

The strains of English Romanticism gave a language to two very different American poets. One was a Quaker from Long Island and Brooklyn who made poems of the young teeming city of New York, and of himself as a common man and a prophet of the new democracy:

> I bequeath myself to the dirt to grow from the grass I love,
> If you want me again look for me under your bootsoles.

—Walt Whitman, 1855

The other came from Congregational stock and wrote small poems about immensity in the village of Amherst, Massachusetts.

> To see the Summer Sky
> Is Poetry, though never in a Book it lie—
> True Poems flee—

—Emily Dickinson, circa 1879

Emily Dickinson died in 1886, and another New England puritan, T. S. Eliot, was born two years later in St. Louis, Missouri. He was going to write some of the lines that launched modernism and the twentieth century:

> Let us go then, you and I,
> While the evening is spread out against the sky
> Like a patient etherised upon a table

—T. S. Eliot, 1917

One version of modernism culminated in an Irish poet living in London:

> O body swayed to music, O brightening glance,
> How can we know the dancer from the dance?

—William Butler Yeats, 1927

Another took root in a young African American poet come to Harlem from the Middle West:

> Tell all my mourners
> To mourn in red—
> Cause there ain't no sense
> In my being dead.
>
> —Langston Hughes, 1933

Post–World War II America brought in a newly charged poetry, sometimes furious and stingingly personal:

> And the villagers never liked you.
> They are dancing and stamping on you.
> They always *knew* it was you.
> Daddy, daddy, you bastard, I'm through.
>
> —Sylvia Plath, 1962

And sometimes, postmodern and post-surreal, an idiom that could include milk-blue skies and whanging girders:

> Still in the published city but not yet
> overtaken by a new form of despair, I asked
> the diagram: is it the foretaste of pain
> it might easily be? Or an emptiness
> so sudden it leaves the girders
> whanging in the absence of wind,
> the sky milk-blue and astringent?
>
> —John Ashbery, 1991

Much of this thousand years of ever-changing language, of new peoples inhabiting it and it inhabiting new peoples, gets summed up by another Irish poet, then a young man making poems out of the troubles in Belfast:

I push back
through dictions,
Elizabethan canopies,
Norman devices,

the erotic mayflowers
of Provence
and the ivied Latins
of churchmen

to the scop's
twang, the iron
flash of consonants
cleaving the line.

—Seamus Heaney, 1975

And here is a way to conclude: a poem that could only have been written in the later part of the twentieth century. You can tell it comes very late in the twentieth century because it borrows from and deconstructs an older poem, John Keats's "Ode to a Grecian Urn," which begins, "Thou still unravished bride of quietness!" and it is about a container John Keats never dreamed of:

Styrofoam Cup

thou still unravished   thou
thou,   thou bride
thou unstill,
thou unravished   unbride
unthou   unbride

—Brenda Hillman, 1999

Rainer Maria Rilke: *Herbsttag*

Rainer Maria Rilke is one of the great poets of the twentieth century. He's also one of the most popular. He's been translated again and again, as if some ideal English version of his German poems haunted so many minds that writers have had to keep trying to find it. Here, for the time of year, are some translations of a poem about the fall. He wrote it in Paris on September 21, 1902.

Autumn Day

Lord: it is time. The summer was immense.
Lay your shadow on the sundials,
and let loose the wind in the fields.

Bid the last fruits to be full;
give them another two more southerly days,
press them to ripeness, and chase
the last sweetness into the heavy wine.

Whoever has no house now will not build one anymore.
Whoever is alone now will remain so for a long time,
will stay up, read, write long letters,
and wander the avenues, up and down,
restlessly, while the leaves are blowing.

—Galway Kinnell and Hannah Liebmann, *The Essential Rilke*
(Ecco Press)

Lord, it is time. The summer was too long.
Lay your shadow on the sundials now,
and through the meadows let the winds throng.

Ask the last fruits to ripen on the vine;
give them further two more summer days

to bring about perfection and to raise
the final sweetness in the heavy wine.

Whoever has no house now will establish none,
whoever lives alone now will live on long alone,
will waken, read, and write long letters,
wander up and down the barren paths
the parks expose when the leaves are blown.

—William H. Gass, *Reading Rilke: Reflections on the Problem of
Translation* (Knopf)

Lord: it is time. The huge summer has gone by.
Now overlap the sundials with your shadows,
and on the meadows let the wind go free.

Command the fruits to swell on tree and vine;
grant them a few more warm transparent days,
urge them on to fulfillment then, and press
the final sweetness into the heavy wine.

Whoever has no house now, will never have one.
Whoever is alone will stay alone,
will sit, read, write long letters through the evening,
and wander the boulevards, up and down,
restlessly, while the dry leaves are blowing.

—Stephen Mitchell, *The Selected Poetry of Rainer Maria Rilke*
(Random House)

Lord, it is time now,
for the summer has gone on
and gone on.
Lay your shadow along the sun-
dial, and in the field
let the great wind blow free.

Command the last fruit
be ripe:
let it bow down the vine—
with perhaps two sun-warm days
more to force the last
sweetness in the heavy wine.

He who has no home
will not build one now.
He who is alone
will stay long
alone, will wake up,
read, write long letters,

and walk in the streets,
walk by in the
streets when the leaves blow.

—John Logan, from "Homage to Rainer Maria Rilke,"
John Logan: The Collected Poems (BOA Editions)

Here is the German text:

Herr: es ist Zeit. Der Sommer war sehr groß.
Leg deinen Schatten auf die Sonnenuhren,
und auf den Fluren laß die Winde los.

Befiehl den letzten Früchten voll zu sein;
gieb ihnen noch zwei südlichere Tage,
dränge sie zur Vollendung hin und jage
die letzte Süße in den schweren Wein.

Wer jetzt kein Haus hat, baut sich keines mehr.
Wer jetz allein ist, wird es lange bleiben,
wird wachen, lesen, lange Briefe schreiben
und wird in den Alleen hin und her
unruhig wandern, wenn die Blätter treiben.

And here, adapted from Stanley Burnshaw's immensely useful book, *The Poem Itself,* is a literal translation:

> Lord, it is time. The summer was (has been) very great.
> Lay Thy shadow upon the sun dials
> and on the (open) fields (meadows) let loose (unleash) the winds.
>
> Command the last fruits to be (become) full (ripe);
> give them another two southerly days,
> urge them on toward perfection (fulfillment), and drive (chase)
> the last (final) sweetness into the heavy wine.
>
> Who now has no house, builds himself none any more.
> Who now is alone, will long remain so,
> will wake, read, write long letters
> and will restlessly wander up and down the tree-lined avenues
> when the leaves are swirling.

SEPTEMBER 26

Rainer Maria Rilke Translated by Galway Kinnell and William Gass

Last week I printed four translations of a poem by the German poet Rainer Maria Rilke. He came to mind because there are two new books about him in the bookstores: a set of new translations by one of our best poets, Galway Kinnell; and a book of translations, essays on the poet, and meditations on the act of translation by one of our best fiction writers, William Gass. Gass's *Reading Rilke: Reflections on the Problem of Translation* (Knopf) contains not only a complete translation of some of his finest poems, including his masterwork, *Duino Elegies,* but also an acute essay on Rilke's life as an artist, a study of his thought, and an essay on translating Rilke that performs line-by-line dissections of sometimes as many as a dozen different translations of some of his most famous lines. Galway Kinnell's poetry, like Rilke's, is haunted by mortality, by a hunger for fullness of life, and a search for the terms on which it might be lived. There are echoes of Rilke throughout Kinnell's work, so it is fascinating to have his own versions of Rilke, made in collaboration with Hannah Liebmann, in front of us in *The Essential Rilke* (Ecco Press).

Readers who have never gotten around to Rilke will find a whole fall and winter's quiet, absorbed, and adventurous work in reading through these two books. No one emerges from reading Rilke entirely unchanged. He aims to go deep, to speak to our deepest and most fugitive sense of the possibilities and limitations of our lives, and, like Picasso or Proust, he's an artist who helps to define the art of this last century. I would add to the shelf of anyone setting out to read him two other translators, the *Selected Poems* (Random House) by Stephen Mitchell, which was published in the 1980s and has become for most people the English versions through which they came to know the poet, and the translations of the two volumes of Rilke's *New Poems* by Edward Snow, published by North Point Press.

Rilke thought that we lived most of our lives behind bars. One of his best known poems is about a caged panther at a zoo. The panther is us. Here is Kinnell's version of the poem:

The Panther
in the Jardin des Plantes, Paris

His gaze has grown so tired from the bars
passing, it can't hold anything anymore.
It is as if there were a thousand bars
and behind a thousand bars no world.

The soft gait of powerful supple strides,
which turns in the smallest of all circles,
is like a dance of strength around a center
where an imperious will stands stunned.

Only at times the curtain of the pupil
silently opens—. Then an image enters,
passes through the taut stillness of the limbs—
And in the heart ceases to be.

Another of Rilke's most celebrated poems comes from a late suite called *Sonnets to Orpheus,* and it contains a phrase that seems to sum up the quest of his poetry. It is something that Apollo, god of the lyre and of lyric poetry, has to tell us: *Gesang ist Dasein,* or in English something like "Singing is being." It means, roughly, that to be alive fully is to find your way to the fullest expression of your being. But are we capable of it? Here is Kinnell's version of the poem:

> A god can do it. But tell me how a man
> is to follow him through the narrow lyre?
> The human mind is cleft. No temple for Apollo
> stands where two heart-ways cross.
>
> Singing, as you reach it, is not desire,
> not suing for a thing in the end attained;
> singing is existence. Easy, for a god.
> But when do we *exist?* And when will *he*
>
> turn toward us the earth and stars?
> It's not, young people, when you're in love, even if
> then your voice thrusts open your mouth,—learn
>
> to forget you once lifted into song. That doesn't last.
> True singing is a different kind of breath.
> A breath about nothing. A blowing in the God. A wind.

Here is Gass:

> A god can do it. But tell me,
> how can a man follow him through the lyre's strings?
> His soul is split. And at the intersection
> of two heart-riven roads, there is no temple to Apollo.
>
> Song, as you have taught, is not mere longing,
> the wooing of whatever lovely can be attained;
> singing is being. Easy for a god.
> But when are we? And when does he fill us

with earth and stars?
Young man, this isn't it, your yearning,
even if your voice bursts out of your mouth.
Learn to forget such impulsive song. It won't last.
Real singing takes another breath.
A breath made of nothing. Inhalation in a god. A wind.

It's like hearing two pianists interpret the same piece of music, and it begins to create in the listener an almost teasing sense of what the unhearable, ideal performance of the poem would sound like. That unhearable performance is also, more or less, what Rilke meant by "true singing," when he urged us to find it in our lives.

OCTOBER 3

Andrew Hudgins

I was out this week walking along a beach and noticed that the migration of birds had really begun. Watching a flock of Canada geese lift off a salt pond and head south, I had the vague thought that seeing them leaving the place where I had seen them all summer feeding in the reeds was like watching the body separating from the soul. And then I remembered where that thought had come from: a single vivid image in a poem that I'd heard Andrew Hudgins read this summer at the Sewanee Writers Conference in Tennessee. What had stayed in my mind was the picture of a flock of grackles rising up out of a chinaberry tree, retaining the shape of the tree for a moment in the air, and then scattering.

The poem comes from his most recent book, *Babylon in a Jar* (Houghton Mifflin). The poem actually describes the event twice. In between the two descriptions, the poet dramatizes the speaker's response and interprets it. It's an interesting pattern—description, interpretation, description. I can see how I got the idea that the poem was an image of the soul peeling off from the body, a mysterious visual enactment of a kind of dispersal, but the interpretation in the poem is more indirect and suggestive than I had remembered. Look at the way it moves from the birds and the trees to

the body and its shadow, and the way the speaker seems to have stumbled
onto some mocking self-knowledge. It's very strange. Here's the poem:

The Chinaberry

I couldn't stand there watching them forever,
but when I moved
                              the grackles covering
each branch and twig
                              sprang
                                          together into flight
and for a moment in midair they held
the tree's shape,
                    the black tree
                                        peeling from the green,
as if
      they were its shadow or its soul, before
they scattered
                    circled and
                                    re-formed
as grackles heading south for winter grain fields.
Oh, it
            was just a chinaberry tree,
the birds were simply grackles.
                                        A miracle
made from this world and where I stood in it.
But you can't know how long
                                        I stood there watching.
And you can't know how desperate I'd become
advancing
                each step on the feet of my
advancing shadow,
                        how bitter and afraid I was
matching step after step with the underworld,
my ominous, indistinct and mirror image
darkening with
                    extreme and antic nothings
the ground I walked on,

                inexact reversals,
        elongated and foreshortened parodies
        of each
                foot lowering itself
                        onto its shadow.
        And you can't know how I had tried to force
        the moment, make it happen
                        before it happened—
        not necessarily this
                    though this is what I saw:
        black birds deserting the tree they had become,
        becoming,
                for a moment in midair,
        the chinaberry's shadow for a moment,
        after they had ceased to be
                        the chinaberry,
        then scattering;
                    meaning after meaning—
        birds strewn across the morning like flung gravel
        until
            they found themselves again as grackles,
        found each other,
                found South
                        and headed there,
        while I stood before
                    the green, abandoned tree.

OCTOBER 10

Heather McHugh

Heather McHugh's new book, *The Father of Predicaments* (Wesleyan University Press), just came into my hands. And it has in it, appropriately enough since we are in hurricane season, a poem about storms.

McHugh writes, typically, a riddling, punning, sometimes almost jangly, almost syncopated iambic verse, but it's organized on the page so that it looks like free verse. Reading her, the eye is doing one thing and the ear is doing another: it makes for a quick, quirky nervous rhythm that is her characteristic sound. Also, her writing is so alert to itself, so alert to language, it's like watching a dancer on a mirrored floor, stepping on her steps. She's practically playing with her words as she writes them down. "Joycean" is the word that comes to mind. There may be something Irish about this almost compulsive playfulness. Here's the poem:

Not So Fast

I thought my life was
my intelligence. But then a dimming overcame me,

then a wind, and then the whole
sound waveletted, aroused.
I was extremely gradual in my
misgiving, as I looked (for things did not
look) up—and there the buffeted

high race of K's revealed, so that a man could
see it for himself, the fabled column in the clouds
(which heretofore I'd only known
from books): and it had one
long eyehole through it
to a blue too light

to trust. (The lightest blue is heaven's kind
of founding oxymoron.) It's not there
for us to understand; it's there for us
to be looked down on through . . .

How clumsily I made my way
upstairs from shore to cover—
where a forest took my thrashing for me.
Still I'd had my awful

eyeful of the future, in which we
are bearing up for life, while it

bears down, a mind for legalism,
slow. It has the time. (Forget
your airs.) It has the grounds.

You see what I mean? The beginning of the poem could be organized as
three lines of iambic pentameter—

I thought my life was my intelligence.
    But then a dimming overcame me, then
a wind, and then the whole sound waveletted,

—as if it were Shakespeare's blank verse, but she's dis-organized it, made
it nervous rather than flowing.

She's describing a storm coming on, but you'd hardly know that she
was talking about a darkening sky from "But then a dimming overcame
me." The effect is more psychological than physical. And you can't be sure
whether "sound" means "bay" or "noise." They both surge in waves, so it
could be both. And then there is the perfectly accurate but slightly sinis-
ter invented word: "waveletted." The next bit is also riddled by wordplay.
The speaker only gradually realizes what the weather is telling her: "as I
looked (for things did not look) up." And then the description of the sky.
For these lines I may need help from my inventive readers:

the buffeted

high race of K's revealed, so that a man could
see it for himself, the fabled column in the clouds

"The buffetted high race of K's"? Like the k's for strikeouts in a baseball
score-keeper's book? Something in the clouds that looks like letter k's?
Anyway, it reveals the stormhead, "the fabled column in the clouds." Hard
to tell—since I've never seen one—whether this is hurricane or cyclone.
"It had one long eyehole through it to a blue too light to trust" may be
the eye of the storm, or some faintly ominous opening in the clouded
sky, or both.

"Heaven's kind of founding oxymoron"? The tender blue sky that is
also a terrifying power? We look up, as if interpretation were also a power?
It's not. Anyway, the speaker retreats from the beach to the bedroom,

"from shore to cover." And there, perhaps from an upstairs window, she sees the forest take the thrashing. And has an "awful eyeful"—this is what I mean by compulsive play; textbooks are full of learned disquisitions on the sublime in art evoking "awe" before the terrible force of nature; McHugh has turned it into an uneasy quip—of the future, everyone's future—when life bears down on us and we try to bear up. More word-play in the face of the awful and inevitable. And the future seems to her remorseless as a lawsuit. It owns the ground, and it has the grounds.

This kind of writing could seem like pure playfulness, but in her it rarely does. McHugh thinks of the world itself as a cunning and danger-ous construction. (This also seems Irish to me.) She isn't trying to outwit it so much as trying to play the game quickly enough to stay alive, like some Oedipus fielding every riddle the Sphinx tosses up. Oedipus in a batting cage. Or a chameleon changing color on a mirror. She's a poet for whom wit is a form of spiritual survival.

OCTOBER 17

Dean Young

Sometimes the world, or your life, seems so confusing, you need a call to order—like a clear account of the history of the world to remind you how you got here. From his new book, *First Course in Turbulence* (Univer-sity of Pittsburgh Press), Dean Young seems to be making such a gesture:

Tribe

The first people came out of the lake
and their god was the raven. Craving
over the mitochondrial plain. The second people
came out of the volcano and their god,
the shark, ate the raven so the first people
turned orange and died. Song gone, dance
done. No one is sure where the third people
came from but they didn't last long.
Somehow they learned to turn themselves

into toads to frighten their enemies
but the toads couldn't pronounce the spells
to turn themselves back into people
and to this day you still hear them trying.
This is where Wagner got his ideas.
Then the shark god gave birth to the coyote
and the whistling ant who mated with a cloud
and gave birth to the hawk and they all
battled and intermarried so the second people
invented the drum as a way of participating.
It was the drumming that brought forth
the fourth people who thought it was important
to always be elsewhere, searching for
some purple root, some flashy feather
for the hat's brim so most of them

were squashed by trucks when they wandered
onto the interstate at night. By then
the second people were pretty sick of
each other and they dreamed of mating
with fish, with lightning in puzzling
contortions, woke up, and to their credit,
wrote everything down. Then they would gather
in their condominiums, sharing descriptions
and disagreeing about the use of color and
whether a shovel could symbolize fear of intimacy.
But then it rained and the earth was covered
with water which was bad but not as bad
as when it gets covered with fire which
everyone knows is going to happen next.
Everywhere you look was once a sea and
in the sea grew gigantic serpents and
in their bellies precious stones and
inside the stones the eggs of another people
and inside these people, well, you get the idea.
Nothing is ever finished and nothing ever
perishes completely, there is always some
residue. Sometimes, in the dust, a cape clasp.

Sometimes, a rat. Everywhere are carved trees,
buried nameplates, initialed cliffs but

the earth, like a fox in a trap, is never done
gnawing itself just as the gods are never done
bickering and swallowing each other, jealous
of our beauty and ability to die.
No claim lasts.
Flags flapping in breeze become breeze.
Eyesight turns into starlight.
And this is how you've come to be
struggling with cellophane, smashing
the ham sandwich within. Human, sometimes
a stone washed up covered with clues. Sometimes
a tree gets knocked over by wind and inside is a flint
but how can you know what to ask or answer
when you don't even know who you are.

Some poems get made out of clarities of seeing, some out of invention
and surprise. Young is a poet of invention and surprise. Taken together,
they make for wit, of course. Sometimes his wit is fierce and dark. He is
a poet, like Baudelaire, like Brodsky, who is inclined to think that a lot of
things, including life itself, are stupid, or at least incomprehensible. Here
is a more characteristic poem. It seems to be a love poem. Notice where
it starts and that it pauses, in its trajectory, to notice the blue tongues
of giraffes and the absolutely functional design of the toilets in jail cells
before it arrives at its astonished noticing of the fact that everything in
our heads depends on the painfully uncertain beating of our hearts:

Mortal Poem

I do not understand why I love you.
The mustard in your hair? Your breasts
like shiny battleships, your thought control?
Reasons seem so insufficient, reason itself
seems insufficient. The sea rushes up

to the beach of no reason, inveigling
chimes for no reason, greenery recumbent
upon the landscape of no reason.

Within the mountain is a valley, within
the blue sky a red one. I don't understand

the weather although I am heavy thralled.
Scraping the windshield made me late, fog
makes me first, cloud shaped like Africa
and I never arrive. Lightning must be
very quick to do its job, otherwise
it'd illumine nothing, pound no chest,
put no lips to unbreathing mouths.

There is an inner weather and an outer weather.
Within the seed is the hundred-year-old tree.
Within the eye is an arrow, the heart a storm
while outside it's warm and bony.
It's a mistake to think

everything is inside one's head. Always
darkness somewhere, giraffes with blue
tongues and who could have thought of that?
Opals dissolve in ordinary water, being
part water themselves. When inside the opal,
I often dream I'm swimming, when inside
you, I'm a flood. When inside the jail cell,

I wasn't in full comprehension although
all seemed one clear instance of form
matched to function: lidless toilet
merged with a slab you can sit
or lie upon, floor with a drain somewhere
toward the middle, all one poured

stone unlike the butterfly.

The anvil must be very hard
to do its job but what flies off
isn't sparks, it's pomegranates,
peach blossoms, sharks, it's the beginning

of the world and we are not the hammer swung
but what's under. O my darling, last night
I woke with pain in my chest but
it is gone this morning.

Young was born in Pennsylvania and went to school in Indiana. For some reason the middle of America—John Ashbery's Rochester, James Tate's Kansas—has produced a number of homegrown surrealists. There's a drawing of the author's on the jacket of the book. It looks like one of those inspired doodles by Paul Klee, a loopy imaginary geometry struck by lightning, a slightly erotic, slightly sinister tangle of forms. It's very much like the feeling of his poems. Here's another, with the same sinuous dream-logic and a sudden, strangely magical conclusion:

The Invention of Heaven

The mind becomes a field of snow
but then the snow melts and dandelions
blink on and you can walk through them,
your trousers plastered with dew.
They're all waiting for you but first
here's a booth where you can win

a peacock feather for bursting a balloon,
a man in huge stripes shouting about
a boy who is half swan, the biggest
pig in the world. Then you will pass
tractors pulling other tractors,
trees snagged with bright wrappers

and then you will come to a river
and then you will wash your face.

OCTOBER 24

John Clare

John Clare was born in Northhamptonshire, in the eastern flatlands of England in 1793, a contemporary of John Keats. His mother was illiterate, his father a scarcely literate agricultural laborer. The children of itinerant farm workers in that time and place were even less likely to become poets than the children of migrant laborers would be in the United States today. Clare's formal education was over by the time he was eleven; at thirteen he had discovered poetry and began to write it while he worked in the fields and at whatever other forms of day labor came his way, lime-burning, driving cattle, digging and setting hedges. When he was twenty-five, he met a bookseller in the market town of Stamford and through him arranged to have a book of poems published. It created a small sensation—here was a peasant poet with a thorough knowledge of the rural landscape, a rich sense of local dialect, and an ear trained by his reading of Spenser and the eighteenth-century nature poets and Wordsworth. Three more books followed. He married and had several children. He had some help for a while from the local aristocracy, and one can imagine what that relationship might have been like. "I must confess," a Lord Radstock, who gave him a small income and much religious advice, wrote, "that I discover in his character a want of gratitude and proper feeling toward the opulent higher orders which has lower'd him not a little in my opinion."

Poetry poured out of Clare. The four published books represent only about a third of the poetry he wrote in his lifetime, and the difficulties of his life were intensified by the onset of madness. He was often and deeply depressed, became delusional (convinced for a period that he was Lord Byron), and was twice incarcerated in asylums. We have his last poems because he spoke them to the keeper of one of these asylums, a literate gentleman who wrote them down. Because Clare wrote in torrents and seems to have revised furiously, the manuscripts of his poems have presented a whole series of problems to modern editors. Since the 1960s two scholars, Geoffrey Summerfield and Eric Robinson, have been getting Clare into print through Oxford University Press and we are getting to see many Clare poems no one but a handful of scholars had seen before. The best reader's edition of their work is *Clare: Selected Poems and Prose* (Oxford, 1966). And here was the dilemma: did they print the poems as edited and punctuated by the 19th century editors or as they appeared in Clare's own hand before they were sent to the printer? And what about the unpublished poems? Did they edit them, as Clare's editors would have, or leave them alone? They chose to reproduce the poems as they appeared from Clare's own hand—though there is evidence that the poet expected the help of his editors with regularizing punctuation and spelling.

Here's a poem to give you a sense of how the issue plays out. It's pure portraiture; not the idealized shepherds and pipe-playing laborers of the upper-class literary tradition, but a portrait of workers and landscape from someone who knew it intimately:

> The thunder mutters louder and more loud
> With quicker motion hay folks ply the rake
> Ready to burst slow sails the pitch black cloud
> And all the gang a bigger haycock make
> To sit beneath—the woodland winds awake
> The drops so large wet all thro' in an hour
> A tiny flood runs down the leaning rake
> In the sweet hay yet dry the hay folks cower
> And some beneath the wagon shun the shower

Here is a version I have punctuated:

> The thunder mutters louder and more loud.
> With quicker motion hay folks ply the rake.
> Ready to burst, slow sails the pitch black cloud
> And all the gang a bigger haycock make
> To sit beneath—The woodland winds awake,
> The drops so large wet all thro' in an hour:
> A tiny flood runs down the leaning rake.
> In the sweet hay, yet dry, the hay folks cower
> And some beneath the wagon shun the shower.

So what would you do? In my experience the unpunctuated poems make you work and in that way bring you close to the poem, but they don't deliver the remarkable music one finds in Clare eventually. It's like hearing a piece of music played tentatively, in rehearsal, and then hearing the performance.

Here are two others poems, as edited by Eric Robinson and Geoffrey Summerfield:

Mist in the Meadow

The evening o'er the meadow seems to stoop
More distant lessens the diminished spire
Mist in the hollows reeks and curdles up
Like fallen clouds that spread—and things retire
Less seen and less—the shepherd passes near
And little distant most grotesquely shades
As walking without legs—lost to his knees
As through the rawky creeping smoke he wades
Now half way up the arches disappear
And small the bits of sky that glimmer through
Then trees loose all but tops—while fields remain
As wont the indistinctness passes bye
And shepherd all his length is seen again
And further on the village meets the eye

Sand Martin

Thou hermit haunter of the lonely glen
And common wild and heath—the desolate face
Of rude waste landscapes far away from men
Where frequent quarrys give thee dwelling place
With strangest taste and labour undeterred
Drilling small holes along the quarrys side
More like the haunts of vermin than a bird
And seldom by the nesting boy descried
Ive seen thee far away from all thy tribe
Flirting about the unfrequented sky
And felt a feeling that I cant describe
Of lone seclusion and a hermit joy
To see thee circle round nor go beyond
That lone heath and its melancholy pond.

Note: Since this note was written, a new biography of John Clare has appeared,
John Clare: A Biography, *by Jonathan Bate (Picador Books). Bate has also edi-*
ted his own selection of Clare's poems, "I Am": The Selected Poetry of John
Clare *(Farrar, Straus & Giroux), which elects to punctuate the poems lightly and*
to correct misspellings. So the controversy continues.

OCTOBER 31

Halloween: John Keats and Lynne McMahon

Halloween is also the birthday of John Keats. Most people know who
Keats was, the young English poet who died in Rome in 1821 at the age
of twenty-six, in despair from a feeling that his work had come to noth-
ing. For millions of tourists, especially English and American tourists, it
has been part of any first visit to Rome to go to Keats's room near the
Spanish Steps and see the place where he died. A friend was with him, the
painter Joseph Severn, and Keats had with him, unopened, the letters of
the young woman he had loved in England, Fanny Brawne. Some of the
tourists stop to read the last enigmatic poem or fragment that he wrote.
It's been titled "This Living Hand." It goes like this:

> This living hand, now warm and capable
> Of earnest grasping, would, if it were cold
> And in the icy silence of the tomb,
> So haunt thy days and chill thy dreaming nights
> That thou wouldst wish thine own heart dry of blood
> So in my veins red life might stream again,
> And thou be conscience-calm'd—see here it is—
> I hold it towards you.

There is a poem about these lines in a new book, *The House of Enter-
taining Science* by Lynne McMahon (David R. Godine). McMahon is a
poet of terrific intelligence and an exact and refined verbal art. Her book
is full of pleasures. But this was the poem that stopped me: it connects this
scary poem to the odd coincidence of Keats's birthday and Halloween.

Anniversary

Strange to think of Keats's birthday
and the American Halloween—there
an oblong of stony damp, here,
the parade and tramp behind

the resurrected dead to beg or threaten
trick or treat. He couldn't eat
the last plates of food, Severn said.
They threw them out the window

onto the cobbled walk.
The concierge wanted them both
thrown out. Poets still write about that,
and Fanny's sad unopened notes

(the handwritten address alone was enough
to crack his heart) and professors
pry open "This Living Hand"
with its ghoulish close which reads as though

All Hallows Eve at last retrieved
its first-born child. Though really
it had never let him go.
Fast fading fast at seven,

at fourteen, at twenty. The future
passed the sentry at his mother's door,
and then poor Tom's a-cold.
The cold warmth on the granary floor

still seems a meager recompense,
that twist of flowers spared by the scythe.
So little of the loss restored.
We were thinking about it tonight

on our meandering course down the road
celebrating this autumn's close.
A holiness of wraiths and creeps,
death-eating Deaths. Our breath

visible in the pumpkin-lighted streets.
The cold traveled centuries to show us that.
We looked, but the dead had all gone back.
No one dressed as Keats.

"Poor Tom's a-cold" is Kent's line from *King Lear*, when he follows the king onto the moor, dressed as a mad beggar. It was a line Keats liked, and when his younger brother Tom died of the tuberculosis that was also going to kill him—which he may have caught while nursing his brother—Keats marked his passing by writing the date of his brother's death beside the phrase in his volume of Shakespeare's plays.

The lines about "The cold warmth on the granary floor" and "That twist of flowers spared by the scythe" refer to the image of autumn in his great ode:

Who hath not seen thee oft amid thy store?
    Sometimes whoever seeks abroad may find
Thee sitting careless on the granary floor,
    Thy hair soft-lifted by the winnowing wind;
Or on a half-reaped furrow sound asleep,
    Drowsed with the fume of poppies, while thy hook
        Spares the next swath and all its twinèd flowers:

Eerie, the idea of the hand in his last scrap of poetry reaching out to us on his birthday: trick or treat?

NOVEMBER 7

Czeslaw Milosz: An Argument About Imperialism

An argument in a cafe. A college professor was remarking that one of the things all of his students knew for sure was that imperialism was a very bad thing. And he found himself thinking, as the post–Cold War world erupted into spasm after spasm of ethnic violence, that there was something to be said for empires. At least they settled some order and tried to command loyalty to something other than the tribal identities that were sending people raging into the streets, murdering their neighbors. Another friend, a journalist, asked him what higher loyalty Indonesia was imposing on East Timor. And the argument ran through Bosnia, Russia and Chechnya, the CIA's support of Pinochet in Chile, England and Northern Ireland, Hutus and Tutsis, Serbs and Albanians in Kosovo, Pol Pot in Phnom Pen.

I found myself thinking of a poem by Czeslaw Milosz about the great ideological wars of the century. Milosz was born in Lithuania in 1911 and wrote his poems, of course, in Polish. When he went off to Paris in the 1930s, to the great capital of the world, he was following the path of hundreds of young men and women, artists, writers, philosophers, future politicians, and revolutionaries from the small, provincial countries who went abroad to get an education or spend time soaking up Europe's capital of art and ideas. The poem I was thinking of is about that. It was written in 1980, when the older man, in Paris again, thinks about the violence of the century he has lived through and what had been for him the glamor of Paris.

Bypassing Rue Descartes

Bypassing Rue Descartes
I descended toward the Seine, shy, a traveler,
A young barbarian just come to the capital of the world.

We were many, from Jassy and Koloshvar, Wilno and Bucharest,
      Saigon and Marrakesh,
Ashamed to remember the customs of our homes,
About which nobody here should ever be told:

The clapping for servants, barefooted girls hurry in,
Dividing food with incantations,
Choral prayers recited by master and household together.

I had left the cloudy provinces behind,
I entered the universal, dazzled and desiring.

Soon enough, many from Jassy and Koloshvar, or Saigon
    or Marrakesh
Would be killed because they wanted to abolish the customs
    of their homes.

Soon enough their peers were seizing power
In order to kill in the name of the universal, beautiful ideas.

Meanwhile the city behaved according to its nature,
Rustling with throaty laughter in the dark,
Baking long breads and pouring wine into clay pitchers,
Buying fish, lemon, and garlic at street markets,
Indifferent as it was to honor and shame and greatness and glory,
Because that had been done already and had transformed itself
Into monuments representing nobody knows whom,
Into arias hardly audible and into turns of speech.

Again I lean on the rough granite of the embankment,
As if I had returned from travels through the underworlds
And suddenly saw in the light the reeling wheel of the seasons
Where empires have fallen and those once living are now dead.

There is no capital of the world, neither here nor anywhere else,
And the abolished customs are restored to their small fame
And now I know that the time of human generations is not like
    the time of the earth.

As to my heavy sins, I remember one most vividly:
How, one day, walking on a forest path along a stream,
I pushed a rock down onto a water snake coiled in the grass.

And what I have met with in life was the just punishment
Which reaches, sooner or later, the breaker of a taboo.

In a note to the poem, in his *Collected Poems* (Ecco/Harper), Milosz writes: "In Lithuania, where the author grew up, many pagan beliefs survived, among them the cult of water snakes, which were associated with the sun. A strict taboo protected a water snake from any harm inflicted by man."

Milosz gets so much history into this poem. He's thinking, I'm sure, about the Marxism, or rather the Stalinism, of Parisian intellectuals in the 1930s. It occurred to me that Ho Chi Minh must have been in Paris at the same time Milosz was, and lots of others who would figure in the history of the century. This poem—Lithuania, like Poland, had been gobbled up by the Russians—comes down on the side of local custom and against empire. Custom, but not tribe. It interested me to read that the water snake is associated with the sun. It argues against the grand ideas, which must be part of what he means by "bypassing Rue Descartes," but not against ideas. The sun, after all, is the source of life. To place a prohibition on our relationship to some aspect of nature seems to be for him a way of setting all the political and tribal passions of the "time of human generations" aside and acknowledging the time of the earth, wondering at the time of the earth.

Poems, of course, are not finally made from ideas. What's so vivid to me in this one is that young man dazed by Paris and the old man's sudden vision of "the reeling wheel of the seasons." An image to think about as the last year of the century turns toward its winter.

NOVEMBER 14

Wallace Stevens

The fact that it is November gives me an occasion to remind you of, or introduce you to, a strange and beautiful poem by Wallace Stevens. It is, as his poems sometimes are, tricky. I suppose it's about the imagination and the world. And it's a tour de force, about as showy a piece of showmanship

as there is in American poetry. As an added bonus, it will also serve as a
surrogate for a Caribbean cruise, so take it slowly:

Sea Surface Full of Clouds

I.
In that November off Tehuantepec,
The slopping of the sea grew still one night
And in the morning summer hued the deck

And made one think of rosy chocolate
And gilt umbrellas. Paradisal green
Gave suavity to the perplexed machine

Of ocean, which like limpid water lay.
Who, then, in that ambrosial latitude
Out of the light evolved the moving blooms,

Who, then, evolved the sea-blooms from the clouds
Diffusing balm in that Pacific calm?
C'était mon enfant, mon bijou, mon âme.

The sea-clouds whitened far below the calm
And moved, as blooms move, in the swimming green
And in its watery radiance, while the hue

Of heaven in an antique reflection rolled
Round those flotillas. And sometimes the sea
Poured brilliant iris on the glistening blue.

II.
In that November off Tehuantepec,
The slopping of the sea grew still one night.
At breakfast jelly yellow streaked the deck

And made one think of chop-house chocolate
And sham umbrellas. And a sham-like green
Capped summer-seeming on the tense machine

Of ocean, which in sinister flatness lay.
Who, then, beheld the rising of the clouds
That strode submerged in that malevolent sheen,

Who saw the mortal massives of the blooms
Of water moving on the water-floor?
C'était mon frère du ciel, mon vie, mon or.

The gongs rang loudly as the windy booms
Hoo-hooed it in the darkened ocean-blooms.
The gongs grew still. And then blue heaven spread

Its crystalline pendentives on the sea
And the macabre of water-glooms
In an enormous undulation fled.

III.
In that November off Tehuantepec,
The slopping of the sea grew still one night
And a pale silver patterned on the deck

And made one think of porcelain chocolate
And pied umbrellas. An uncertain green,
Piano-polished, held the tranced machine

Of ocean, as a prelude holds and holds.
Who, seeing silver petals of white blooms
Unfolding in the water, feeling sure

Of the milk of the saltiest spurge, heard, then,
The sea unfolding in the sunken clouds?
Oh! C'était mon extase et mon amour.

So deeply sunken were they that the shrouds,
The shrouding shadows, made the petals black
Until the rolling heaven made them blue,

A blue beyond the rainy hyacinth,
And smiting the crevasses of the leaves
Deluged the ocean with a sapphire blue.

If you have read this far, you will not be surprised to find that the
fourth section begins like this:

IV.
In that November off Tehuantepec
The night-long slopping of the sea grew still.
A mallow morning dozed upon the deck

And made one think of musky chocolate
And frail umbrellas. A too-fluent green
Suggested malice in the dry machine

Of ocean, pondering dank stratagem.
Who then beheld the figures of the clouds
Like blooms secluded in the thick marine?

Like blooms? Like damasks that were shaken off
From the loosed girdles in the spangling must.
C'était ma foi, la nonchalance divine.

The nakedness would rise and suddenly turn
Salt masks of beard and mouths of bellowing,
Would—But more suddenly the heaven rolled

Its bluest sea-clouds in the thinking green,
And the nakedness became the broadest blooms,
Mile-mallows that a mallow sun cajoled.

V.
In that November off Tehuantepec
Night stilled the slopping of the sea. The day
Came, bowing and voluble, upon the deck,

Good clown .... One thought of Chinese chocolate
And large umbrellas. And a motley green
Followed the drift of the obese machine

Of ocean, perfected in indolence.
What pistache one, ingenious and droll,
Beheld the sovereign clouds as jugglery

And the sea as turquoise-turbaned Sambo, neat
At tossing saucers—cloudy-conjuring sea?
C'était mon esprit bâtard, l'ignominie.

The sovereign clouds came clustering. The conch
Of loyal conjuration trumped. The wind
Of green blooms turning crisped the motley hue

To clearing opalescence. Then the sea
And heaven rolled as one and from the two
Came fresh transfiguring of freshest blue.

I've written elsewhere about my discovery of this poem, and about
the night, when I was in college, that a group of us—six or eight—sat
huddled in an old car in the parking lot of a beach on the California coast
in a lashing rain storm—so that we could see the white of the breakers in
the surf—and passed around a bottle of wine, and took turns reading the
stanzas of this poem to each other over and over. It was my only experi-
ence of being intoxicated by Wallace Stevens.

The trick of the poem, of course, is that it acts out one of Stevens's
pet ideas about reality. In the poem the nouns and the basic sentence
structure are the physical world; the adjectives and the subtle variations
in the rhythms of the sentences are the way the imagination apprehends
the world, and for Stevens the world is the endless play of those adjectives
over the adamant nouns of our experience.

For you, this November, the idea would be to read the whole thing and
then go outside to see how many worlds there are.

NOVEMBER 21

Thanksgiving: Daniel Halpern

Anyone who has had a newborn arrive in their life knows how power-
ful and hard to describe the emotions are. Twentieth-century poets have
mostly stayed away from them. They are too frail. They are not mammal
grief and rage, even though they can turn into grief and rage. (That's what
King Lear is about.) And the example of the tradition of domestic and
familial poetry in Victorian America has not encouraged us. It made the
subject seem impossible to approach without sentimentality. Language
makes the distinction: we speak of anger and desire as "feeling," the ten-
der and uneasy stuff around the helplessness of infants, and the impulse
to protect children we call "sentiment." And it's probably well that we
do. Because they are frail emotions, and they are capable of turning into
something quite savage. Nevertheless it is a deep thing, the wonder (and
fear) at the arrival of a newborn child, and the process of—hard to know
how else to say it—falling in love that parents go through with this crea-
ture given into their care. How do you talk about it?

Daniel Halpern, in his new book *Something Shining* (Knopf), takes the
subject on. He's my editor, and an old friend, and a poet I've been read-
ing for twenty years or more. I've always thought of him as a poet on the
model of the Roman poet Horace, with a poised and immensely civilized
mind for the life we live, its large and small panics and decorums, and a
civilized balance in his verse, in which orderliness can sometimes seem
sinister and wry, and sometimes seem a gift, the kind of gift social beings
can give to one another, like a well-set table. Reading him has, over the
years, made for very good company, this intelligence that is reasonably
disenchanted, keeps an eye on the decades as they pass, the telling particu-
lars in the social habits of a generation, its ardors, suavities, and defeats.

And now this book that requires another kind of poise. How do you
write about the whole business of becoming a parent, and about the way
this attachment, this profound and life-defining tenderness and wonder,
grows in us. He goes straight to it, and succeeds, I think. Have a look:

After the Vigil

They turn up, no longer nameless,
their bodies clear, so nearly pure
they appear in morning light transparent.

They turn up and one day look at you
for the first time, their eyes sure now
you are one of theirs, surely here to stay.

They turn up wearing an expression of yours,
imitating your mouth, the smile perfected
over years of enduring amusing moments.

They turn up without a past, their fingers,
inexact instruments that examine what carpets
their turf, what they inherit through blood.

They turn up with your future, if not in mind
very much in the explosive story of their genes,
in gesture foreshadowing the what's-to-come.

They turn up with your hair—albeit not much
of it—something in the color, the curl of it
after the bath, its bearing after sleep.

They turn up already on their own, ideas
of their own, settling on their own limits,
their particular sense of things.

They turn up and we have been waiting,
as they have without knowing. They turn
into this world, keeping their own counsel.

Here's a section from one called "Her Body":

The Eyes

We believe their color makes some kind of difference,
the cast of it played off the color of hair and face.

But it makes no difference, blue or brown,
hazel, green, or gray, pale sky or sand.

When sleep-burdened they'll turn up into her,
close back down upon her sizable will.

But when she's ready for the yet-to-come—
oh, they widen, grow a deep cool sheen

to catch the available light and shine
with the intensity of the newly arrived.

If they find you they'll hold on relentlessly
without guile, the gaze no less than interrogatory,

fixed, immediate, bringing to bear what there's been
to date. Call her name and perhaps they'll turn to you,

or they might be engaged, looking deeply into the nature
of other things—the affect of wall, the texture of rug,

into something very small that's fallen to the floor
and needs to be isolated and controlled. Maybe

an afternoon reflection, an insect moving *slowly,*
maybe just looking with loyalty into the eyes of another.

A Peruvian Poet: César Vallejo

Several weeks ago I printed various translations of Rainer Maria Rilke's great sonnet *"Herbsttag,"* along with the original German text. To my surprise I received at least two dozen new translations of the poem in the mail from readers, many of them quite wonderful. It confirmed my own experience of reading poetry in translation. You glimpse the original, or your idea of the original, behind the English of the translation, and the idea of it haunts you. It's the impulse, often enough, that starts translation.

So here's another opportunity and another autumn sonnet, this time one of the best-known poems in Latin American literature, *"Piedra Negra sobre una Piedra Blanca,"* "Black Stone upon a White Stone," by the great Peruvian poet César Vallejo. This time I'm going to give you first a literal translation. My Spanish is primitive, so I have borrowed it from one of my favorite books, *The Poem Itself* (Simon & Schuster, 1960) by Stanley Burnshaw. In the book Burnshaw offers, as an alternative to poetic translations, word-by-word translation of a whole range of modern poems in French, German, Spanish, Portuguese, and Italian, with a grammatical commentary. Here is his version of the Vallejo poem:

> I shall die in Paris with heavy showers,
> on a day of which I already possess the memory.
> I shall die in Paris—and I'm not dismayed—
> perhaps on a Thursday, like today, in the autumn.
>
> It shall be a Thursday, because today, Thursday, as I prose
> these lines, my forearms have gone bad
> and, never before, in all my road
> have I felt myself so lonely as today.
>
> César Vallejo is dead; everybody kept hitting him
> even though he has done nothing to them;
> they hit him hard with a stick, and hard,

> also, with a rope; his witnesses are
> the Thursdays and the bones of his arms,
> the loneliness, the rain, the roads . . .

In his commentary Burnshaw points out several odd things about the flavor of the language. The *aguacero* of the first line is "heavy showers." The *lluvia* of the last line is "rain." In line five, he uses the curious medieval verb *prosar* for the composing of poetry. In line six, he uses the somewhat medical word *húmeros,* literally "humerus," for the bones of his arm, and *me he puesto a la mala* is colloquial, a way of saying "ache" or "hurt." And line seven is also strange; *todo mi camino* comes where one expects "all my life" and thus gives you something like "in all the road of my life." Line ten—the one line that varies the twelve-syllable pattern—uses a present subjunctive, *haga nada* instead of the conditional *hiciera nada* that a Spanish reader might expect; a literal translation would be "without his doing them." And, in the same line, *le pegaban,* "they used to hit him," is a past tense form, and it's followed by a present tense verb: the effect of the tense "everybody (used to) hit him without his doing them. They hit (present) him hard . . . " The word *palo* translated here as "stick" could also mean "club."

The Spanish text looks like this:

Piedra Negra sobre una Piedra Blanca

> *Me moriré en Paris con aguacero,*
> *un día del cual tengo ya el recuerdo.*
> *Me moriré en Paris—y no me corro—*
> *tal vez un jueves, como es hoy, de otoño.*
>
> *Jueves será, porque hoy, jueves, que proso*
> *estos versos, los húmeros me he puesto*
> *a la mala y, jamás como hoy, me he vuelto,*
> *con todo mi camino, a verme solo.*
>
> *César Vallejo ha muerto, le pegaban*
> *todos sin que él les haga nada;*
> *le daban duro con un palo y duro*

también con una soga; son testigos
los días jueves y los huesos húmeros,
la soledad, la lluvia, los caminos . . .

The poem was published in a posthumous collection of his poems, *Poemas Humanos,* in 1939. One of the haunting things about it is that he did die in Paris. His life had not been easy. He grew up in an Andean village outside of Lima and went to the university in the capital, where he was jailed for his political activities. He left Lima for Paris in 1923, where he lived in poverty and practiced his art. He was intensely moved and engaged by the Spanish Civil War and threw himself into the defense of the Spanish republic with furious energy, often carrying messages and money back and forth from Paris to Barcelona. It's thought that this wore him down. In any case, he died of a fever of unknown origin, perhaps the recurrence of a childhood illness, in Paris in 1937.

Here is a version I've made of the poem:

Black Stone on White Stone

I will die in Paris on a rainy day,
on a day I can already remember.
I will die in Paris—and I don't mind—
perhaps on a Thursday in autumn, like today.

It will be a Thursday, because today, Thursday, as I write
these lines, the bones in my arms ache badly,
and never before, in all my road, have I felt
myself as lonely as I do today

César Vallejo is dead, everyone kept hitting him,
even though he had done nothing to them.
They hit him hard with a stick, and hard

also with a rope; his witnesses
are the Thursday and the bones of his arms,
the loneliness, the rain, the roads . . .

This is doing it the easy way, which has been typical of late twentieth century translation. I ignored the rhymes. I mostly ignored the eleven syllable line, the *endesilabo* of the Romance language sonnet. I ignored the grammatical strangenesses, and just tried to find a clear way through the main line of the poem, letting the timing of the phrasings in the stanzas, and the imagery, and the intense melancholy carry it. But I know I did not get Vallejo's poem. Perhaps you will try.

DECEMBER 5

Bad Words: Stephen Berg

There is a piece I had in mind to print around Labor Day, and I have been hesitant about it. It contains a few words not normally seen in family newspapers. Words that can't normally be seen in family newspapers have either to do with sex or the bathroom. It is a peculiarity of the English language that writers and family newspapers have to work with, that there is very little middle ground in the language between words that seem rude and words that seem excessively scientific or euphemistic. For the most common private acts we have no comfortable public language. And so the writer makes choices. And editors make choices. Until recently the typographical convention, where the rude words were concerned, was to use an intermitting dash. "Oh, s—t!" he said. And there is a story about Tallulah Bankhead in the early 1950s, meeting Norman Mailer at a party. Mailer was then newly famous for his novel of World War II, *The Naked and the Dead,* in which he had gone to great and somewhat tortuous lengths to render the speech of combat soldiers accurately. But he bowed to the conventions of the time, so his characters were always "fugging" this and "fugging" that. The great actress, introduced to the young novelist, studied him cooly. "Oh, yes," she said, "you're the young man who can't spell f—k." (You see that I, unlike Bankhead, bow to the convention of the family paper.)

The words in question here are bathroom words, and since we have had a whole summer of movies so filled with bathroom humor that the critics have begun to theorize about it, it seemed to me suddenly absurd not to print a serious piece of writing when it took the subject that the bathroom jokes have such a good time with—human dignity—seriously. It comes from a wonderful recent book by the Philadelphia poet Stephen Berg. It's called *Shaving* (Four Ways Books), and it is a collection of prose poems. The prose poem is a form that is hopeless to try to define. It usually consists of short prose pieces written by a poet in the spirit of poetry. The form originated with the French poet Charles Baudelaire. Baudelaire wrote formal verse—the French alexandrine—of great elegance and force. In the middle of the nineteenth century he experimented with short prose—in something like the spirit of *feuilleton,* the short prose sketches of city life and its passing styles that had become popular in Paris newspapers—and published a book called *Paris Spleen*. Berg has adopted Baudelaire's method to his own Philadelphia and found a casual demotic language for his subjects.

Here is the poem about work and labor unions:

Doors

I walk in unzipping my fly, enter a stall, let my pants drop, sit on the cool black plastic horseshoe-shaped toilet seat, pants at my ankles, elbows on knees, head down, and leave the green steel door open when this guy, about sixty, comes in and I look up just as he pops out his dick to piss in one of the urinals, glancing back at me over his shoulder. I think my bare crotch must offend him the way his eyes skid over me. I think he thinks, "Why doesn't that creep close his door?" so I jerk my knees out of the way, swing it around, blank gray, flip up the chrome latch tongue into its keeper and hear—"You were probably too young to remember but seeing you like that reminded me of what it was like in the Ford plant in Chester in the early 30s—unions, you know, people don't understand why they exist—they had rows of toilets and Ford ordered all the doors taken off so you could see if the man in the stall was really taking a shit or just goofing off. At the head of each row they stationed some jerkoff to watch and clock in and out every single worker from the second his ass hit the seat to the second he left the stall." In front of me, my blank door. His shoes scraping the stone floor, the pneumatic men's room door closing *wsss wsss wsss.*

And here, to give you a sense of what Berg does with the form, is another piece. Older readers will remember the subjects he puts together, the linoleum "rugs" of the Depression years and the vanished world of radio, and all readers will recognize his underlying theme, the terror and wonder in ordinary things.

On Blue Linoleum

It comes back often when it snows or when it's cold—the cheap marbleized shiny deep blue linoleum "rug" my folks bought for my bedroom instead of a wool rug, two wide yellow and red bands about an inch apart decorating the edge, which almost touched the walls. It never seemed clean because, when the dawn sun slanted across it so it glowed, you'd see dust, the gauziest layer, you could always pick out scuffs and smears dulling the waxed surface. I never could get used to it. It was scary at night, like having heaven for the floor of your own room. Isn't that crazy? Think of it—you're about eight, lying in bed, lost, listening to Jack Benny or Sky King materialize from behind the brown plastic fins masking the speaker of the radio, rapt in those programs and the ceiling, the known limit of a ceiling, its glass-hatted fixture glistening in the center, bursts of canned laughter, King's engine gunning, Benny's plaintive wry ingenuous "Raah-chester . . . ," and you envision infinity beneath you, you see what you'll step into if you need to pee or want to raid the refrigerator. On braver nights, you lie there, tuning out the world, door closed, the sky-floor all around you, in a bed, in the universe, not yet free enough to plummet or float through space that has no beginning or end, no objects, nothing to stop you: then, you peer over the bedside, once, twice, and stare hard and make out flecks of indefinite color beckoning, convinced they are stars, stars just beginning to reach us or stars so young they barely can be seen.

DECEMBER 12

Seamus Heaney's *Beowulf* as an Ecological Epic

I've just read the advance galleys of an extraordinary book. Farrar, Straus & Giroux is publishing a new translation of the founding work of literature in the English language, the Old English epic *Beowulf*. The translator is the Irish Nobel laureate Seamus Heaney. Heaney's poems of the bogs and peats and soaked turfs of the farm country around Belfast brought him to the world's attention, and so did his language. He is a poet in whom—as the critics have remarked—the gutteral weight of Anglo-Saxon consonants is married to a watery quickness in Celtic vowels. His most famous book, *North,* is a work of excavation. In the time of the worst troubles in Belfast, he turned his attention to archaeology, to the bones mercilessly preserved in the green, carbon-rich earth of the north country, and he used language like a spade to meditate on the ancestral roots of human violence.

So—a translation of *Beowulf* by him is an event. And *Beowulf* is a real poem, not an archaeological document. It was written somewhere near the end of the first millennium by one of the Germanic descendants of the northern peoples who raided and then colonized the British Isles, a Christianized pagan who knew the oral traditions and heroic poetry of the Scandinavian past and fashioned them into a poem that is, in some ways, an elegy to that past. It takes its title from a legendary warrior-hero, Beowulf, who belongs to the Geatish people of southern Sweden, and it tells the story of three of his famous battles. At the beginning of the poem he travels to Denmark where a kingdom is being ravaged by some earth-monster of an elder imagination, a giant bog creature named Grendel. Beowulf kills Grendel, and this arouses the rage of a still older power of the earth, the monster's mother, whom he also faces and defeats. Cast in the mold of the warrior-poetry of clans, shields, swords, and drinking halls, it reads from our vantage point almost like an allegory of that earlier, fearful sense of the human relation to the earth—as if the fire in the mead hall, and the skill of brewing mead, and the fire-based skills of working metals into weapons were the only things that stood between human tribes and a terrifying outer darkness.

The temptation to read it as an ecological poem is deepened by the final battle. Beowulf returns to his own land and rules for fifty years of intermittent peace and tribal warfare. Then, we are told, some thief goes deep into the earth and pilfers the riches of an older, perished civilization, the buried treasure-goods of some people exhausted by endless tribal warfare. The gold is wrapped in the coils of an earth-dragon. The dragon, once stirred into anger, begins to take his revenge, and the old king gathers himself once more to face her. He faces the monster three times, and in the last encounter he kills her—with his sword, that glittering artifact of human technological superiority—and himself receives a fatal wound. The conclusion of the poem is a description of Beowulf's funeral.

Someone has remarked that the irony of the old western movies was that every time the good lawman killed the bad outlaw, he was digging his own grave. Once the wild west was tamed, there was no place for him in it. He existed as a licit wildness. The story of Beowulf and the dragon carries a similar paradox. But the Beowulf poet was conscious of this irony and is therefore able to convey its tragic sense. Beowulf and the dragon belong to the same world. They die at the same time. And the Christian poet, years past the first tellings of the legend, understands that it is the end of one thing and the beginning of another. The story of the hero and the dragon would survive for another five hundred years. So would the warrior-hero, dressed up in the chivalric code of knighthood, until Cervantes's *Don Quixote* finished him off.

The final form of the Beowulf legend is the story of St. George and the dragon. St. George is a Christian knight and the dragon, female, a thing of the earth, is sin. But it is really an echo of the older tale, a dream of strength and valor to set against fear of the powers of the earth. The new era, in which the earth seemed less and less outside human control and understanding, has been, as Cervantes understood, about our terror of ourselves.

So *Beowulf* is a poem of the end of the first millennium. It is also—both for its themes of intra-tribal violence and the troubled human relation to the earth—strangely contemporary. Here is Seamus Heaney's rendering of the funeral of Beowulf:

> The Geat people built a pyre for Beowulf,
> stacked and decked it until it stood four-square,
> hung with helmets, heavy war-shields
> and shining armour, just as he had ordered.

Then his warriors laid him in the middle of it,
Mourning a lord far-famed and beloved.
On a height they kindled the hugest of all
funeral fires: fumes of woodsmoke
billowed darkly up, the blaze roared
and drowned out their weeping, wind died down
and flames wrought havoc in the hot bone-house,
burning it to the core. They were disconsolate
and wailed aloud for their lord's decease.
A Geat woman too sang out in grief;
with hair bound up, she unburdened herself
of her worst fears, a wild litany
of nightmare and lament: her nation invaded,
enemies on the rampage, bodies in piles,
slavery and abasement. Heaven swallowed the smoke.

And here, from the introduction, is Heaney's own comment on this passage: "The Geat woman who cries out in dread as the flames consume the body of her dead lord could come straight from a late-twentieth-century news report, from Rwanda or Kosovo; her keen is a nightmare glimpse into the minds of people who have survived traumatic, even monstrous events and who are now being exposed to a comfortless future. We immediately recognize her predicament and the pitch of her grief and find ourselves the better for having them expressed with such adequacy and dignity and unforgiving truth."

The book won't be in bookstores until February. It will make for some good nights of winter reading.

DECEMBER 19

Snow: Emerson, Lowell, Dickinson, Longfellow, Whittier, and Stevens

The winter season is upon us, and I have been visiting with the elders—looking in the old American poets to see what they had to say about it. One of the things I noticed is that all of the nineteenth-century poets of

New England had something to say about snowfalls. Here's Ralph Waldo Emerson:

The Snow Storm

Announced by all the trumpets of the sky,
Arrives the snow, and, driving o'er the fields,
Seems nowhere to alight: the whited air
Hides hills and woods, the river, and the heaven,
And veils the farm-house at the garden's end.
The sled and traveler stopped, the courier's feet
Delayed, all friends shut out, the housemates sit
Around the radiant fireplace, enclosed
In a tumultuous privacy of storm.

Come see the north wind's masonry,
Out of an uneven quarry evermore
Furnished with tile, the fierce artificer
Curves his white bastions with projected roof
Round every windward stake, or tree, or door.
Speeding, the myriad-handed, his wild work
So fanciful, so savage, nought cares he
For number or proportion. Mockingly,
On coop or kennel he hangs Parian wreaths;
A swan-like form invests the hidden thorn;
Fills up the farmer's lane from wall to wall,
Maugre the farmer's sighs; and, at the gate,
A tapering turret overtops the work.
And when his hours are numbered, and the world
Is all his own, retiring, as he were not,
Leaves, when the sun appears, astonished Art
To mimic in slow structures, stone by stone,
Built in an age, the mad wind's night-work,
The frolic architecture of the snow.

Parian refers to a white marble from the island of Paros in Greece: it's mocking because the snow hangs classical wreaths on chicken coops. *Maugre* —
I don't know if the word was still in colloquial use in nineteenth-century

Massachusetts or if this is a scholarly man's idea of playfulness—is an old English word for "despite."

This poem I came across in the new anthology by Robert Pinsky and Maggie Dietz, *Americans' Favorite Poems* (Norton), selections by a wide range of Americans who responded to the poet laureate's invitation to send him their favorite poems with comments on why they found them memorable. It is by James Russell Lowell:

The First Snow Fall

The snow had begun in the gloaming,
And busily all the night
Had been heaping field and highway
With a silence deep and white.

Every pine and fir and hemlock
Wore ermine too dear for an earl,
And the poorest twig on the elm tree
Was ridged inch deep with pearl.

From sheds new-roofed with Carrara
Came Chanticleer's muffled crow,
The stiff rails softened to swan's-down,
And still fluttered down the snow.

I stood and watched by the window
The noiseless work of the sky,
And the sudden flurries of snow-birds,
Like brown leaves whirling by.

I thought of a mound in sweet Auburn
Where a little headstone stood;
How the flakes were folding it gently
As did robins the babes in the wood.

Up spoke our own little Mable,
Saying, "Father, who makes it snow?"
And I told of the good All-Father
Who cares for us here below.

Again I looked at the snowfall,
And thought of the leaden sky
That arches o'er our first great sorrow,
When the mound was heaped so high.

I remember that gradual patience
That fell from that cloud like snow,
Flake by flake, healing and hiding
The scar that renewed our woe.

And again to the child I whispered,
"The snow that husheth all,
Darling, the merciful Father
Alone can make it fall!"

Then, with eyes that saw not, I kissed her;
And she, kissing back could not know
That my kiss was given to her sister,
Folded close under deepening snow.

Carrara is the name for a white Italian marble. (I don't know who was borrowing from whom. Emerson and Lowell read one another.) *Auburn* is the famous cemetery. One of the fascinating things about this book—that sets it apart from any other anthology I know—is the comments on the poems by the readers who suggested them. This poem, for example, was selected by Dorothy Stanaitis, a retired librarian from Gloucester, New Jersey, who wrote: "My father was the first one to wake up in our house. He was eager to greet each day. One of his great pleasures was to announce an overnight snowstorm by reciting, 'The snow had begun in the gloaming.' Then he would watch his five children leap from bed and run to the window to see for themselves. Early one winter morning in later years I received a wake-up call. I answered the phone groggily and heard my father's voice: 'The snow had begun in the gloaming.' My father had been gone for seven years. There have been many snowfalls since then, but I still get tears in my eyes when I wake up to the white world without his voice reciting James Russell Lowell's 'The First Snowfall.'"

Here is one by Emily Dickinson:

It sifts from Leaden Sieves—
It powders all the Wood.
It fills with Alabaster Wool
The Wrinkles of the Road—

It makes an Even face
Of Mountain and of Plain—
Unbroken Forehead from the East
Unto the East again—

It reaches to the Fence—
It wraps it Rail by Rail
Till it is lost in Fleeces—
It deals Celestial Vail

To Stump, and Stack—and Stem—
A Summer's empty Room—
Acres of Joints, where Harvests were,
Recordless, but for them—

It Ruffles Wrists of Posts
As Ankles of a Queen—
Then stills its Artisans—like Ghosts—
Denying they have been—

The snow around the posts like—what? lace? skin?—something around the ankles of a queen is certainly the most peculiar image so far. And it seems typical of Dickinson that she would, in the last two lines, record with such accuracy the moment when the snow stops falling.

Here is her much-admired Longfellow on the same subject:

Snow-Flakes

Out of the bosom of the Air,
    Out of the cloud-folds of her garments shaken,
Over the woodlands brown and bare,
    Over the harvest-fields forsaken,

Silent, and soft, and slow
Descends the snow.

Even as our cloudy fancies take
    Suddenly shape in some divine expression,
Even as the troubled heart doth make
    In the white countenance confession,
    The troubled sky reveals
    The grief it feels.

This is the poem of the air,
    Slowly in silent syllables recorded;
This is the secret of despair,
    Long in its cloudy bosom hoarded,
    Now whispered and revealed
    To wood and field.

And here's a bit from John Greenleaf Whittier's "Snow-Bound":

Unwarmed by any sunset light
The gray day darkened into night,
A night made hoary with the swarm,
And whirl-dance of the blinding storm,
As zigzag wavering to and fro,
Crossed and recrossed the winged snow:
And ere the early bedtime came
The white drift piled the window-frame,
And through the glass the clothes-line posts
Looked in like tall and sheeted ghosts.

So all night long the storm roared on:
The morning broke without a sun;
In tiny spherule traced with lines
Of Nature's geometric signs,
In starry flake, and pellicule,
All day the hoary meteor fell;
And, when the second morning shone,
We looked upon a world unknown,

On nothing we could call our own.
Around the glistening wonder bent
The blue walls of the firmament,
No cloud above, no earth below,—
A universe of sky and snow!

The twentieth century was considerably more terse. Here's Wallace Stevens, downriver in Hartford, Connecticut:

It was evening all afternoon.
It was snowing
And it was going to snow.
The blackbird sat
in the cedar-limbs.

DECEMBER 26

Christmas: Ira Gershwin and Cole Porter

One of the things I liked about living in England in the 1970s was Boxing Day. It's the name the English gave to the day after Christmas. No one is quite sure where it came from. Possibly there was a time when the villages held holiday boxing matches. It has come to seem to mean the day you lounge around in a litter of boxes and recover from Christmas. In the 1970s the BBC celebrated Boxing Day by showing a day-long festival of old American musicals. In the winter of 1976 they did musicals based on the songs of George and Ira Gershwin and Cole Porter. It was also a day when one had endless invitations to drop in at other people's houses. We made a round of the local villages in Cambridgeshire with names like Little Shelford and Long Melford and Cherry Hinton. That year it was an icy cold day with huge clouds scudding over the flat, muddy East Anglian landscape that Thomas Constable had painted with such accuracy for the piled, looming grandeur of the clouds, and a North Sea wind his paintings suggested that was, however, cruelty itself.

I approved of the idea of a second day of celebration to recover from the first day of celebration. The social round could be intense. There was ale and toasted cheese at the flat of an Hungarian literary scholar in Cambridge. It was supposedly the flat in which Ted Hughes and Sylvia Plath had lived briefly and seemed, I was willing to think after a couple of pints, haunted by their presence. A Swedish poet out in a village called Whittlesford had a roaring fire, three or four kinds of pickled herring, and a choice of strong tea or little shot glasses of single malt whiskey. If the drive between parties was long, you could also stop in at the pubs. The heater in our English Ford wasn't especially effective, and our kids loved the pubs with their coal fires and steaming pork pies, so we made a few stops. As the designated driver, I nursed mulled ciders. Everywhere we went, we would hear, from a television set somewhere in the room, fragments of the lyrics of Ira Gershwin and Cole Porter. Occasionally a group would gather around it and sing along. So our day was punctuated by bits and pieces of those songs and their inventive lyrics.

> They laughed at me wanting you,
> Said I was reaching for the moon;
> But oh, you came through—
> Now they'll have to change their tune.

> *

> Maybe I shall meet him Sunday,
> Maybe Monday—maybe not;
> Still I'm sure I'll meet him one day—
> Maybe Tuesday
> Will be my good news day.

> —Ira Gershwin

> You're a rose,
> You're Inferno's Dante,
> You're the nose
> On the great Durante.

> —Cole Porter

They all laughed at Christopher Columbus
When he said the world was round;
They all laughed when Edison recorded sound.

—Gershwin, again

If she then wants an all-by-herself night,
Let her rest ev'ry 'leventh or "Twelfth Night"

*

It's the wrong time and the wrong place,
Though your face is charming, it's the wrong face

*

Even overeducated fleas do it
Let's do it, let's . . .

—Porter

'S awful nice! 'S paradise—
'S what I love to see!

—Gershwin

I remember at the party in Whittlesford a Mexican scholar explaining that in Mexico City the shot glasses of whiskey (or tequila) were called *caballitos,* "little horses." This led to jokes about "one-horse open sleighs" and "laughing all the way." And this led, via the television, to an impressive rendition in fluent English with trilled r's of "I Got Rhythm."

It seems, in retrospect, an odd way to spend an English Christmas. I thought about it last week because I had spent a day shopping on Madison Avenue in New York. In every store some of those songs were playing in the background, Fred Astaire versions and Billie Holiday versions and Ella Fitzgerald versions. It called up the city of the 1920s and 1930s as a magical place and time. Much of the magic, it seemed, had to do with the wit of a playful or unexpected rhyme. Strange that a New York that was already a fantasy of the young lyricists of the time has become our fantasy, the Christmas poetry of a consumer culture. In the electronics store, some of the lyrics even seemed prophetic:

> the radio and the telephone
> and the movies that we know
> May just be passing fancies—
> And in time may go,
> But oh,—
>
> —Gershwin

New Year's Day:
Tessa Rumsey and Harryette Mullen

So what is the work of the new century going to look like? Here, for the new year, is the work of two young poets. Get ready for a ride. They aim to be alive in their language, but they do not aim to be clear in the way that many of the poets of the 1960s and 1970s, in revolt against what seemed like the academic appropriation of high modernism, of the difficulties of Ezra Pound and T. S. Eliot, aimed to be clear. This new work comes from several different directions—surrealism, semiotics, the jump-cut rhythms of video and film, an impulse to make language rather than story or personal history do the work of poetry. One critic has called this vein "the new difficulty," and it has sometimes looked to models like the Jewish poet Paul Celan, who fractured the language to find a way to use it after the Shoah; or the Peruvian poet César Vallejo who, in one of his books, *Trilce,* partly written when he was jailed in Lima for his political activities in the late 1920s, wrote poems in a riddling and fractured Spanish; or the American poet John Ashbery, experimenting with language the way the abstract expressionist painters had experimented with paint.

The first is Tessa Rumsey, whose first book, *Assembling the Shepherd,* has just appeared from University of Georgia Press. Surrealism doesn't quite describe her method. But she's inventing in language; she's a poet capable of writing, "Fish be ruby-weeping" or "no one knows who wind pitches for." This poem assembles its own half-mythological world. It seems to be trying to trace the shape of some ancient and buried grief:

Poem for the Old Year

January. The archer aims at himself.
His target is the eye of a fish. River
is frozen. Field rises in mist of lost
desire and steams the sealed sky open.
Fish be ruby-weeping. Fish be nailed
through scale onto door of silver birch.
Over the mountain beaten boy searches
for his teeth inside a clump of brambles.
The sound of thorns through his skin
is *mercy*. The sound of a beautiful fish
being nailed to a door is *mercy, mercy*.
Nobody knows the origin of music,
or who wind pitches for between rock
and rock like a bronco heart kicking
in its cage. Breeze seduces bow. Bow
abandons arrow. Boy finds shelter
in thicket and hears music of his breath
through ugly, twisted thistles. Come
home. It's time to begin again. A boy
is nailed to the door and a fish is aimed
at an archer, mountain is weeping rubies
onto frozen river while wind grinds
two new teeth. Who are you
inside the music of another's suffering?
When I was a nail I loved only
the hammer. When I was a breeze I died
on a door. When I was a fish
I swam without knowing not yet, or last
breath, or shore.

The second comes from Harryette Mullen's *Muse & Drudge*, from
Singing Horse Press in Philadelphia. It was published in 1995. It's written
in quatrains, four-line poems or stanzas, sometimes rhyming, sometimes
not. What Mullen does is invent, play with language, play with ideas, make
all the sounds she can discover. It's an exuberant performance. Here are
some stanzas from the end of it. Notice that every stanza invites you to

read it as a separate poem, something between a blues and an epigram, and that you then have to do the work of seeing how each stanza connects to the next:

> blessed are stunned cattle
> spavined horses bent under their saddles
> blessed is the goat as its throat is cut
> and the trout when it's gutted
>
> Jesus is my airplane
> I shall feel no turbulence
> though I fly in a squall
> through the spleen of Satan
>
> in a dream the book beckoned
> opened for me to the page
> where I read the words
> that were to me a sign
>
> houses of Heidelberg
> outhouse cracked house
> destroyed funhouse lost
> and found house of dead dolls
>
> two-headed dreamer
> of second-sighted vision
> through the veil
> she heard her call
>
> they say she alone smeared herself
> wrote obscenities on her breast
> snatched nappy patches from her scalp
> threw her own self in a heap of refuse
>
> knowing all I have dearly bought
> I'll take what I can get
> pick from the ashes
> brave the alarms

another video looping
the orange juice execution
her brains spilled milk
on the killing floor

JANUARY 9

Charlotte Smith

Here is a chance for you to decide for yourself one of the cultural issues
of our time. The issue is whether or not the sonnets of a woman named
Charlotte Smith deserve to be included in anthologies of English lit-
erature. That, anyway, is what the issue seemed to boil down to, when I
listened to a group of literature professors arguing on a morning talk
show. They kept using Charlotte Smith as an example—of a really inter-
esting poet passed over because she was a woman, and of a really mediocre
poet suddenly put into the company of Wordsworth and Keats because
she was a woman.

No one on either side read or quoted a single line of her poetry, even
while they dueled about its value. So here is the question. Charlotte Turner
Smith was born into the English gentry in 1750 in London. Her mother
died when she was three. When her father remarried, she was fifteen and,
according to one biographer, "plunged into a ruinous marriage to the
dissolute son of a wealthy West Indian merchant." This sounds, so far, like
a subplot of Jane Austen's *Mansfield Park.* Then it turns into Dickens. She
had twelve children. She worked as an accountant in her father-in-law's
shipping firm. When he died, he left his financial affairs in such a mess
that the lawsuit to settle them went on for forty years. In the meantime,
Charlotte's spendthrift husband ran up debts that landed them in a debt-
or's prison for a few months in 1783. Once she was free, Charlotte fled to
France to avoid her husband's creditors. She published her first book of
poems in 1784, while she was still in prison. Later she supported her eight
surviving children by writing novels with titles like *Emmeline, the Orphan
of the Castle* and *Ethleinde, or The Recluse of the Lake.* She wrote long poems,
more sonnets, children's books, translated French literature, and produced
one play. She died in Sussex in 1806.

Here are three of her—intensely melancholy—poems. The first comes from 1789:

Written in the Church Yard at Middleton in Sussex

Pressed by the moon, mute arbitress of tides,
    While the loud equinox its power combines,
    The sea no more its swelling surge confines,
But o'er the shrinking land sublimely rides.
The wild blast, rising from the western cave,
    Drives the huge billows from their heaving bed,
    Tears from their grassy tombs the village dead,
And breaks the silent sabbeth of the grave!
With shells and sea-weed mingled, on the shore
Lo! their bones whiten in the frequent wave;
    But vain to them the winds and waters rave;
They hear the warring elements no more:
While I am doomed—by life's long storm oppressed,
To gaze with envy on their gloomy rest.

This is the moody, turbulent style of the period. Jane Austen makes fun of this taste for melancholy a little in *Persuasion* in the figure of the widowed sea captain who likes brooding poetry. Here's one from 1797— nearer Austen's own time—about sounds from a ship heard on shore. It calls up that era of naval war between England and Napoleonic France, when for civilians the life of a port must have felt both a bit romantic and a bit dangerous:

Written Near a Port on a Dark Evening

Huge vapors brood above the clifted shore,
    Night on the Ocean settles dark and mute,
Save where is heard the repercussive roar
    Of drowsy billows, on the rugged foot
Of rocks remote; or still more distant tone
    Of seamen in the anchored bark that tell
The watch relieved; or one deep voice alone
Singing the hour, and bidding, "Strike the bell."

All is black shadow, but the lucid line
    Marked by the light surf on the level sand,
Or where afar the ship-lights faintly shine
    Like wandering fairy fires, that oft on land
Mislead the Pilgrim—Such the dubious ray
That wavering Reason lends, in life's long darkling way.

And here, from the same year, she imagines a shepherd on a seaside cliff on a summer evening watching a naval battle in the distance:

The Sea View

The upland shepherd, as reclined he lies
    On the soft turf that clothes the mountain brow,
Marks the bright Sea-line mingling with the skies;
    Or from his course celestial, sinking slow,
    The Summer-Sun in purple radiance low,
Blaze on the western waters; the wide scene
    Magnificent, and tranquil, seems to spread
Even o'er the Rustic's breast a joy serene,
    When, like dark plague-spots by the Demons shed,
Charged deep with death, upon the waves, far seen,
    Move the war-freighted ships; and fierce and red
    Flash their destructive fire.—The mangled dead
And dying victims then pollute the flood.
    Ah! thus man spoils Heaven's glorious work with blood!

So—what do you think? The issue—at least for me—has to do with writing. There are some period clichés—the storm is "a wild blast," the shepherd feels "a joy serene"—in the poems. There is also some vivid description. A poem wants to be fresh and alive, to catch something of life or make available to consciousness something that wasn't there before. Would you put Charlotte Smith in your anthology? I think of the young Keats hoping that he could do something, someday, that would put him "in the company of the English poets."

JANUARY 16

Rita Dove

When Rita Dove was a young poet living in Europe, she wrote several poems about women saints. They are to be found in her second book, *Museum* (Carnegie-Mellon):

Catherine of Siena

You walked the length of Italy
to find someone to talk to.
You struck the boulder at the roadside
since fate has doors everywhere.
Under the star-washed dome
of heaven, warm and dark

as the woolens stacked on cedar
shelves back home in your
father's shop, you prayed
until tears streaked the sky.
No one stumbled across your path.
No one unpried your fists as you slept.

I thought of this poem—and the figure of a woman with a fierce inner life—when I read a poem from her most recent book, *On the Bus with Rosa Parks* (Norton) last year. Here it is:

Rosa

How she sat there,
the time right inside a place
so wrong it was ready.

That trim name with
its dream of a bench
to rest on. Her sensible coat.

Doing nothing was the doing:
the clean flame of her gaze
carved by a camera flash.

How she stood up
when they bent down to retrieve
her purse. That courtesy.

This stunning small poem does so much to capture the spirit of the time and of great-souled Rosa Parks in a few words. It made me think about the Catherine of Siena poem because of the connection between the saint and the quiet revolutionary. They are both very determined spirits. It also made me think how much Rita Dove's poems are about the right to a vivid inner life. One of her most moving poems on this subject comes from her Pulitzer Prize–winning collection, *Thomas and Beulah,* a sequence of narrative poems about an ordinary and remarkable African American family. Beulah, in this poem, is neither saint nor activist, but a woman in a life full of the demands of nurturing, trying to hold onto some corner of herself that belongs to her:

Daystar

She wanted a little room for thinking:
but she saw diapers steaming on the line,
a doll slumped behind the door.

So she lugged a chair behind the garage
to sit out the children's naps.

Sometimes there were things to watch—
the pinched armor of a vanished cricket,
a floating maple leaf. Other days
she stared until she was assured
when she closed her eyes
she'd see only her own vivid blood.

She had an hour, at best, before Liza appeared
pouting from the top of the stairs.

And just *what* was mother doing
out back with the field mice? Why,

building a palace. Later
that night when Thomas rolled over and
lurched into her, she would open her eyes
and think of the place that was hers
for an hour—where
she was nothing,
pure nothing, in the middle of the day.

It's a space we all require—people with a religious passion, people caught in the turmoil of social change or in the steady drizzle of a daily life, young people trying to carve out for themselves the space to become artists, as Rita Dove did twenty years ago brooding over the lives of saints.

This is my last appearance in this space. I'm going to try to give myself more time for the work of making poems. I've been doing this column weekly for four years and I will probably miss it. I know I will miss the responses of readers, and this is a chance to express my gratitude. The letters, suggesting topics or poets, offering alternative interpretations, correcting my not-always secure hold on the facts, telling stories that the poems each week stirred up, offering poems and translations in response to the ones printed here, have brightened my days. I'm leaving you in good hands. Rita Dove is not only a Pulitzer Prize–winning poet and a novelist and a playwright and a former Poet Laureate, but also she's what the poet Wallace Stevens said modern life requires: a figure of capable imagination.

As my granddaughter has taken to saying, "So long. Have a good thousand years."

Epilogue: Ezra Pound

I began this book with a poem of winter by Wallace Stevens. I will end it with a spring poem by another modernist master, Ezra Pound. Some of Pound's poems are so full of obscure and not-so-obscure cultural references that he once referred to them, collectively, as "the Ezraversity." People who study him, mostly poets, do so because he seems worth the trouble, and one of the ways he is worth the trouble is the sheer brilliance of his verbal music. But we also study him because, as disastrously wrong-headed as he often was, he was after something. One of the projects of his poetry involved culling from powerful imaginations of the past and from deep lores in old cultures the element of an imaginative vision of life on earth in the modern world. Some part of that project—for him—as for almost all of the modernists—had to do with renewing our imagination of the power of art. Another had to do with renewing our imagination of the earth.

Here, from *The Cantos*—it is a section of Canto 39—is a poem of spring. It has Old English in it; it has the Italian landscape south of Genoa in it; it has the rhythms of the old Greek and Roman nature poems in it; and it has also a scrap of late medieval Italian song and of a Roman wedding song from the Latin, a wedding song because the myth of nature is a sexual myth:

> Aprile and Merche
>   With sap new in the bough
> With plum flowers above them
>   With almond on the black bough
> With jasmine and olive leaf,
> To the beat of the measure
> From star up to the half-dark
> From half-dark to half-dark
>   Unceasing the measure

Flank by flank on the headland
 With the Goddess' eyes to seaward
By Circeo, by Terracina, with the stone eyes
 White toward the sea
With one measure, unceasing:
 "Fac deum!" "Est factus."
Ver novum!
 Ver novum!
Thus made the spring,
Can see but their eyes in the dark
 Not the bough that he walked on.
Beaten from flesh into light
Hath swallowed the fire-ball
A traverse le foglie
His rod hath made god in my belly
 Sic loquitur nupta
 Cantat sic nupta

Dark shoulders have stirred the lightning
A girl's arms have nested the fire,
Not I but the handmaid kindled
 Cantat sic nupta
I have eaten the flame.

Circeo and Terracina were places on the Italian coast near Spoleto where Pound was living. The goddess here must be Aphrodite, goddess of sexual love; it's she who presides over the violence of the spring quickening. There was, the commentators tell us, an old Roman temple on the spot, and Pound had imagined its restoration. "Given the material means," he wrote, "I would replace the statue of Venus on the cliffs of Terracina." And, lacking the funds, he puts her there in this poem, and he sets all of creation dancing to the earth's diurnal measure.

Pagan was the punk of the 1910s and 1920s. From the satyrs in the undergraduate stories of E. M. Forster to the dances of Isadora Duncan and Josephine Baker to the novels of D. H. Lawrence, it was part of the rebellion against the Puritanism of evangelical Christianity in England and America to believe, seriously or half-seriously, in the resurrection of polytheism, of the world experienced as a play of magical and contending powers. Pound took the idea quite seriously. He also believed that sexual and intellectual and spiritual force were versions of the same thing, in the way, he said, that heat and light were the same energy transmitted at different frequencies. So, when the poem seems to move toward some kind of mystery cult or sexual ritual, an experienced reader of *The Cantos* knows that the poem is very near the center of Pound's enterprise, intellectually as well as spiritually. He is talking as much about new art or new understanding as he is about sexuality or natural fertility.

"Fac deum! Est factus" is "Make the god! He is made." "Ver novum!" is "New spring!" "A traverse le foglie" is an Italian phrase, "through the leaves"—the commentators haven't identified the source. "Sic loquitur nupta" is "thus the bride speaks." "Cantat sic nupta" is "thus the bride sings."

That cry—"Fac deum"—must refer to some fertility ritual that was thought to evoke and perhaps literally to bring to being the divine power in nature. The modernists were great readers of the generation of classical scholars who took an interest in old European agricultural rituals, of the kind in which each year involved the death-of-the-year god and each spring his rebirth. And they were inclined to see the Christian story as a version of that myth. So for Pound, who loved the pagan elements in Roman Catholicism, there is an element of the Annunciation story in this, probably, and the Incarnation, the word made flesh. I can't make out everything in that stanza. The "they" whose eyes can be seen in the dark are, my guess is, the ritual dancers. The "he" who walks on the bough is the god of spring in the form of a blossom. And after that—in the next lines—the poem seems to shift from sexual to intellectual magic:

> Beaten from flesh into light
> Hath swallowed the fire-ball

If the word can become flesh, in ritual the flesh can become word, can be beaten into light. There is a dose of macho at the end of the poem that seems to evoke a Roman wedding song. "His rod hath made god in my belly" is a bit much, but it isn't untrue to the many incarnation stories. The last lines bring us to Pound's deepest interest in the ritual: that it was about transformation and renewal at every level, about any time in our lives when we step into the pulse of life, as if into fire or the current of a river, and are altered by it. It is about any transfiguration. And in that way it is as much about the act of reading as it is about anything else. To read, to read deeply, and to be changed by what we read is to have eaten the flame, which is an argument that these essays, I hope, have been making.

Poets are flawed instruments. To live in Italy, as many English and American expatriates did in the 1930s, where the pound and the dollar went very far, and the weather was so mild, and the Renaissance still flowered on the walls of dark little churches, and pre-Christian Europe still seemed alive every time the wind came up in the olive trees, and you could smell the sea and walk down when the evening sky was full of swifts to eat an exquisitely prepared dinner in a casual trattoria—it must have been very pleasant indeed. But you had to be able to swallow Mussolini. And Pound did. He became an enthusiastic fascist and a cocksure and virulent anti-Semite (even as he nurtured into existence a school of young Jewish American poets in New York through his letters and his magazine, *The Exile.*) He had leisure to repent these views after he was arrested by the U.S. Army in 1944 for treason and committed to St. Elizabeth's Hospital in Washington, D.C., on the grounds that he was too crazy to stand trial—a fiction arranged by friends like Ernest Hemingway and Robert Frost who used their influence to save him from hanging. After his release, in his very last years, he returned to Italy, and he died there.

The instincts of most of the modernists were not especially democratic. They wanted, in the spirit of the 1920s, to shake up democratic complacencies, and they were, therefore, not hesitant to write poems that implied learning and required work. They believed profoundly and sometimes despairingly in the transforming power of art in every life. They thought that great art, great music and literature required great readers and listeners, free in the circuit of their own minds and willing to labor at understanding. It's one of the reasons why, in Joyce as well as Pound, the figure of the Odyssean journey was so important. Pound's friend T. S. Eliot articulated this perhaps most memorably at the end of that other modernist landmark, *Four Quartets:*

> We shall not cease from exploration
> And the end of all our exploring
> Will be to arrive where we started
> And know the place for the first time.
> Through the unknown, remembered gate

When the last of earth left to discover
Is that which was the beginning;

These lines were written in London during the German bombing or just after, and that must be one of the reasons why their central impulse is deeply conservative and comforting. It is probably just as likely the case that the end of all our exploring will be some place far from where we started and quite unexpected. Exploration has in it an element of risk, and one often pays for risks.

Ver novum!
  Ver novum!
Thus made the spring,

Note: Currently all readers of Pound rely on a scholarly dictionary of the poem, A Companion to The Cantos of Ezra Pound, *by Carroll F. Terrell, to gloss these references and to enter into the mental landscape of this poet with a late nineteenth-century classical education and vehement literary convictions.*

Copyright Acknowledgments

William H. Gass. Reprinted by permissions of Alfred A. Knopf, a division of Random House, Inc. "Autumn Day" from *The Selected Poetry of Rainer Maria Rilke* by Rainer Maria Rilke. Translation copyright © 1982 by Stephen Mitchell. Reprinted by permissions of Random House, Inc. "The Waking" from *Collected Poems* by Theodore Roethke. Copyright © 1953 by Theodore Roethke. Reprinted by permission of Doubleday, a division of Random House, Inc. "Opus from Space" from *Eating Bread and Honey* by Pattiann Rogers. Copyright © 1997 by Pattiann Rogers. Reprinted by permission of Milkweed Editions. "Poem for the Old Year" from *Assembling the Shepherd* by Tessa Rumsey. Copyright © 1999 by Tessa Rumsey. Reprinted by permission of University of Georgia Press. *Sijo* translation from *The Bamboo Grove: An Introduction to Sijo* by Richard Rutt © 1971, printed by the University of Michigan Press. "The Lovers" from *Pieces of Shadow: Selected Poems of Jaime Sabines* by Jaime Sabines. Translation copyright © 1996 by W. S. Merwin. Reprinted by permission of Marsilio Press. "The Wedding Feast at Cana" from *Dark and Perfect Angels* by Benjamin Alire Saenz. Copyright © 1995 by Benjamin Alire Saenz. Reprinted by permission of the author. Selections from *Does Your House Have Lions?* by Sonia Sanchez. Copyright © 1998 by Sonia Sanchez. Reprinted by permission of Beacon Press. Excerpt from *Myths & Texts* from *No Nature: New and Selected Poems* by Gary Snyder. Copyright © 1993 by Gary Snyder. Reprinted by permission of Random House, Inc. "Sea Surface Full of Clouds" from *The Collected Poems by Wallace Stevens*. Copyright © 1965 by Wallace Stevens. Reprinted by permission of HarperCollins Publishers, Inc. "Explanation" and "The Snow Man" from *Collected Poetry and Prose* by Wallace Stevens. Copyright © 1997 by Wallace Stevens. Reprinted by permission of Random House, Inc. "Night in Day" from *Below Cold Mountain* by Joseph Stroud. Copyright © 1998 by Joseph Stroud. Reprinted by permission of Copper Canyon Press, www.coppercanyonpress. org. "Death, Great Smoothener" and "Question" from *Nature: Poems Old and New* by May Swenson. Copyright © 1994 by the Literary Estate of May Swenson. Reprinted by permission of Houghton Mifflin Company. "The String Diamond" from The *Redshifting Web: Poems 1970–1998* by Arthur Sze. Copyright © 1994 by Arthur Sze. Reprinted by permission of Copper Canyon Press, www.coppercanyonpress.org. "Sanctuary" from *Dark Sky Question* by Larissa Szporluk. Copyright © 1998 by Larissa Szporluk. Reprinted by permission of Beacon Press. "The Mystery" from *Encompassing Nature: A Sourcebook*. Edited by Robert Torrance. Translation

Index

"A Quoi Bon Dire," 85
"Advance of the Father, The," 184
"After the Vigil," 251
Agha, Shahid Ali, 53
Aguilar-Carino, Maria Luisa, 95
Alberti, Rafael, 131
"[All night by the rose, the rose,]," 84
Allbery, Debra, 208
Amichai, Yehuda, 116
"And Did Those Feet," 208
"Anniversary," 241
"Anything Rarer Than an Angel," 83
Ashbery, John, 97, 219
"[As kingfishers catch fire]," 147
"Assembler," 209
"At Ease," 176
Atwood, Margaret, 55
Auden, W. H., 120
"Autumn," 106
"Autumn Day," 221
"Aware," 195

Battle of Kosovo, The, 189
Beatty, Paul, 175
"Belgrade," 164
Beowulf, 259
Berg, Stephen, 256
Bidart, Frank, 19
Bishop, Elizabeth, 80, 173
"Black Stone upon a White Stone," 253
Blake, William, 207, 217
"Blue," 3
Bly, Robert, 102
Borson, Roo, 106
"[Boy comes by my window, A]," 10
"Boy in a Snow Shower, A," 123
Bradstreet, Anne, 216
Brown, George Mackay, 123

Brown, Lee Ann, 187
Brown, Sterling, 99
"[Brythnoth broke out brand from
    sheath]," 211
"By Candlelight," 35
"Bypassing Rue Descartes," 243
"Byways," 7

"Cafeteria," 188
"[Can a swarm of these tiny insects]," 11
Canterbury Tales, The, 213
"Canto 39," 281
"Catherine of Siena," 277
"Celebration," 194
Chaucer, Geoffrey, 213
"Chinaberry, The," 228
"Christopher Robin," 115
Clare, John, 237
"Conversation with a Mouse, A," 103
Converse, Harriet Maxwell, 109
"Crow's Nerve Fails," 37
"Cuckoo Song, The," 212

"Daystar," 278
"Death, Great Smoothener," 90
"Deep Measure," 151
"Definitions at 3:15," 188
Dickinson, Emily, 200, 218, 265
"Discourse," 188
Does Your House Have Lions?, 29
Donne, John, 215, 216
"Doors," 257
Doty, Mark, 117
Dove, Rita, 182, 277
"Downfall of the Kingdom of Serbia,
    The," 191
"Drunkard, A," 14

Eady, Cornelius, 64
"Earthly Love," 201
"Ebony Chickering, The," 51
"Echo," 14
"Eel, The," 143
Eliot, T. S., 218, 284
Emerson, Ralph Waldo, 69, 262
"Emperor," 82
"Episode in a Library," 82
"Everything Is Going to Be All Right,"
    46
"Explanation," 5
"Eyes, The," 252

"Familiar," 95
"Farragut North," 27
"Field Guide to Southern Virginia," 160
"First Rule of Sinhalese Architecture,
    The," 157
"First Snow Fall, The," 263
"First time I saw you, The," 136
"For My People," 125
"For the Father of Sandro Gulotta," 129
"For the Union Dead," 71
"Four Quartets," 284
"[Fowles in the frith]," 213
"Friend, A," 15
"Friend at Midnight, The," 98
"From My Dentist's Window," 116
"From the Porch," 34
Frost, Robert, 47, 74

Gander, Forrest, 160
"Garment, The," 200
Gershwin, Ira, 267
"Ghazal," 53
"Gift, The," 178
Glück, Louise, 9, 199
"Grand Miracle, The," 44
"Great Lord Danube," 163
Gregerson, Linda, 60

"Half-and-Half," 206
Halpern, Daniel, 250
Han Shan, 63
Heaney, Seamus, 220, 259
"He or She That's Got the Limb, That
    Holds Me Out on It," 75

Herbert, George, 133, 216
Herbert, Zbigniew, 81
"Her Body," 252
"Herbsttag," 221
Herrick, Robert, 215
Hillman, Brenda, 220
Hopkins, Gerard Manley, 146
Horace, 39
"House on a Red Cliff," 156
"Houston, 6 P.M.," 22
Howe, Fanny, 183
Howe, Marie, 30
Hudgins, Andrew, 227
Hughes, Langston, 153, 219
Hughes, Ted, 37
"Hymn: Sung at the Completion of the
    Concord Monument, April 19, 1836,"
    69

"In Carrowdore Churchyard," 46
"In Memory of W. B. Yeats," 120
"Innocent One, The," 104
"In Terror of Hospital Bills," 93
"Invention of Heaven, The," 236
"[It sifts from Leaden Sieves]," 265
"[It was evening all afternoon]," 267
"[I've never kept sheep]," 108
"[I wake and feel the fell]," 147

Jeffers, Robinson, 48
Jonson, Ben, 138
Justice, Donald, 90

Karr, Mary, 44
Keats, John, 217, 240
Koethe, John, 32
Komachi, Lady, 63
Komunyakaa, Yusef, 85
Ko Un, 13

"Lady Bird," 20
"Lady Freedom Among Us," 182
Larkin, Philip, 130
"Last Day of August, The," 205
"Last Time, The," 31
Laughlin, James, 6
Laux, Dorianne, 51
"Learning," 115

"Least You Could Do, The," 6
Lee, Li-Young, 177
Levertov, Denise, 16, 193
Lewis, Janet, 127
"Like Summer Hay," 128
"Line Drive Caught by the Grace of
    God," 60
"Little Bit of Soap, A," 64
"Little Summer Poem Touching the
    Subject of Faith," 84
Longfellow, Henry Wadsworth, 265
"Love Incarnate," 21
"Love (III)," 134
"Lovers, The," 171
"Lovesong," 38
Lowell, James Russell, 263
Lowell, Robert, 70
"Lute Music," 135

"Magi, The," 9
Mahon, Derek, 45
Matthews, William, 18
McHugh, Heather, 229
McMahon, Lynne, 240
Mew, Charlotte, 84
Midsummer Night's Dream, A, 56
Milosz, Czeslaw, 114, 243
"Mist in the Meadow," 239
Mitchell, Joni, 3
Montale, Eugenio, 142
"Moonless Night, A," 15
Mörling, Malena, 167
"Morning in America," 33
"Mortal Poem," 234
"Mower, The," 130
Muldoon, Paul, 136
Mullen, Harryette, 272
Muse & Drudge, 273
"My Picture Left in Scotland," 139
"Mystery, The," 63

"Night at the Opera, A," 18
"Night in Day," 66
"[Nightingale on the flowering plum,
    The]," 136
"Not So Fast," 230
"[Nou goth sonne under wode]," 212
Nye, Naomi Shihab, 205

"O!," 115
"Objects," 82
"On Blue Linoleum," 258
"Once Only," 195
Ondaatje, Michael, 156
"One Art," 80
"One Kind Favor," 65
"Opus from Space," 140
"Opus Posthumous III," 150
"O Taste and See," 16
"Oven Bird, The," 47

"Pansy," 189
"Panther, The," 225
"Pantoum of the Great Depression," 91
"Paradiso," 65
"Passover," 42
Pastan, Linda, 41
"Pasture, The," 74
Paz, Octavio, 49
"Peony," 189
Pessoa, Fernando, 107
"Piedra Negra sobre una Piedra Blanca,"
    254
Plath, Sylvia, 34, 219
Plumly, Stanley, 26
"Poem for the Old Year," 272
"Poetry," 188
Popa, Vasko, 162
Porter, Cole, 133, 267
Pound, Ezra, 281
Powell, D. A., 76
"Private Fall, A," 102
"Promise, The," 31

"Question," 88
"Questions of Travel," 173
"Quote Unquote," 176
"Quotidian, The," 144

Rankine, Claudia, 144
"Red," 131
"Red Clay Blues," 154
"Resurrection," 155
Rexroth, Kenneth, 134
Rich, Adrienne, 165
Rilke, Rainer Marie, 221, 224
"Ripples," 15

"Road-side Dog," 114
Roethke, Theodore, 79
Rogers, Pattiann, 140
"Romantic," 55
"Rosa," 277
"Roses Entwined, The," 213
Rumsey, Tessa, 271

Sabines, Jaime, 170
Saenz, Benjamin, 180
Sanchez, Sonia, 29
"Sanctuary," 67
"Sand Martin," 239
Sappho, 62
"[Scraps of moon]," 194
"Sea Surface Full of Clouds," 246
"Sea View, The," 276
"Seeing the Unseen," 17
"Seven Laments for the War Dead," 116
Shakespeare, William, 56, 196, 215
"Shanked on the Red Bed," 75
"Shattered Head," 166
"Shooting Star, A," 15
"[Silence in the hall]," 117
Smith, Charlotte, 274
"Snow-Bound," 266
"Snow-Flakes," 265
"Snow Man, The," 4, 17
"Snow Storm, The," 262
Snyder, Gary, 87
"Song of Myself," 24
"Song: To Celia," 139
"Song to Sumerian Inanna, A," 62
Sonnets to Orpheus, 226
"Southern Road," 100
"South of the Mind," 187
"Step," 158
Stevens, Wallace, 3, 17, 245, 267
"Straight Talk from Plain Women," 202
"Streets in Shanghai," 112
"String Diamond, The," 78
Stroud, Joseph, 66
"Styrofoam Cup," 220
"Subway Exchange," 187
Swenson, May, 88
Swift, Jonathan, 216
Sze, Arthur, 78
Szporluk, Larissa, 67

Tennyson, Alfred Lord, 149
"[Tha Byrthnoth braegd, bill of
    scaethe]," 210
"Thanksgivings, The," 109
"[This is the year the old ones]," 16
"This Living Hand," 240
"[Thunder mutters louder and more
    loud, The]," 238
"To Extract Objects," 83
"To Sestius," 41
"To Waken an Old Lady," 48
Tranströmer, Tomas, 111
"Tribe," 232
Twichell, Chase, 104
"2 A.M.," 107
Two Gentlemen from Verona, 196
"Two Poems about President Harding,"
    94

Vallejo, César, 23, 253
Vaughn, Henry, 216
"Verge, The," 105
"Vulture," 48

"Waking, The," 79
Walker, Margaret, 124
Wang Ping, 155
"We Are Here," 168
"Wedding Feast at Cana, The," 180
"Weightless, Like a River," 105
Wesley, Charles, 217
"[Western wind, when wilt thou
    blow?]," 133
Wheatley, Phyllis, 217
Wheeler, Susan, 74
"When I Was Living Near the Ocean,"
    170
"When You're Lost in Juarez, in the
    Rain, and it's Easter Time Too," 149
"[Where shall we find the ninth song?],"
    11
Whitman, Walt, 24, 218
Whittier, John Greenleaf, 266
"Whoso List to Hunt," 214
"Why That Abbott and Costello Vaude-
    ville Mess Never Worked with Black
    People," 176
Williams, Sherley Anne, 202

Williams, William Carlos, 48
"Wind and the Rose, The," 82
"Wind and Water and Stone," 50
"Woebegone," 86
"Wolf Land, The," 163
"Words," 187
Wright, Charles, 148
Wright, James, 92
Wright, Richard, 152
"Written in the Church Yard at
    Middleton in Sussex," 275

"Written Near a Port on a Dark
    Evening," 275
Wyatt, Thomas, 214

Yeats, William Butler, 9, 218
Yi I, 11
"You Look Outside," 169
Young, Dean, 232
"You Were Never Miss Brown to Me,"
    203

Zagajewski, Adam, 21